Mountains

Mountains

A
Natural
History and
Hiking Guide

Margaret Fuller

WILEY

Wiley Nature Editions

JOHN WILEY & SONS, INC.

New York • Chichester • Brisbane • Toronto • Singapore

Publisher: Stephen Kippur
Editor: David Sobel
Managing Editor: Frank Grazioli
Editing, Design, and Production: G&H SOHO, Ltd.

Library of Congress Cataloging-in-Publication Data

Fuller, Margaret.
    Mountains: a natural history and hiking guide / by Margaret
Fuller.
        p.   cm.   — (Wiley nature editions)
    Bibliography: p.
    ISBN 0-471-62080-7 (pbk.)
    1. Mountain ecology.   2. Mountaineering.   3. Hiking.   I. Title.
II. Series.
QH541.5.M65F85 1989
508.314′3—dc19   88-27539
                                                                    CIP

Printed in the United States of America

89   90   10   9   8   7   6   5   4   3   2   1

To my husband, Wayne, and my children,
Doug, Leslie, Neal, Hilary, and Stuart

Foreword

I don't know anyone more experienced with mountains than Margaret Fuller. Since 1972 she has hiked some 3000 miles of Idaho's trails, often with her husband, Wayne, and one or more of their five children. Her careful observations are recorded in three excellent trail guides: *Trails of the Sawtooth and White Cloud Mountains, Trails of Western Idaho,* and *Trails of the Frank Church— River of No Return Wilderness,* considered backcountry bibles by new and experienced hikers alike.

In *Exploring Mountains,* Margaret combines research with her field experience, answering almost every question mountain visitors might ask. For example, why is the sky so blue up here? What makes one side of a range look so different from the other? How can delicate alpine wildflowers exist in such harsh conditions? How do frigid winds twist pines into dwarfed carica- tures? How do mountain goats, ibex, and other species of wild- life survive? And what about the earth itself? How has it come to be reworked into jutting peaks and rounded valleys?

As she leads us on an armchair tour of the world's mountains, Margaret explains complex things clearly and succinctly—per- haps in the same way she used to help her children understand what they were seeing along the trail. She often does this visu- ally, comparing such unfamiliar things as how alpine plants respond to photosynthesis with familiar ones like a bicycle tube stretching as it's inflated. Explanation extends from the per- sonal (why we experience cabin fever and why headaches plague weekend climbers) to the cosmic (how mountains are made and what causes weather). Her backpacking how-to's are as thorough as you'll find anywhere and offer insights for parents who want to share high-country adventures with their children.

Margaret also is sensitive to the problems associated with mountains: from the ethics of "no-trace camping" to the dangers of acid rain and the deforestation of the Himalayas. She expects her readers to take these matters as seriously as she does. One reason she writes is to develop a "constituency" for mountains

and their fragile ecosystems. Her premise is, the more we understand the alpine environment and how it works, the less likely
we'll be to inadvertently destroy it.

Since 1972 I've lived in Idaho, a state blessed with the most
unroaded mountain backcountry in the lower 48 states. All my
life, I have depended on mountains—their solid, familiar presence; their unique plants and animals; their clear air and ex-
traordinary vistas—for spiritual renewal and to give me a sense
of the relative importance of things.

The psalmist says, "Lift thine eyes to the hills, whence cometh
thy help." Those of us who follow this advice know that mountains are, indeed, a source of salvation. In this book Margaret
Fuller expands our understanding and enjoyment of this re-
markable terrain while increasing our respect for the forces
creating it.

Diane Ronayne, editor of *Idaho Wildlife*
Boise, Idaho

Preface

This book introduces the natural history of the mountains of the world in language every amateur can understand. Its aim is to inspire you to observe mountain geology, weather, plants, animals, and ecology for yourself. This learning will add a new dimension to your mountain trips.

You will also learn about hiking methods and mountains of the world. Chapter 1 tells about the most rugged mountain environment, the alpine tundra. Chapters 2 and 3 present the environment of the mountains, including weather.

Chapter 4 discusses how plates of the earth's crust create mountains when they collide. Chapter 5 explores the effects of heat, erosion, and water on mountains.

Chapter 6 examines the relationships of mountain plants and animals in networks called *ecosystems*. Chapter 7 outlines the ways mountain ecosystems have been classified or placed into zones. You learn that mountains are biological islands; they contain plants and animals found on only one mountain or range.

To help you enjoy mountains, Chapter 8 gives basic information on backpacking, including how to plan a safe trip, what food and equipment to take, and the basics of no-trace camping. You'll learn that in some parts of the world, little equipment is required because foot travelers stay at mountain huts, but the same principles of safety and planning apply.

Do you need new places to go on your next vacation? Chapter 9 locates each mountain range in the world and its highest peaks.

You might be surprised to learn of some of the places that have high mountains, such as the Canary Islands off the coast of Morocco.

The Appendix lists organizations that conduct mountain trips emphasizing natural history, education programs on mountain environment, and sources of maps and guidebooks. It also offers sources of information on trails for the handicapped.

This book is the first detailed natural history of mountains that locates each range. Learning mountain natural history will add enjoyment to hiking and backpacking trips. It may encourage you to find new places and take more trips. It may inspire a renewed respect for mountains that will make you work to preserve their environments for future generations.

ACKNOWLEDGMENTS

I would like to thank the following people for research, photographic and editing help: Nana Clark, David Sobel, and Frank Grazioli of John Wiley & Sons, Inc.; David Sassian of G&H SOHO Ltd., New York; Marilyn M. Harlin, professor of botany, University of Rhode Island; Cecil D. Andrus, governor of the state of Idaho; James R. Fazio, professor of wildlands recreation management, University of Idaho; Mary Kelly, executive director, Idaho Conservation League; Daniel M. Cohen, chief curator, Life Sciences Division, Natural History Museum of Los Angeles County; Mary Higdem of the geology department of the College of Idaho, Caldwell, Idaho; Scott Kiser of the National Weather Service, Boise, Idaho; Butch Harper of the Ketchum Ranger District, Sawtooth National Forest; Elaine Leppert and Terri Andes of the Caldwell, Idaho, library; Ellen Koger of the Boise State University Library; Jane Huston of the Idaho State Library; Joann Osburn of the Weiser, Idaho, library; the staff of the Terteling Library, College of Idaho; the members of the Westminster Camera Club, Canyon County, Idaho; and the members of the Idaho Writer's League in Weiser, Idaho; also Mary Kennan, Judy Ferro, Wallace Cathcart, Leslie Magryta, and Wayne, Doug, Neal, Hilary, and Stuart Fuller. I would especially like to thank Diane Ronayne, editor of *Idaho Wildlife*, for writing the Foreword, and Marie Guise for drawing the flower and tree sketches.

Contents

Introduction

When you explore mountains you enter a unique and fragile environment. It is more than a place of granite pinnacles, sapphire lakes, and emerald meadows. It is the home of plants and animals, from the glacier lily to the bristlecone pine to the golden eagle. This home is increasingly threatened by civilization.

Civilization cuts the forests of many watersheds for timber and fuel. It builds roads and mines that scar and erode the hillsides. Its crowds seek out the last refuge, trampling flowers underfoot and disturbing animals.

The environment of mountains is fragile because the mountain growing-season is so short that damage to plants and trees takes hundreds of years to repair. Studying this environment will inspire you to get out and explore. So you can learn how to be a careful guest, this book gives instructions on how to hike and camp without causing damage.

When you explore mountains, you will see many interesting things. For example, at a timberline lake called Cirque Lake in Idaho's White Cloud Mountains, the turquoise water is milky. Gravel ridges surround this 10,040-foot-high lake in front of pleated white cliffs. Pines the size of small bushes climb one of these ridges, and other dwarfed trees stand near the lower end of the lake (Figure I.1).

Mounds of turf make walking difficult along the lakeshore. Rocks litter this turf, and flowers sprinkle it with pink, white, blue, and yellow. One kind of plant has green needles, but pink, bell-shaped flowers instead of cones (Figure I.2). A pink snowbank extends from the turf up onto one of the gravel ridges.

Among rocks near this snowbank cling tiny, pillow-shaped plants. Between these plants wander narrow piles of dirt three inches high. Among boulders nearby, small furry animals run back and forth crying "peep, peep!"

Three 50-foot-deep pits dent the top of another gravel ridge. A pond, still partly frozen in early August, fills the bottom of

Figure I.1.   Whitebark pines grow in stunted krummholz form above Cirque Lake in Idaho's White Cloud Mountains.

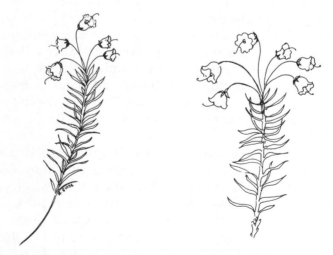

Figure I.2.   Heaths grow at or near timberline all over the world. Their needlelike leaves with curled edges help them retain water in dry mountain environments.
Courtesy of Marie Guise.

each of these pits. Gray striped layers of ice hide between rocks on the side of these ponds.

Above the ridges the sky is so dark it looks violet. When you sprawl on the turf you find that a chilly breeze disappears. While lying there you also notice unexpected sunburn on top of your tan.

Do you wonder why the trees here are the size of bushes? Or why the gravel ridge has pits? Does that ice belong to a glacier? Why is the lake milky? Why does the turf have mounds in it? Why does the wind lessen when you lie down? What kind of an animal is that ball of fur, and why does it run back and forth so much? Why is the snowbank pink? This book attempts to answer these questions and others you may have about mountain environments.

So what is a mountain? A basic definition is that a mountain is a section of land dramatically higher than the land around it. Usually a mountain is grouped with others into ranges, chains, and systems.

This book will help you understand mountains, whether you are climbing the hill in back of town or trekking in the Himalayas. The information will help you enjoy a biology or geology course or any mountain trip more, because it is fun to know things like this: Insects bask in the sun inside mountain flowers to keep warm, because the flowers focus the sunlight like reflectors do. Your reading will probably inspire you to go see mountains firsthand.

To get the most out of these trips you must first learn to observe. The process is a sharpening of the eye, similar to the one artists undergo when they learn to draw by first sketching single objects.

To help sharpen your eyes, take along field guides to identify trees, flowers, birds, mammals, or insects. The Audubon and Peterson series are both informative and easy to use. In many cases a picture in a field guide will pinpoint identification. Start with brightly colored, distinctive flowers and work up to mushrooms as you become more skillful. It is helpful to write down the characteristics of what you see or keep a log. These notes plus a photograph or sketch will aid you in finishing identification at home. Taking a field guide to a museum of natural history and comparing specimens with the pictures in the guide will help fix in your mind the appearance of different species.

Taking pictures is easier, but sketching will sharpen your eyes the most rapidly. It is more fun to start with a single flower or leaf and then work up to trees and animals. In a sketch you can emphasize certain characteristics that might not be clear in a photograph.

Some equipment is helpful in the field. You can take notes easily with a pocket-size tape recorder. Because plants are best identified by their flowering parts, take along a magnifying glass. On an automobile trip a microscope allows you to see the very small as well as the large. Binoculars will help you observe birds and distant wildlife.

Use all your senses to identify things. For example, the bark of ponderosa and Jeffrey pines in the western United States is vanilla-scented. Also, some birds have distinctive songs. With a sensitive tape recorder you may be able to record those songs and later compare them with a birdsong record.

Classes, reading, and field trips will increase your knowledge and awareness. You can take courses at local colleges or through community education, or you can join a bird-watching or natural history club. A camera club can instruct you in nature photography. Magazines like *Natural History, Audubon, Sierra,* and *National Wildlife* are also valuable sources.

ONE

Above the Forest: The Alpine Tundra

Imagine you are climbing above a lake at timberline. As the wind picks up, you stop to put on your jacket. You notice that the highest tree is almost all deadwood, sanded smooth by the wind, and that only scattered clumps of flowers and tufts of grass cling between the rocks.

The timberline divides two major life zones: alpine tundra and forest. Above this line only herbaceous plants, lichens, mosses, and flattened shrubs grow. Because the plant cover resembles that of the Arctic tundra, botanists call the area above the timberline *alpine tundra*. Tundra covers 9.1 million square miles of the Northern Hemisphere and 500,000 square miles of the Southern Hemisphere. Forty percent of this is alpine tundra.

Mountaintop environments are more hostile even than the Arctic. Alpine tundra has half as long a growing season as the mountain forests below, twice as much wind, and less precipitation. There is also high solar radiation, reduced oxygen, and seasonally frozen ground. The ground freezes because winters are so cold. Theoretically, temperature decreases 5.5°F for every 1000 feet of gain in elevation when no water vapor is present and 3.0°F when the air is saturated with moisture. The real rate is between these extremes and averages 3.5°F per 1000 feet. The contrast between summer and winter is greater here than it is anywhere else. As a result, fewer species live on the tops of mountains than in the Arctic. And few animals stay year-round.

KRUMMHOLZ TREES

The dwarfed trees you saw at the timberline lake are known as *krummholz* (German for "crooked wood"). They mark timberline on many mountains. Dwarfed by exposure to ice, sand, and wind-driven snow, they sometimes form mats dense enough to walk on. Their branches often extend from the windy side to the shelter of the lee side. Because roots can grow from any branches bent to the ground, a clump of krummholz can spread in the lee of its own crown or that of a big rock. The trees grow only as tall as the depth of the snow because wind and cold kill any sprouts above the snow's insulation. They rarely produce seed; instead, new trees start from the rooting of branches or from seeds that blow up from below timberline or are carried up by birds.

The dwarfed trees on tropical mountains are called *elfin forest*. These tiny, gnarled trees are covered by epiphytes (air plants such as orchids) and grow from a forest floor carpeted with mosses. At lower elevations are larger, though still dwarfed, trees. Blanketed with mosses, climbing ferns, and epiphytes, these trees are called *cloud forests* because the high humidity in their environment creates continual mist. Above the elfin forest are plants, grasses, and shrubs that stay green most of the year in spite of freezing temperatures every night.

Unlike the vegetation on tropical mountains, some shrubs above timberline in the Northern·Hemisphere are deciduous, and the plants and grasses turn green only in summer. Krumm-holz trees here are usually conifers, which fare better than other types in this environment. A conifer is any woody plant bearing seeds on woody or papery scales that form a cone; pines, firs, junipers, spruces, larches, and yews are all conifers. Because the sap in conifers contains sugar it freezes at a lower temperature than that of deciduous trees. Conifer sap also protects the trees against attacks by insects, which are repelled by its pungent taste. Protected by wax, conifer needles present less surface to wind and cold than leaves do. Sprays of needles can also catch water from mist and let snow through, and the trees' flexible limbs let snow slide off without breaking. Some conifers, such as subalpine fir and mountain hemlock, have narrow crowns with short branches and so accumulate little snow.

In the United States alpine larch, mountain hemlock, and

whitebark and bristlecone pine often form krummholz. Larches, common throughout krummholz in the Northern Hemisphere, are one of five genera of deciduous conifers. They do well in the alpine environment because they don't have to manufacture substances to keep their needles from freezing. The needles, which grow in clusters of 20 from spurs on the branches, are an intense lime green in spring, then turn to gold in the fall.

In the eastern United States the trees are stunted below timberline, so the band of krummholz is wider than it is in the west. In northern New England, for example, krummholz trees form a thick and extensive mat. In the western United States, *flagged trees*—whose branches grow on the side away from the wind— often replace krummholz at a more abrupt timberline. Sometimes frost drought kills the top of a flagged tree and a branch on the lee side becomes its new top.

TIMBERLINE

Scientists believe that timberline occurs where the growing season is too short for young leaves or needles to grow thick enough to withstand frost drought. Frost drought usually occurs in spring and early summer, when temperature inversions warm and dry out the needles. Because their channels and the soil are still frozen, the trees are unable to replace the water they've lost. Thus timberline results from summer cold and wind, not winter cold.

Two lines form the boundaries of the alpine timberline: the upper limit of the forest, called timberline, and the upper limit of trees and shrubs over two feet tall, called the *tree limit*. Between these two lines may be krummholz, elfin forest, or a parkland of scattered flagged trees. Or the two lines may coincide. Ecologists call the narrow transition zone between two vegetation types (in this case, timberline and the tree limit) an *ecotone*.

Nighttime temperature inversions cause trees to grow higher on peaks and ridges than they do in valleys and ravines. Usually, air is cooler the higher you go, but when cold air is trapped in a valley by the warm air above, a temperature inversion occurs. You may have noticed that timberlines are lower in cloudy areas, such as along the Pacific Coast. In general, timberlines are higher just north and south of the equator and become lower as you go toward the poles. In the southern Rockies, for example, timberline is 11,500 feet, whereas near the Canadian border it is only 7500 feet. In addition, timberlines in inland areas are higher than those on coasts because these areas have more sunny days, which compensate for colder temperatures. Trees also grow higher on larger and higher mountain ranges because there is more rock to radiate heat. Deserts often have both high timberlines and low ones below which no trees grow because of heat and dryness. Where it is both dry and cold, the lines are close together and, because it is too cold for drought-tolerant trees, only one or two tree zones occur.

FROZEN SOIL

Prolonged below-freezing temperatures in alpine tundra can cause *permafrost*, the permanent freezing of underlying soil, but it is not extensive above alpine timberline because of the insulation of snow. Permafrost occurs only where the annual average temperature is below 20°F.

In summer, the top layer of soil in alpine tundra melts. Where there is much moisture it turns soupy and creeps downhill, forming lobe-shaped gravel terraces. Water expands 9 percent when it freezes, so the freezing and thawing of this top layer causes *frost heaving*. Frost heaving occurs as follows: 1. When the temperature drops slowly below freezing, water freezing on the surface of the saturated ground forms ice needles. The needles grow because ice, which is lighter than water, rises. 2. The growing needles draw water and soil particles from below, causing uneven freezing and elevating the ground into *frost hummocks*. Needle ice and frost hummocks form where the soil freezes only in winter as well as where there is permafrost. All you need is wet soil and below-freezing temperatures.

Plants on the frost hummocks grow in a cycle. When a hummock rises above the snow, the plants growing on it will die. By summertime, the dead plants no longer can hold the soil on the hummock, and without this insulation the frozen soil below melts. On cold nights and in winter, the water resulting from the melting freezes and heaves rocks in the hummock to the surface and down its sides. With the loss of soil and rocks, the hummock shrinks enough to be under the snow level again. Eventually plants again invade the hummock.

How can needle ice heave rocks out of the hummock? Rocks absorb more heat than soil does, so more ice melts under them. When this extra water freezes into needle ice, more ice accumulates under the rocks than between them. Eventually, these growing ice needles raise the rocks to the surface, where they slide off the hummocks on all sides to form circles. On a slope the rising ice needles push the rocks up perpendicular to the slope. When the needles melt the rocks fall downhill in regular patterns. These circles and patterns are called *patterned ground.*

WIND

Wind blows oftener on mountains than at lower elevations for two reasons. First, mountains are high enough to reach at times into the prevailing winds, winds caused by the earth's rotation and air circulation. Second, solar warming of the uneven ground sets up an air circulation system in which air flows upslope in the daytime and downslope at night. Wind also blows harder on mountains because wind squeezed into a narrow place, like a mountain pass or the space between a mountain and a cold air mass aloft, speeds up in much the same way that rivers speed up in gorges.

Wind intensifies the effect of cold temperatures because it carries away the respiration heat of animals and plants. The reduction of effective temperature by wind is called *wind chill.* A wind chill factor table is given on page 158.

ALPINE PLANTS

Alpine plants have adapted to a severe environment in many ways. To take advantage of the warmth and wind protection found underground, they have larger root systems than they have leaves and stems. Their stems and branches are flexible so that they don't break in wind or under snow. Because friction slows wind close to the ground, alpine plants characteristically hug the ground (Figure 1.1). Flowering plants here bloom in intense, dark colors that attract insect pollinators and absorb heat.

Figure 1.1.   To conserve heat, alpine plants in temperate climates throughout the world grow close to the ground. These are on Mount Egmont, New Zealand.
Courtesy of Neal Fuller.

Both mountain and desert plants must tolerate extreme differences in temperature. Alpine plants can keep warm because their dark leaves absorb heat and are often insulated with fuzz. Some plant hairs are white outside to reflect heat back into the leaf and black inside to absorb the heat reflected. Other hairs are hollow, so the air in them provides extra insulation. One example of a tundra plant with hairy leaves is the edelweiss, found in the Alps. It has so many hairs on its leaves that the leaves are white. Also white with shorter hairs are the thickened bracts around the tiny yellow flower clusters.

Hairs also enable alpine plants to conserve moisture. Alpine plants have short, thin stems with few branches and small leaves that often cover the stems. To conserve water, leaves may be thickened for water storage or may have a waxy surface, scales on the underside, curled edges, or their *stomata* indented. (Stomata are the openings in the leaf surface that take in carbon dioxide and give off oxygen and water vapor.)

Figure 1.2.   On Mount Washington, New Hampshire, *Diapensia*, an arc-tic-alpine shrub of mat form, grows at the southern limit of its range. It grows so slowly it takes a seedling 30 years to spread into a three-inch circle.

Alpine plants often grow in mats, or cushions, which trap so much heat that a plant's temperature may be 20°F warmer than the surrounding air (Figure 1.2). An example is moss campion, a cushion plant with hundreds of pink flowers. The warmth of the mat or cushion attracts the insects needed for pollination. Cushion plants have a single long taproot, while mat plants attach themselves to the ground at several places. The even smaller *rosette plants* place their leaves flat on the ground. Plants such as yarrow, which grow at various altitudes, are shorter at high elevations (Figure 1.3).

Some alpine plants can produce their own heat, which en-ables them to melt their way up through snow. Marsh marigolds can even flower under the snow.

Figure 1.3.   Plants that grow only at higher elevations on temperate mountains tend to be short to conserve heat. The yarrow, which grows in lowlands as well as on mountains, is shorter at higher elevations.
Courtesy of Marie Guise.

PREPARING FOR WINTER

Where winters are cold, as in alpine tundra, plants undergo hardening, a series of changes in response to autumn frosts. These changes which prepare plants for winter dormancy are so effective that plants which wouldn't survive temperatures lower than 25°F in the summer are able to tolerate temperatures of −40°F in winter. Have you ever tried to transplant a shrub from a nearby mountain to your garden and found that it didn't grow? This is because plants at different altitudes have become accustomed to the conditions at those altitudes in a process similar to hardening.

Several types of winter dormancy are triggered by shortened day length, low temperature, and drought. Perennials die back in winter and grow each spring from the roots. Deciduous plants lose their leaves and lower their metabolism. Grasses and sedges stay partly green all year so they can photosynthesize whenever it is warm enough. To survive winter, woody plants stop growing, lose their high water content, add woody material to cell walls, close their stomata, and concentrate their sap. Concentrated sap, which freezes at a lower temperature than regular sap, acts as antifreeze.

PHOTOSYNTHESIS

Plants work harder at high altitudes. They photosynthesize more rapidly at low temperatures and high light intensity than low-altitude plants. Plants of the same species contain less chlorophyll per unit volume on mountaintops than they do in the Arctic because less is needed to photosynthesize in the intense sunlight.

Alpine plants receive 50 percent more ultraviolet radiation than plants at sea level. The light at high altitudes is so intense that alpine plants can photosynthesize during a snowstorm (as researchers studying bluegrass in Wyoming discovered). No wonder you got sunburned through your tan at such altitudes.

Some of the most interesting alpine plants have white or pale flowers shaped like dish antennas. These act as reflectors that concentrate heat on pistils and stamens, which are often insulated with fuzz. The stems rotate the flowers to follow the sun. The temperature inside the flowers may be 10° to 32°F warmer than outside. An example is the *pasqueflower*, found in the mountains of the western United States. Researchers have discovered that insects like to sit inside the flowers of another of these plants, the dryad, even at night.

Hair protects leaves from too much solar radiation. Solar energy at high altitudes is intense because there are fewer air and water vapor molecules and dust particles to filter the sunlight. Alpine plants in the tropics receive more solar radiation than any others because the rays of the sun shine vertically all year and the ozone layer that helps filter sunlight is thinner over the equator.

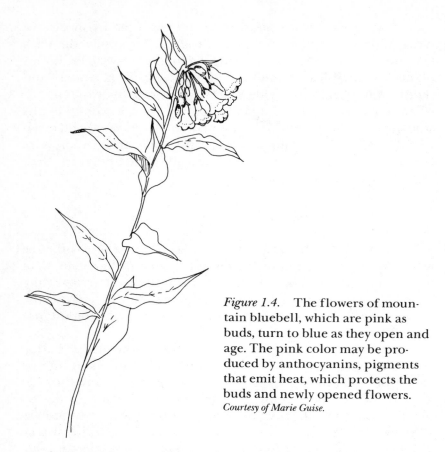

Figure 1.4.   The flowers of mountain bluebell, which are pink as
buds, turn to blue as they open and
age. The pink color may be produced by anthocyanins, pigments
that emit heat, which protects the
buds and newly opened flowers.
Courtesy of Marie Guise.

In some leaves, such as those of alpine sorrel, red or purple
pigments called *anthocyanins* screen out this excess ultraviolet
light and convert some of it to heat (Figure 1.4). In most alpine
plants, the green pigment, chlorophyll, masks the anthocyanins
in midsummer. Intense light and low temperatures favor the
formation of these pigments from carbohydrates. Autumn cold
destroys the chlorophyll, revealing the red color of anthocyanins and the yellow of carotene.

Some plants are able to pipe light into the soil by using fiber
optics. What is fiber optics? It is the transmission of light along a
fiber or thin rod of transparent material. Light shining into the
rod reflects from one side of the rod to the other in such flat
zigzags that it parallels the walls of the rod and travels along it.
This is an especially useful adaptation in alpine areas because
of the short growing season. With fiber optics, plant tissues can

guide light from the tops of seedlings to underground. Thanks to piped light, the seed leaves can begin photosynthesis before they emerge from the ground.

TIMING OF FLOWERS

Have you ever wondered why gentians bloom so late in the summer and how they know to start blooming then? Sensitivity to day length, called *photoperiodism*, makes the flowers bloom in the best conditions (Figure 1.5). To determine when to flower,

Figure 1.5.   Shooting star is an example of a plant that blooms in spring as soon as the days are a certain length.
Courtesy of Marie Guise.

plants use two varieties of pigments called *phytochromes* to mea-sure light. Phytochrome r absorbs red light, and phytochrome fr absorbs far-red light, which has a longer wavelength than true red. In the daytime, light changes phytochrome r into phy-tochrome fr; at night the darkness allows phytochrome fr to change back to phytochrome r. In this way the pigments give the plant a chemical message of the number of hours of daylight.

Some flowers, such as sagebrush buttercups, can bloom only after 13 to 15 hours of daylight. This keeps them from blooming when the weather is cold enough to damage the blossoms but allows them to bloom before their communities dry out. Other flowers, such as alpine asters, wait even longer, until day length has reached its maximum and shortened to a certain length. This allows plants living where snowbanks melt late to grow before they flower. Because water from snowmelt often lingers late in the meadows where gentians live, it is sometimes not dry enough for them to start growing until midsummer. By flower-ing late even in dry years, more gentians will have a chance to produce flowers in wet years.

SHORT GROWING SEASON

Alpine plants have developed several adaptations for the short alpine growing season. Many plants grow mostly under-ground. One moss campion in Colorado grew only a third of an inch in ten years, put out only two leaves a year, and flowered only after ten years, but the taproot of the same plant was five feet long.

Most alpine plants are either perennial or reproduce vege-tatively. Alpine tundra is hostile to seedlings, so plants that reproduce vegetatively have an advantage. Some, like grasses, mints, and sedges, have underground sprouting stems, called *rhizomes*. Others grow miniature plants called *bulbils* in their leaf axils (bases of the leaves) or in place of flowers. The bulbils take root when they fall from the parent plants. Still other alpine plants put out stems or runners, called *stolons*, that take root at points called nodes. Some use layering, which occurs when branches take root where they touch the ground. Others develop bulbs and corms, enlarged buds with fused leaves. In the axils of these "leaves" new bulbs grow. The plants also use these struc-tures to store food along with their roots.

Plants that do produce flowers and seeds produce them in abundance, to ensure that some seedlings survive. The flowers are unusually large relative to the size of the plants, so as to attract pollinators. Seeds germinate in spring, when water is available, the temperature is between 20° and 30°F, and the day is the right length. In contrast, lowland plants don't start growing until it is between 40° and 50°F. Seeds of alpine plants may take four years to germinate. This long period ensures the plants' survival: Because only a few seeds germinate in a year with bad conditions, some will be left for a better year.

Another adaptive strategy developed by some alpine perennials is to produce next year's flower buds at the end of the preceding summer, when the plants have plenty of carbohydrates on hand. These buds enable the plants to bloom earlier the following summer than they could without them.

ALPINE TUNDRA AND ARCTIC TUNDRA

If you go to the Arctic you will notice that Arctic and alpine tundras have similar plants but different conditions. All the extra light the Arctic tundra receives from the midnight sun makes a great difference in the Arctic environment. The alpine environment is harsher, with cold nights and days during the growing season; it has more wind, snow, rain, and solar radiation but less oxygen and carbon dioxide. In addition, steep topography makes alpine tundra drier than the Arctic. Alpine plants use carbon dioxide more efficiently than Arctic plants do because less is available. And whereas alpine animals show definite daily cycles, Arctic animals show none because of the continuous summer daylight.

Several plant and animal species, called *Arctic-alpine species*, are the same in both areas. These species moved south during the ice ages to escape from the advancing ice. After the ice melted, they moved up onto mountaintops, along mountain ranges, and back into the Arctic.

If you go to the Canadian Rockies you will see more Arctic-alpine species than farther south. Many Arctic species are restricted to the Arctic because they are unable to stand the day–night temperature change during the growing season.

Most alpine species evolved from desert, grassland, or forest species that migrated up the mountains and were isolated by climatic change. A few plant families, such as gentians, heaths, and composites, are represented by species in most alpine areas. Some species have a wide range, such as the purple saxifrage of the Alps and North America

SIMILAR ALPINE PLANTS

Biologists have found that in different parts of the world some mountain plants resemble each other. These plants demonstrate convergence, which is the development in unrelated plants or animals of resemblances resulting from adapting to similar environments. Several treelike alpine plant species with thickened flower stalks grow in Hawaii, the Andes, Africa, and Southeast Asia. These giant woody plants are not considered trees because they grow above the timberline of normal-shaped trees and shrubs. These alpine plants have thickened woody stems and leaves attached directly to the stems. The few types whose stems branch resemble the Joshua trees of the American southwestern deserts.

One family of these giants, the *Espletias*, grows in the mountains of Venezuela. They have rosettes of large brown or white wooly leaves and unbranched trunks. As the trunks grow taller the lower leaves die and hang down, keeping the stems warm. The plants put out a single stalk, about a foot wide and up to 35 feet tall, of yellow flowers.

Another giant plant, the *puja*, related to and resembling the pineapple, is found in the Andes and grows at elevations as high as 13,000 feet. Pujas are bromeliads, a plant family found only in Central and South America. They have a rosette of sharp-edged leaves and when 150 years old form a flower stalk a foot thick and 15 to 30 feet tall with thousands of greenish yellow or blue flowers. A flowering puja resembles a giant ear of corn on top of a pompon of swords.

In East Africa there are two main types of giant plant, *lobelias* and *groundsels*. The flower stalks of giant lobelias, containing small blue or purple blossoms and resembling giant hairy or scaly candles, grow up to 25 feet tall from a basal rosette. The leaves of one species contain a reservoir of water that is secreted by the plants each night and later freezes. The secretion lowers the water content of the plant tissue enough for them to avoid freezing. Lobelias also secrete pectin, which helps keep the water from evaporating.

The treelike groundsels, up to 25 feet tall, grow as high as 14,800 feet and have bundles of long metallic leaves that resemble pompons on top of each branch. Groundsels branch from the points where they put out flower stalks. Beginning at age 30, the plants produce yellow daisylike flowers. Some species of groundsel, such as *Senecio keniodendron* found on Mount Kenya, close their woolly leaves at night, keeping them 10°F warmer than the surrounding air.

ALPINE COMMUNITIES

Within the alpine tundra there are several different biological communities in different environments. Three of these environments are cliffs, talus, and scree. A slope of rocks most of which are bigger than a fist which accumulate at the base of cliffs is called talus. Scree is composed of smaller rocks, gravel, and sand.

On cliffs and boulders the black, gray, green, or orange patches you see are usually lichens, of the crustose type. Two other types, fruticose and foliose, grow on trees and on the ground, especially in moist areas. Lichens are made up of a fungus and an alga growing in symbiosis. The fungus is dependent on the alga. There are more than 17,000 different combinations. Although lichens photosynthesize best at 5°F, they are able to photosynthesize at temperatures as low as −10°, in part because one of the foods they store, a sugar alcohol, prevents freezing. Crustose lichens live for up to 4500 years, so they spend little energy making new plant material. They attach themselves so firmly to rocks that they can't be removed whole without breaking the rock.

By taking refuge in cracks in rocks or in the shelter of boulders, plants can live at greater heights than they can in the open. One such plant, *Stellaria decumbens* (a stitchwort), has been found at 20,130 feet in the Himalayas.

Two alpine birds that take advantage of cliffs and rock outcrops are lammergeiers and wall creepers. Lammergeiers, vultures that fly as high as 30,000 feet, were once found in the Alps but now remain only in Spain, Greece, and Central Asia. Black-

Figure 1.6. Pikas, which live in Asia and North America in boulder fields at elevations up to 20,000 feet, cut and dry plants and grasses for winter food and insulation.
Courtesy of New York Zoological Society.

ish brown with buff-colored breasts and orange throats, they have diamond-shaped tails and narrow wings with a nine-foot wingspread. Tufts of black bristles below their bills give them the nickname bearded vultures. Lammergeiers eat bone splinters and marrow, cracking the bones open by dropping them on rocks.

Using long, sharp claws, wall creepers climb the cliffs of Europe and Central Asia looking for insects. These gray birds with bright crimson under their wings and large white spots on their wings and tail edges flit from place to place like butterflies. They nest in inaccessible cracks in rocks up to 9000 feet.

The pika, a small furry animal often mistaken for a rodent but related to the rabbit, lives in boulder fields at elevations of up to 20,000 feet (Figure 1.6). There are a dozen species in Asia, two in North America, and many subspecies. Hikers in rocky areas in the mountains of these continents may hear the pika's cry, usually a shrill *peep, peep!*

Fur on the bottom of the pika's feet and the ability to close its nostrils help it withstand the cold. During summer pikas cut hay, mostly plants rather than grasses, and store it in burrows and haystacks for winter use. Each day they add to the haystack only what will dry that day. In winter they use the hay they haven't yet eaten to keep themselves warm.

If you saw a larger, fatter animal sitting up and whistling at you along the trail, it was probably a marmot. Marmots, related to squirrels, live in boulder fields and burrows with entrances hidden by rocks. They are much larger than pikas—up to 24 inches long—and hibernate in winter. Marmots live in Eurasia as well as North America.

Another community in the progression from boulder fields to turf is the stone field called a *fellfield* (Figure 1.7). In fellfields cushion and mat plants cover less than half of the dry, rocky soil. Since wind blows the snow away soon after it falls and water runs off rapidly, these areas have early-blooming flowers and summer drought.

In contrast, snowbed communities cluster in concentric rings around late-staying snowbanks. Plants requiring the longest growing season are found in the outermost circle and plants requiring the least, like mosses, are in the middle. Being able to survive cold is not as important as growing fast here.

Figure 1.7.   In alpine tundra, dry rocky areas less than half-covered with plants are called fellfields.

Before they melt, many snowbanks develop a microscopic community within them, often called pink snow. The community is made up of green algae with gelatinous red coats plus microscopic fungi, ciliates, rotifers, protozoa, and bacteria which eat pollen and organic debris blown up from below. There are 100 species of snow algae worldwide. The intensity of the red pigment hematochrome depends on day length. Using this pigment the algae concentrate enough of the sun's radiation to register on a Geiger counter. The algae need liquid water, so pink snow is found only when snowbanks warm up in spring and summer. If you could watch the algae under a microscope, you might see the little tails called *flagellae* that develop during the summer as the snow begins to melt. They use these tails to swim up to the surface of the snowbank. Pink snow makes snowbanks smell like watermelon, but it causes diarrhea if eaten.

Pink snow is not the only life in snowbanks. Jumping spiders, glacier fleas, and springtails live in snowbanks at 22,000 feet in the Himalayas, eating pollen and tiny insects blown up from below. Springtails freeze to the snow each night and melt loose in the daytime; the springlike organs on their abdomens enable them to become unstuck from the snow and to jump 15 feet. Black snow worms occur in western North America, and there are even microorganisms in the snow on top of Mount Everest, at 29,028 feet.

Another alpine community, evergreen *heaths*, is low shrubs or mat plants that often have tiny pink or white bell-like flowers and small narrow leaves in whorls. In tropical alpine areas the heaths are so enormous they resemble trees. Heaths grow in wet places with few soil nutrients. They can live in nutrient-poor environments because mycorrhizae, or the fungi on their roots, help them by growing filaments which act as auxiliary root hairs.

Still another community of alpine plants is found along streambeds, lake margins, and in marshes. These plants need more moisture than those in other spots. Willows, sedges, heaths, mosses, and saxifrages like these wet places.

Alpine meadows are communities that cover well-drained basins. When sedges, rather than grasses, dominate, the meadows are called *sedge meadows*. There are a thousand species of sedge, the genus *Carex*. You can distinguish sedges from

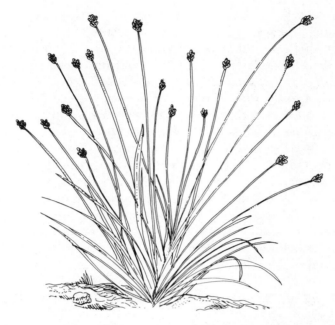

Figure 1.8. Sedges resemble grasses, but their stems are solid and triangular instead of round and hollow.
Courtesy of Marie Guise.

grasses by their triangular stems (Figure 1.8). Pocket gophers
live in dry meadows and montane voles in sedge meadows.

Pocket gophers make narrow dirt piles by packing the dirt
from their tunnels into tunnels they dig in the snow. When the
snow melts the mounds of dirt are exposed. These tiny rodents
cause vegetation cycles in meadows by eating the roots of sedges
and cushion plants. Their burrowing pushes up soil that
smothers the plants. When the sedges and cushion plants die,
taller plants the gophers don't eat invade the area, and so the
gophers leave. Then the sedges and cushion plants grow back.

WINTER DORMANCY

Alpine animals change their activities according to the time
of day or the season. They may leave their community in winter
or go into winter dormancy, the reduced metabolism that occurs
under shelter during food shortages and cold temperatures.
Bears undergo only a slight dormancy, but true hibernators,

such as marmots, experience great reductions in breathing, heart rate, and body temperature.

If you dug up a hibernating ground squirrel you might think it was dead (Figure 1.9). Fully hibernating rodents maintain a body temperature near freezing and breathe only once a minute, with a heart rate of two or three beats per minute. When hibernation begins these functions decrease gradually over several days. The process may be hastened by inhalation of carbon dioxide, which collects when the animals are in their den. Researchers have found that chemicals from the blood of hibernating woodchucks induced a 50 percent drop in heart rate and a 10 percent drop in body temperature in monkeys. Because Arctic ground squirrels living at a constant temperature and with constant amounts of light, food, and water show periodic torpor, some biologists believe that the trigger for hibernation must be genetic. Hibernating animals wake up a little to warm

Figure 1.9.   True hibernators like ground squirrels undergo great reductions in breathing, heart rate, and body temperature during hibernation.
Copyright, Jan Boles, Snake Basin Photography.

themselves when it becomes cold enough to freeze them. So the animals will be in an active state the longest practical time, the timing of hibernation varies with altitude.

Cold-blooded mountain animals are also dormant in winter. Did you know that frogs can be frozen and still live? A researcher discovered that three different frogs could survive for five days while partly frozen at 21° to 28°F. When warmed they showed no damage because their tissues contained glycerol, a type of antifreeze. Fish, amphibians, and reptiles also have temperatures near and below freezing while dormant in winter.

Insects make antifreeze too. Alpine insects are usually dark-colored to absorb heat, small, and wingless. The dark colors of alpine insects, birds, and butterflies also protect them against ultraviolet radiation. High-altitude insects include flies, beetles, grasshoppers, and butterflies. It is too cold for most bees, so flies pollinate many flowers. Because of the short growing season, alpine tundra insects often take two or three years to reach adulthood.

MIGRATION

Last winter when you rode the ski lift at Jackson Hole you saw only a few tiny animal tracks because not many animals or birds live permanently in alpine tundra. Pikas, meadow voles, marmots, ptarmigans, and Rocky Mountain goats are year-round residents, but most alpine animals migrate south or to lower elevations in winter. Mountain vegetation zones are narrow, so animals need to go only a short distance before they reach food and shelter. Some animals seek shelter within their own communities on lee slopes, under boulders, in depressions, within krummholz trees, and even in snowbanks. Some go only a short distance down the mountain, but others go far.

Unlike humans, birds don't flock south in winter to escape the cold. They migrate to find enough food to keep up their high metabolism. A biological clock makes migratory birds restless twice a year. Change in day length, rainfall, or temperature sets the exact time. Because birds keep flying as long as the restlessness lasts, those with long migrations have longer periods of restlessness. The direction birds fly during each part of their migration is determined by genes.

The brains of some species of birds contain compasses of magnetic particles that help them find this direction, while the eyes of others orient them to the sun and stars. Odors and sounds of wind and waves help the birds find exact places. Researchers have found particles of magnetite, a magnetized mineral, in the heads of pigeons and in the wings of migratory butterflies.

Day length triggers the beginning of most migrations in birds. Migrations vary from the mile or so traveled by some chamois and bighorn sheep to the 11,000-mile journeys of Arctic terns. Why do these birds fly nearly halfway around the world? Some ornithologists believe that continental drift may have lengthened what was once a short journey. Other long migrations may be connected to the extensive ice cover of the ice ages. Many species tend to use the same route as a flyway because of favorable winds and food sources. Many birds crash, become lost, are blown off course, or freeze to death. To prepare for the tremendous exercise of migration birds often eat enough to double their weight.

WINTER PROTECTION

Several alpine animals disguise themselves in order to avoid predators. Some have different disguises in winter; for example, ptarmigans and weasels turn white. Laboratory experiments with weasels suggest that shortened day length triggers the change in color. Other animals are better off keeping the same color year-round. Rocky Mountain goats, for example, are white to blend with snow and light-colored rock. If their coats were black they would absorb more solar radiation but would also radiate it back faster.

Alpine animals also put on insulated jackets in winter, just as you do. Animals such as pikas, weasels, snowshoe hares, voles, and Rocky Mountain goats that are active in winter grow dense winter coats. Cold, not day length, triggers the growth of this thicker fur.

But feathers are warmer than fur. Some birds even grow thicker winter feathers. Birds also snuggle together in flocks, fluff up their feathers to make them thicker, and tuck their heads under their wings. Some mountain birds nest underground, where it is warmer.

If you gained weight from eating holiday goodies, your body may have just been trying to keep warm. Another provision for cold weather is to eat more in order to fuel an increase in metabolism, which helps keep animals warm. Birds can increase their metabolism three or four times to cope with cold temperatures.

Another way animals adapt to cold is by controlling blood circulation. In some animals arterial blood warms venous blood returning from the feet, nose, and ears. Because the veins and arteries are parallel, the venous blood in turn cools the arterial blood, so that when it goes again to the feet, nose, and ears, less heat will be lost.

Groups such as the Andes Indians, who have lived in high mountains for generations, have greater blood circulation and shorter arms and legs for it to circulate to. Blood circulates more rapidly in the hands and feet of Eskimos, so higher blood circulation is an adaptation to cold, not altitude.

Cold-blooded animals also acclimatize to seasons. Brook trout will choose to swim in water of 68°F in summer but only 46°F in winter. If kept at a constant temperature, they lose this ability. Some reptiles can move black pigments to their backs to absorb more heat in the cold of high altitudes. In the tropics reptiles using this method survive near the snow line.

Another adaptation alpine animals have developed to withstand their hostile habitat is to breed at times that allow young to be born when forage will be available for the longest time. The animals adapt to the shorter growing season by having fewer but larger litters.

EFFECTS OF ALTITUDE

Alpine animals must also overcome the lack of oxygen and carbon dioxide caused by the low air pressure at high altitude. At sea level air pressure is 15 pounds per square inch, but at 18,000 feet it is only 8.5 pounds per square inch. The reduced pressure causes only 67 percent of the sea level amount of oxygen to enter the blood of an animal at 10,000 feet.

Did you get a headache on your backpacking trip to high altitudes? If so, it was probably caused by altitude sickness. This misery often strikes residents of low elevations when they go up to alpine tundra. For some people, headache and lassitude may occur 5000 feet above the elevation of their homes. Most experience sleeplessness, nausea, vomiting, irritability, severe headaches, impaired memory, and difficulty in concentrating beginning 10,000 to 13,000 feet above where they live. With a 15,000 foot increase coordination may be impaired. Above 18,000 feet humans deteriorate rather than becoming acclimatized. Other animals, however, can live at even higher elevations. For example, some yaks live permanently at 19,800 feet.

Altitude affects blood cells and cell membranes, allowing fluid to enter the tissues from the blood. When fluid accumulates in lung tissue it interferes with getting enough oxygen and causes pulmonary edema. When water enters brain tissue it causes swelling, headaches, and in severe cases a life-threatening condition called cerebral edema. Those who develop these conditions will die unless they are removed to a lower altitude *immediately*. Even if the condition is not fatal, the cerebral edema may cause brain damage.

Over time lowlanders at high altitudes develop increased blood circulation and more red blood cells and capillaries. Kidneys also adjust the level of carbon dioxide in the blood.

Those living at high altitudes undergo permanent changes. They have larger lungs, hearts, and chests and more blood, with most of the gain in red corpuscles. Their hearts beat more slowly, for example, at 50 instead of 72. Indians in the Andes have more hemoglobin. Sherpas in Nepal have normal hemoglobin and more but smaller red blood corpuscles than normal. The smaller size of individual cells increases the total surface area available for absorbing oxygen.

High-altitude animals also undergo permanent changes. Rodents in the Andes make more myoglobin, the substance that delivers oxygen to the muscles, than rodents at low altitude. Changes in altitude affect birds little because they have rich hemoglobin and their lungs are larger and more efficient than those of other animals. Air flows continuously through their lungs just as water flows through fish gills, enabling birds to fly at extreme altitudes. For example, a bar-headed goose was seen flying over Everest at over 29,000 feet. Another high altitude bird is the Andean condor, a vulture that nests above 10,000 feet in caves and on ledges all along the Andes but is commonest in Chile and Peru. Condors eat carrion and prey on other animals and birds. Mostly black with bare heads and necks, they have a ten-foot wingspan that enables them to soar at 20,000 feet.

TYPICAL ANIMALS

A few animals are especially well adapted to the North American alpine tundra. Pikas, marmots, and pocket gophers have already been discussed.

Another is the grouselike *ptarmigan*, which, as mentioned earlier, turns white in winter (Figure 1.10). Its legs and feet are covered with feathers, which grow thicker in winter. Each feather frond is hollow and so insulates more than if it were filled with pigment. Ptarmigans nest in ground depressions, under bushes, or in the shelter of rocks. In winter they burrow into the snow to keep warm. Bacteria in their crops enable them to eat lichens, leaves, and twigs in winter.

If you have seen a small dark bird bobbing its head on the shore of a mountain lake, it was probably a *water ouzel*, or *dipper*.

Figure 1.10. The white feathers that cover the grouselike ptarmigan in winter make it invisible to predators.
Courtesy of Bob and Ira Spring.

Using their wings to keep them under water, these dark gray, eight-inch birds run along the bottom of streams looking for insect larvae, crustaceans, or fish fry. Their constant bobbing gave them the nickname dipper. They live near rushing water and make dome-shaped nests of moss in the bank or behind waterfalls, which they are able to fly through. Dippers wear feathers so oily and thick they can feed under water all year (Figure 1.11). Dippers are not the only birds that bob at mountain lake edges. *Water pipits* also do so. Resembling sparrows with thinner bodies, these pipits often eat insects frozen into snowbanks.

Another well-adapted animal is the *meadow vole*, or *field mouse*. The most common alpine animals, meadow voles resemble small rats up to ten inches long but with snub noses. They burrow under the snow, make narrow runways in the grass, and cache hay for winter. Females bear up to eight young every five weeks. In years with plentiful food, overpopulation occurs. Excess numbers lead to fighting, little breeding, and tearing up of the vegetation in a frenzy that causes an abrupt population decline.

Goats, sheep, and especially goat-antelopes are common in alpine tundra around the world. They are especially well adapted to where they live because their hoofs allow them to climb up and down cliffs.

Figure 1.11. The feathers of dippers are so oily that these birds are able to search for insects on the bottoms of mountain streams all year.
Courtesy of Bob and Ira Spring.

Figure 1.12. Bighorn sheep live in dry, rugged country, some of it above timberline, but spend winter at lower elevations.
Courtesy of Yellowstone National Park

An example is the *bighorn: Ovis ammon* of Eurasia and *Ovis canadensis* of Siberia and the Rockies. North of the Peace River and in Alaska lives a related species, the white *Dall sheep*, which has white hair and gold horns. In the southern part of their range these sheep are charcoal gray and known as *Stone sheep* (Figure 1.12). Some bighorns live above timberline all year and some below timberline in rugged dry areas. In winter those at higher altitudes descend. Short legs, broad haunches, and shoulders and hoofs with spongy centers help bighorns climb well. They mark their paths with scent from glands on their feet, and the young learn the paths by following them. As soon as they are born the lambs can climb rocks, and by the time they are two weeks old they can go 30 miles a day. Bighorns will eat grass but prefer shrubs. They will dig up arrowleaf balsamroot to eat the roots (Figure 1.13). In winter two or three will work together to

Figure 1.13.   The roots of arrowleaf balsamroot are a favorite food of bighorn sheep.
Courtesy of Marie Guise.

dig away the snow. Only those rams with horns the same size will fight. The two-inch-thick bone of their skulls absorbs the tremendous force of their heads and horns crashing together.

In European mountains the ibex, a stocky, chocolate brown wild goat, lives at the highest elevations, eating herbs, sedges, lichens, and grasses. The forty-inch-long horns of the males weigh so much that they sometimes prop them up when resting. Their rubberlike hoofs contain pads that cling to rocks. Eight different races of ibex live in the Caucasus, Central Asia, and in Africa, each with differently shaped horns (Figure 1.14).

The chamois, a goat-antelope with small curved horns, inhabits European mountains and the Caucasus. Chamois change from yellow-brown in summer to black in winter. They winter in forests below 7500 feet but go above timberline in summer. Their concave hoofs can be spread apart for traction. Males mark their territories with scent from a horn gland.

In gorges between 7000 and 13,000 feet in Afghanistan and the western Himalayas lives the *markhor*, a 200-pound goat with

5-1/2-foot corkscrewlike horns. Markhors are iron gray in winter and red-brown in summer.

In the Pamirs from 13,000 to 18,000 feet lives the argali, or Marco Polo sheep, a wild sheep related to the bighorn. Forming a double outward spiral up to 75 inches long, the gray horns of argalis may have curls 30 inches across.

Living at timberline in the Himalayas is the Himalayan tahr, a goat-antelope with 15-inch horns. The manes of the tahrs reach their knees, which are calloused because they are used to help the animals climb.

Wild yaks, related to bison, dwell in the Tibetan highlands. Bulls may weigh 1800 pounds, have three-foot horns, and black fur that reaches the ground. The tongues of these yaks have barbs to help them pull up the tufts of short grasses they live on.

Figure 1.14.   The ibex lives at higher elevations than the chamois and is found in Asia and Africa as well as Europe.
Courtesy of Swiss National Tourist Office.

A final example of an alpine animal is the Rocky Mountain goat. For many, seeing these goats is often the high point of a wilderness trip in the Rockies. Like the chamois of the Alps, the Rocky Mountain goat is intermediate between goats and antelope and is a ruminant with four stomachs. Heat from fermenting food in its rumen helps keep it warm. It also relies on an eight-inch-long outer winter coat (Figure 1.15). This falls off in summer, but even the remaining undercoat is so warm that the goat digs into snowbanks to cool off. A fondness for dust baths turns the animal's white coat dirty gray by late summer.

Both sexes have short, black hollow horns, which form growth rings as they grow. Males often live alone, but females and kids graze in small groups. If a nanny doesn't get enough to eat, the fetus dies and her body reabsorbs it. Cougars and eagles prey on these goats, and eagles will shove the kids off cliffs.

Rocky Mountain goats make well-marked trails across slopes and can turn around by rearing up if necessary. They can jump but usually climb up or down the easy way, going up to 1000 vertical feet in 20 minutes. How can they climb so well? Their split hoofs act as pincers going up or downhill and as traction

Figure 1.15.   Rocky Mountain goats, which live above timberline all year, keep warm with eight-inch-thick winter coats and heat produced by the food fermenting in their rumens.
Courtesy of Glacier National Park Photo Archives

devices when spread apart going downhill. Claws on their ankles also aid traction. Rough-surfaced pads project above their hoofs, in contrast to the concave hoofs of deer, antelope, and bighorn sheep.

These goats eat grasses, mountain mahogany, lichens, and even conifer needles. When snow falls they usually descend a short distance but stay near cliffs to eat the plants on snow-free faces.

If you saw the environment of these goats in winter it would be hard to believe that an area so cold, snow-covered, and barren will be alive in summer with scurrying pikas, rust- and cream-colored butterflies, and pink, blue, and yellow wildflowers. The next chapter will explore the causes of alpine tundra characteristics and those of mountain forests in more detail.

TWO

Solar Energy, Water, Wind, and Soil In Mountains

Most hikers realize that mountains have cold air, intense sunlight, and low oxygen. So they prepare for harsh weather by taking water, warm clothes, rain gear, a long-sleeved shirt, and sunburn cream. They camp at the trail head before the trip, then climb slowly to prevent altitude sickness. The careful ones avoid trampling the grass and flowers. As they pitch their tents to catch the morning sun, they may realize that heat and light from the sun are the most important factors in the mountain environment.

Life depends on this solar energy. You use some of your energy to climb to the alpine tundra, but everything has energy. Energy is a basic property of matter, either from location (such as a boulder perched on a hill) or from radiation, like that of the sun. Without solar energy plants could not make food by photosynthesis. This energy helps seeds germinate, seedlings grow, and plants flower and form seed. It causes winds that affect temperature and water supply. At high altitude solar energy is 50 percent stronger than it is at sea level in midsummer. It is so intense because there are fewer air, water, and dust particles to scatter the sunlight.

Do you ever wonder why the sky is dark blue on high mountains? The blue color of the sky darkens with altitude because there are fewer particles in the air. The sky is blue in the first place because the particles scatter more blue light, which is the shortest wavelength, than light of other wavelengths.

Light scattering also causes the *alpenglow*, the pink, orange, or gold tints you see on the highest peaks for a few minutes after sunset. When the sun is near the horizon the greater number of particles near the earth's surface scatter its light more than when the sun is high, completely scattering all colors except those at the red end of the spectrum. The sunset light from farther west causes the alpenglow, first from the direct light of the setting sun and then from reflection of the bright colors off any sunset clouds.

Solar energy is so intense mountain plants can even photosynthesize when the air is below freezing because the sun warms the leaves to a temperature above freezing. With the help of chlorophyll, the green pigment in leaves, plants use sunlight to make food by photosynthesis. In this process they make carbohydrates and oxygen from carbon dioxide and water.

RESPONSE TO DARK-LIGHT CYCLES

The daily timing of plant and animal activities to the rising and setting of the sun is especially important in mountains because nights are so much colder than days.

Dramatic changes in mountain plants occur in response to this dark-light cycle. The morning light that falls on a leaf activates hormones that cause water to flow into the guard cells on either side of the porelike stomata. The inflow of water opens the stomata as the inflow of air into a bicycle tube enlarges the hole in the center of the tube if it is stretched lengthwise while being inflated.

Similar changes in the water content of the cells at the base of leaves or petals open the leaves or flowers of some plants during the day and close them at night. The water content is altered by light-sensitive pigments, which change the number of potassium ions the cell membrane lets through. Lower water content relaxes the flowers or leaves, and higher water content stiffens them.

Just as you install storm windows and snow tires, plants prepare for the great reduction in the amount of radiation in winter. In the fall chlorophyll breaks down in the leaves of deciduous trees and shrubs, and much of the nutrients are reabsorbed into the branches and trunks. Also a photosensitive pigment triggers hormones that stop growth and cause the cells at the bases of the leaves to die. Another thing that happens before the leaves die is that lengthening nights cause leaves to produce more sugars. From the sugars some plants make red and purple pigments, the anthocyanins mentioned in the last chapter. In leaves without anthocyanins other pigments, called *carotenoids*, tint the leaf orange or yellow. All plants contain carotenoids, which are thought to protect cells from ultraviolet light, but chlorophyll masks their colors in summer.

Response to sunrise and sunset fine-tunes the biological clock, but the basic mechanism is unknown for most species. The fact that timing of activities can be transferred from one moth to another by exchanging brains indicates that brain cells must help keep time, at least for moths. Also, some reptiles, such as the tuatura lizard of New Zealand, have a third eye, or vestiges of one, that is known to set their biological clocks.

Scientists now think that winter depression may occur because a vestigial third eye is present in humans and senses the shortened days. They also believe this eye, the pineal body in the human brain, helps time our activities.

Reproductive activity may be associated with spring because of the increase in daylight. For example, the amount of singing done by male songbirds depends on the amount of the male sex hormone, testosterone, in their bodies. In the spring when they produce more of this hormone the amount of singing increases.

By annual timing to the sun's progression nature sees to it that animal babies are born when they have the best chance to live. Long-day breeders have short gestation periods, breed in late winter, and give birth in the spring. Short-day breeders are the large animals with long gestation periods. They breed in the fall and give birth the following spring or summer. Timing of birth is especially important for mountain animals because of the cold and the short growing season in their environment. Plants and animals also can time activities over spans of several years. Bamboos, for instance, flower at intervals of several years, which seems to have a protective function, at least for the species eaten by the giant panda. This animal, which lives a solitary life in the mountains of China's Szechuan and Kansu provinces at elevations between 6500 and 15,000 feet (most live in the Qin Ling Mountains), spends at least ten hours a day eating bamboo. The bamboo species it eats flowers only once every 120 years, so that when flowers do appear the animals are not used to eating them, and so many appear at once that they are not able to eat them all. Because bamboo dies after flowering, the flowering of this species introduces a time of famine for the giant panda.

TEMPERATURE

Any hiker who has had hypothermia and lived to tell about it knows that temperature is another critical factor for plants and animals, especially in mountains.

Luckily, the earth's atmosphere allows sunlight to filter through to heat the ground but keeps the heat from radiating back out by absorbing some of it. Thus the atmosphere functions as a warm, insulating blanket. Water vapor holds this heat in the air and prevents it from becoming too hot. High altitudes are cold because lower air pressure means that there are fewer air and water molecules to hold the heat.

This radiation of heat is not the same as the reflection of light. Have you ever had a headache or sore eyes from being out in the mountain sun? That happened because the sunlight is strong at high altitudes, and the two surfaces common in mountains—snow and light-colored rock—reflect the sunlight intensely. The fraction of sunlight reflected by such surfaces is called *albedo*. The emission of heat by an object after it has been heated or when heat is a part of the object is called *radiation*. Surfaces that radiate heat well also absorb it well. For example, fresh snow reflects 90 percent of visible light but absorbs and then emits almost all of the heat it receives.

Similarly, during the day white granite rock keeps the heat it absorbs but reflects back light and ultraviolet rays. At night it slowly radiates the heat back to the atmosphere. So, if you want to warm up on a cold evening, snuggle up to a boulder. Dark objects absorb and then radiate heat especially well. For example wells form in the snow around trees because the trees absorb heat and radiate it into the snow.

Did you ever wonder why it is hottest in the late afternoon? The reason is that early in the day the earth's surface absorbs solar energy faster than it reradiates it.

How well objects absorb and radiate heat affects temperatures. Plants and animals are distributed according to the lowest temperatures they can stand at the critical parts of their life cycles. At low temperatures lack of water affects them more than it does at high temperatures.

The thin air around mountains gives the sun greater heating power than it has in lowlands. Furthermore, mountains have little water vapor to prevent heat loss at night. This means that day-night temperatures differ more in mountains than elsewhere. Deserts have similar, but smaller, temperature differences.

Plants have adapted to the greater heating power of the sun in both places. Sunlit leaves can get as hot as 120°F on a warm day, so some trees, like oaks, have lobed leaves to increase the surface in contact with the air for cooling. To dissipate heat, leaves on the outside of the tree crowns are smaller, thicker, hairier, and more lobed than those on the inside.

Animals, on the other hand, cope with temperature changes by seeking or avoiding the sun, changing color, regulating circulation as described in the last chapter, and increasing or decreasing their metabolism. Animals in cool areas tend to be larger than those in warm regions since they have less surface area (skin) per pound to keep warm than smaller animals. They also have shorter legs and smaller noses and ears—areas that are hard to keep warm. Species of warm-blooded animals in cold, dry areas are paler than related species in warmer, wetter areas because white or pale skin keeps the heat of metabolism from radiating to the atmosphere rapidly. The warmth of the sun is too slight for these animals to obtain any advantage by being dark and thus able to absorb its heat. Cold-blooded animals, however, benefit from the warmth of the sun in cold climates. Insects in these areas, for example, are apt to be black so they can absorb heat.

WIND

Wind increases with elevation, making temperatures feel colder. Wind is caused by the interaction of the force of the earth's rotation with air-pressure differences resulting from temperature differences.

Prevailing winds increase as they are forced over or around mountains. Isolated peaks are windier; so are peaks with smooth rocks and little vegetation. A mountain range is most windy when it runs north and south and so is perpendicular to the prevailing winds. In the higher latitudes of both hemispheres (toward the poles) the prevailing winds are westerly; in middle latitudes they are easterly. Wind causes the most hostile conditions in mountain environments. It sweeps the snow off ridges and piles it elsewhere into deep drifts that don't melt until late summer.

Have you ever noticed that the wind at a campsite blows one way all day and the opposite direction at night? This happens because air circulation has a daily cycle. As the sun heats mountain slopes in the morning, the slopes heat the air near the ground. This warm air weighs less than the cool air, so it flows up the slopes. As it does so the air above the valleys sinks to replace the air that has moved up the slopes. This air then flows up the valleys to replace the risen air, producing a wind called the *valley wind* (Figure 2.1).

At night the air above the mountain slopes cools, sinks, and flows back down into the valleys and then down the valleys, producing the *mountain wind*. The air over the valleys that descends at night is often drier than the air that blew up the mountains since it may have shed its water in a thunderstorm as it rose. As a result, a big valley may be drier than the mountains

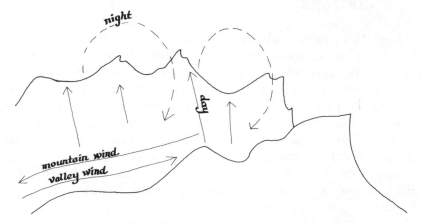

Figure 2.1. When the morning sun heats the air above mountains, it becomes lighter and rises. At the same time cooler air from below flows upslope to replace the warm air. Then at night, when the air above the mountains cools, it flows downslope.

above. Glaciers cool enough air so that a cold wind blows from them day and night, stunting the trees below them. On a mountain range near a coast, the land-sea breeze, similar to the mountain-valley wind circulation, intensifies the daily wind. The sea breeze flows from sea to land in the daytime and back again at night.

Wind blows away water vapor that collects outside leaf stomata in still air and thus dries leaves. But wind also benefits plants and animals by cooling them in hot weather and spreading pollen spores and winged or plumed seeds.

Some seeds are aerodynamically designed. For example, by using a wind tunnel a researcher learned that the design of a cone of a particular pine enables it to pick up more pollen grains of its own species than of others. Pine needles at the base of the cones also help direct the pollen. The air spirals along the cone axis in vortices and eddies toward the separations of the cone scales.

Wind also helps determine where plants grow by blowing snow off some slopes and into drifts on others. Since mountains receive moisture mostly as snow, its amount and timing are vital to plants and animals.

MOISTURE

Luckily for people who want to be near ski areas but don't like to shovel snow, mountains get more precipitation than neighboring lowlands. This is because the moisture in the warm air that rises over mountains condenses as it rises. When the air descends on the far side of the mountain, it has already lost its moisture on top, so this side gets less precipitation. The descending air is also warmed by the compression of higher air pressures at lower altitudes. So the lee side of a mountain range is not only drier but also warmer than the windward side. Because cool air holds less water vapor than does warm air, the highest slopes of mountains in the tropics are drier than middle altitudes. Elsewhere, precipitation usually increases with height because of the rise in strength of prevailing winds with elevation.

Dew, the moisture that condenses on your sleeping bag if you sleep without a tent, adds to precipitation. *Dew* is water vapor that has condensed from the air on the soil surface or has risen from the soil and then condensed. When it condenses dew warms the air; when it evaporates, it absorbs heat. Since heat is always absorbed when water vaporizes and given off when water condenses, water helps moderate temperatures.

Water also has several effects on plants and animals. It is able to dissolve substances like carbon dioxide and oxygen. It controls chemical reactions in plants and animals. Its surface tension helps water rise in the roots of plants by capillary action; in this process water molecules stick to each other and to the walls of the tubes within the plants. Water also provides insulation and stiffening.

Energy to move water through mountain plants comes from the evaporation of water molecules from the stomata in the leaves. This evaporation causes fluid in the guard cells to be more concentrated. Since water tends to flow from a solution of less concentration to one of greater concentration, it flows from the leaves into the stomata. Here it evaporates, a process called *transpiration*. Water then rises from the soil to replace that which has moved to the stomata.

Because of the high solar radiation and low humidity in their environment, plants on high mountains transpire more water vapor than those in lowlands. Mountain plants have adapted to this additional transpiration by developing features that help them resist water loss, such as hairy or waxy leaves. Extensive roots and water-storage structures also help the plants conserve water. Some, such as the pujas of South America, have stomata that open only at night. These plants take in carbon dioxide at night and turn it into malic acid, then in the daytime they remove carbon dioxide from malic acid by photosynthesis and use the CO_2 to make carbohydrates.

One plant that resists drought well is the creosote bush, which grows in deserts and on lower mountain slopes in the American Southwest and Mexico. Creosote bushes need only an inch or two of rain a year, so they can grow where it is too dry for cactus. After a rain new hairy leaves with a sticky surface emerge, making the bushes smell like creosote. Recently a researcher discovered that a group of creosote bushes in the Mohave Desert all spread by expanding in a great ring from the same bush, beginning 11,700 years ago. This suggests that creosote bushes are the oldest living plants in the world.

Mountains located in the great desert belts of the world are warmer and drier than most mountains, even though, like most mountains, they are colder, wetter, and windier than the lowlands around them. The characteristic weather of an environment is its climate and climate helps determine the kind of soil in a region. Because rock weathers slowly and plants grow slowly in the cold environment of mountains there is often little soil, but whatever soil there is helps determine what plants grow.

SOIL

Soil, which takes from 100 to 20,000 years to form, is composed of mineral particles, plant and animal material, water, and air. Long winters in mountains mean plants grow slowly and produce little humus, so soil takes longer to form than it does in lowlands. Freezing and thawing, dissolving of minerals by the weak carbonic acid of rainwater, and decay of organic material help form soil. Other factors are slope, rock type, and orientation to the sun and wind.

Scientists classify soils by their layers, called *horizons*, which are created when soil particles move downward. On the surface is the *O*, or *organic horizon*, a dark layer of organic material often called *humus*. Below it is the *A horizon*, which contains coarse-grained mineral soil and some organic material near the top. Below the A horizon the firm and fine-grained *B horizon* contains humus, clay, iron, and aluminum leached from above. The *C horizon* contains weathered rocks, with bedrock below it.

SOIL TYPES

Scientists use several systems to classify soil, some based only on soil form and structure and others based on climate and vegetation as well. A mountain contains several types of soil from its base to its summit.

Azonal soils, often occurring in high mountains, may have no horizons. These dry soils, containing little organic matter, often host lichens, mosses, and cushion plants.

Mountain meadow soils, up to 32 inches deep, occur where there is good drainage. The A horizon is fine-textured and dark brown or black, and the B horizon is coarse-textured and gray-brown.

Wet soils have a peaty A horizon on top of waterlogged B and C horizons. During the growing season the melting of frozen ground and the lack of drainage make these soils wet. These soils occur in bogs, wet forests, and Arctic and alpine tundra. Thick mosses, such as sphagnum, and a thick layer of decayed vegetation cover wet soils. Iron compounds cause them to be gray, black, or dark brown when waterlogged, but red near any air pockets.

Grassland soils grade into mountain meadow soils at higher elevations. They have different names according to the type of grass or the amount of precipitation. These soils lack the O layer. The black, deep, and spongy A layer contains earthworms and animal burrows. The C layer has weathered calcium-containing rocks that form a white hardpan impervious to water.

Podzols are the coarse-textured, well-drained soils in coniferous forests, some deciduous forests, and areas dominated by heaths. Minerals and clays are leached to the lower horizons in a process called *podzolization*, so the soils are acid. There is a thin O horizon, a black or grayish upper A horizon, and a pale lower A horizon. The leached minerals color the B horizon red-brown, dark brown, or black.

Brown forest soils occur in deciduous forests. The soil microorganisms and earthworms convert litter to soil rapidly, so these soils have little litter and a narrow O horizon. Organic matter stains the only soil horizon, the upper A, black.

Desert soils, sometimes called gray soils owing to their color, have little organic matter and faint horizons. In Mediterranean climates and in the humid subtropics iron oxides accumulate at the surface of several kinds of reddish soils. These soils are sometimes found in foothills, such as in California.

When the upper B horizon of tropical soils is exposed to air it hardens permanently to a red, bricklike material called *laterite*. Here, high temperatures cause fast decay of organic matter. Leaching by heavy rain removes silicates and metals and leaves clays, sand, and iron and aluminum oxides behind. The trees contain most of the soil nutrients. At higher elevations leaching changes these soils to the podzols found in temperate forests.

Figure 2.2.   Nitrogen-fixing bacteria on the roots of plants like alder convert nitrogen from the air into the nitrites and nitrates needed by plants.
Courtesy of Marie Guise.

NITROGEN

The most important nutrient tropical soils lack is nitrogen. Plants need it to make chlorophyll, enzymes, and proteins but are unable to use it unless it is in the form of nitrites, nitrates, or ammonium. Nitrites and nitrates are "fixed" from free nitrogen by nitrogen-fixing bacteria in nodes in the roots of certain plants, such as legumes like alder and lupine (Figure 2.2).

Nitrogen is just one of several nutrients plants need. Most nutrients occur as *ions*, electrically charged particles, in the soil water. Scientists divide nutrients into two groups, the *macronutrients* and *micronutrients*, according to the quantities the plant needs. Nitrogen, phosphorus, potassium, and calcium are in the macronutrient group.

pH

In addition to nutrients, the soil must have the proper balance of acidity and alkalinity, called *pH*, for plants to grow. They don't like vinegar any better than you do.

Acid rocks and decomposing organic matter produce acid soil. Evaporating water and decomposing alkaline rocks produce alkaline soil. A pH of 7 is neutral, neither acid nor base. A decrease of one point in pH means a tenfold increase in acidity. Plants prefer slightly acid water (a pH of 6.5).

When you put all the environmental factors together, what determines where species will live? The range of conditions organisms can stand is called their *tolerance*. When conditions approach the limit for one factor, being near the limit of another factor is likely to hurt the plant. For example, cold will do more damage to a wilting plant than it will if the plant has plenty of water (Figure 2.3).

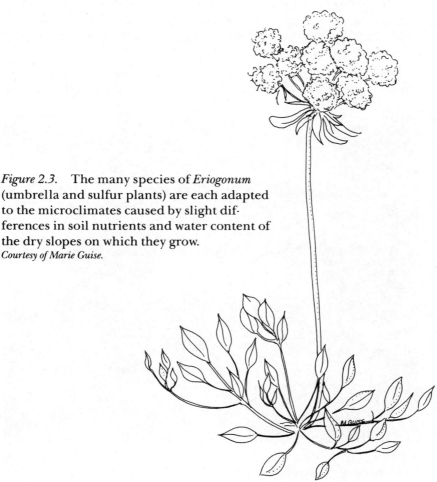

Figure 2.3.   The many species of *Eriogonum* (umbrella and sulfur plants) are each adapted to the microclimates caused by slight differences in soil nutrients and water content of the dry slopes on which they grow.
Courtesy of Marie Guise.

MICROCLIMATES

Plants vary in how well they tolerate differences in conditions in the same areas. Have you ever noticed the contrast between a mountain's forested north slopes and its grass-covered south slopes? North and south slopes differ greatly in temperature and moisture. These differences, called *microclimates,* are caused by differences in orientation to the sun and wind. Southwest slopes are the warmest and driest. Types of rock and soil nutrients present also affect what grows on certain slopes (Figure 2.4).

These vegetation differences can be dramatic, especially in semidesert mountain ranges. On the north slopes of the Owyhee Mountains of southwestern Idaho dense stands of Douglas fir grow, but on the south slopes only sagebrush and scattered clumps of mountain mahogany are found.

Another microclimate occurs on valley floors and in hollows and ravines. It is much colder at night on a valley floor than on

Figure 2.4.   Alpine tundra flowers seek shelter in the warm microclimate next to a krummholz tree.

Figure 2.5. Because it is 20° F warmer inside the large hollow stems of cow parsnip than it is in the cold, wet meadows where it grows, the stems can photosynthesize when it is too cold for the leaves to do so.

the slopes above. This is because wind blowing down from the mountains into the valleys at night pushes the warm air upward.

This wind also makes hollows as shallow as 3 feet damper and as much as 20°F colder than surrounding areas. Some of these frost pockets are subalpine wet meadows where plants with hollow stems, like cow parsnip, may grow. In the daytime it is 20°F warmer inside these stems than it is outside, allowing the insides of the stems to photosynthesize when it is too cold for the leaves to do so (Figure 2.5). Cow parsnip stems are purple, so probably contain anthocyanins, the heat-producing pigments, to make them even warmer.

Plants and animals show many other adaptations to the mountain climate. Some of these reduce their need for energy. For example, the needles of bristlecone pine trees, which grow at 12,000 feet in California's White Mountains, sometimes stay on the trees for 30 years. Long needle life means the trees spend little energy to make new needles.

Another example of an adaptation to cold climate is cone color. White fir (*Abies concolor*) may have yellow, green, or purple cones, but at high elevations it tends to have purple cones, which are colored by anthocyanins, the heat-producing pigments. In the North American West conifers growing at the highest elevations, except for limber pine, usually have purple cones.

FIRE

The harshest condition mountain plants and animals have to adapt to is recurring fire. If you have ever seen an area that has burned in a forest fire, you may know that some plants benefit from fire. This is because fire releases seeds and nutrients and kills harmful insects and fungi. Burning the soil speeds the growth of *chaparral*, a group of fire-adapted shrubs and plants. Fire also helps maintain grassland and shrub-covered areas, which benefits wildlife. Repeated burning causes fire-adapted species like lodgepole pine to dominate.

If fires are not recurring, burnable materials accumulate that can cause *crown fires*, which burn the whole forest. These can be prevented by allowing frequent fires to burn underbrush and deadwood. When conditions permit, foresters now allow lightning fires in wildernesses to burn, but so much material has built up that these fires tend to get out of control, especially in drought years.

AIR POLLUTION

Fire is not the only cause of widespread forest destruction. If you hike in some areas of the eastern United States you will see stands of trees that have died because of *acid rain*, which is caused by air pollution. (Rain becomes acid when it combines with sulfur dioxide or nitrous oxide). Acid rain has been blamed for the death of fish in the Adirondacks and in Sweden and the death of trees in the Appalachians and Germany's Black Forest, where a third of the trees have died. Because of acid rain, lakes in the Adirondacks are 40 times as acid as they were 50 years ago. While limestone buffers many lakes against acid rain by making the water alkaline, most other types of rock do not provide this benefit.

Researchers have found other alarming symptoms caused by acid precipitation. One discovered that since 1965 80 percent of the spruces on Camels Hump in the Green Mountains of Vermont have died. Another discovered that many Frazer firs and red spruces above the 6350-foot level on Mount Mitchell, the highest peak in the Appalachians, are losing needles and dying. Here the rain and mist contain lead, ozone, and excess nitrogen, and the rime ice is more acid than vinegar.

A study by the National Academy of Sciences found that 75 percent of the acid rain in the Northeast is caused by the release of sulfur compounds into the atmosphere, and two-thirds of this sulfur is emitted by coal-fired electrical plants. The researchers found that while in the air sulfur dioxide takes four days to oxidize, so it can travel thousands of miles. They also found that it kills mosses, lichens, and eastern white pines.

Factories have been around a long time, but acid rain is recent. Before the 1950s dusty, basic ash escaping from chimneys counteracted the acid in smoke but modern filters, which make the air clearer, take out this neutralizing ash. Acid rain is also caused by automobile exhaust, which contains large amounts of nitrogen oxides. Methods of removing sulfur and nitrogen oxides from smoke and exhaust are known but expensive.

Acid rain injures plants in several ways. Excess nitrogen makes trees grow in late fall when they should be dormant, so new growth freezes. Acid combines with nutrients in the soil to cause them to wash away and makes poisons that interfere with root-cell division. Acid also damages leaves and kills soil organisms. In lakes it kills fish, which suffocate from extra mucus, and the zooplankton the fish and water birds eat. Acid rain affects mountains more than it does lowlands because mountains get more precipitation, much of which comes from valley air that has risen and cooled.

Acid rain is not the only troubling thing in our atmosphere. We worry that freon from aerosol cans and nitrous oxide from smog and fertilizer may be destroying the ozone layer, which protects the earth from excess ultraviolet light. We also worry that the amount of carbon dioxide in the air has increased 17 percent since 1860. Photosynthesis and other natural processes take up half of the carbon dioxide that is emitted, but this amount is decreasing because humans are destroying the world's forests at the rate of 1 percent a year.

Carbon dioxide in the atmosphere reflects solar energy radiated by the earth back to earth again. Scientists worry that increased carbon dioxide in the air will make the earth warmer, a possibility called the *greenhouse effect*. If the earth warms, more water from the oceans will evaporate into water vapor, and that vapor will add to the greenhouse effect. When this vapor condenses into clouds it will cool the earth by blocking the sun's rays and causing precipitation, but not enough to counteract the warming.

Air pollution in an area varies with the weather: the temperature, cloud cover, humidity, precipitation, and wind speed. As you know, these factors can make a mountain trip either pleasant or miserable, so the next chapter continues our look at mountain environments with a discussion of their weather.

THREE

Mountain Weather

In order to adequately plan for the weather you are likely to encounter on a mountain trip, it is helpful to know something about meteorology, the science of weather. The weather comes from the interaction of world air circulation patterns with local conditions. Everyone has an idea of what weather is, but scientists define it as the temperature, moisture, air pressure, wind speed, and direction at a particular time.

WORLD AIR CIRCULATION

By heating the earth unevenly, the sun causes world air patterns that determine our weather. When sun-heated air rises at the equator and cooler air flows along the surface to replace it, the result is worldwide winds.

Air moves from regions of higher pressure to regions of low pressure. Because it is warmer and less dense than cold air, low-pressure air rises. This rising air pulls air along the surface from the high-pressure areas, where dense cold air is sinking.

You notice air pressure—created when air molecules collide with a surface—mostly when you have a flat tire, but air presses on you all the time. Air pressure is expressed as metric millibars or in inches of mercury within a tube. Low pressures occur at the center of storms, so we measure air pressure with barometers to help predict weather.

The heated air at the equator rises and spreads north and south. By the time this air reaches 30 degrees north and south latitudes most of it has cooled enough to sink back to the surface, where it is pulled back toward the equator by the air

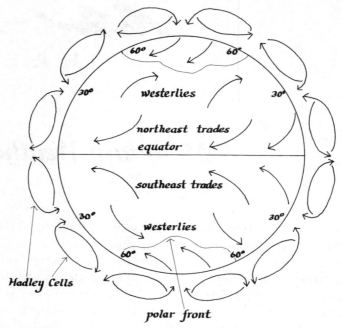

Figure 3.1. The fact that the sun heats the air above the equator and causes it to rise is a major cause of world wind circulation.

rising there. Some heated air continues aloft toward the poles, making two more rotations, called *Hadley cells* (Figure 3.1).

The earth's rotation deflects the winds blowing north and south in these cells with the *Coriolis force*. The Coriolis force exists because points near the pole travel only short distances in the same time that points at the equator travel the full distance around the earth. Thus as an object moves across the earth's surface the earth rotating beneath it bends the object's path into a curve. Because the earth rotates counterclockwise—from west to east—in the Northern Hemisphere, the Coriolis effect deflects objects moving toward the poles to the east and those moving away from the poles to the west. Note that if you are standing in the Northern Hemisphere the earth rotates counterclockwise, but in the Southern Hemisphere it rotates clockwise even though it is still rotating in the same direction, from west to east. In the Southern Hemisphere you are upside down relative to the Northern Hemisphere, so the effect is just as if you turn your wristwatch upside down—its hands go counterclockwise relative to your viewpoint.

You can illustrate the Coriolis effect yourself by quickly turning the lid of a cooking pot by its knob flat on a table while you draw lines on it with a marker with your other hand. First try to make a straight line from the knob to the outside, then try to draw a straight line from the outside to the center. Note the curved lines that result. (Scrub the lid right away afterward so the lines won't become permanent decorations.)

The air sinking in the first of the Hadley cells at 30 degrees is dry; it lost its moisture by precipitation as it rose above the equator. As the air sinks and becomes denser, higher pressure compresses it and warms it. Because warm air holds more moisture than cold air, it has less relative humidity. Relative humidity is the amount of water in the air, given as a percentage of the maximum it could hold at a particular temperature. Air with a low relative humidity has a drying effect on its surroundings. The sinking dry air causes great deserts, such as the Sahara, at 30 degrees north and south latitudes.

At the equator, where air converges and rises, rain falls frequently. The wind aloft blowing north and south is returned along the surface from 30 degrees latitude by the northeast and southeast trade winds. These winds, moving away from the poles, are deflected by the Coriolis force to blow *toward* the northwest and southwest, but they, like all winds, are named by the direction they blow *from* rather than the direction they blow *to*.

At 50 degrees, in a second zone of convergence, the prevailing "westerly" winds, blowing at an angle from the deserts, meet cold winds from the pole called *polar easterlies*. These converging winds rise in stormy areas known as the *polar fronts*. At the poles a second zone of sinking air creates high pressure and dryness.

A strong true westerly wind (blowing from west to east) caused by the earth's rotation blows everywhere on the globe. The Coriolis force diverts much of the air that rises at the equator and flows north and south from it into these westerlies. In the two bands in each hemisphere—at the equator and at 50 degrees, where this diversion occurs—the westerlies are so strong that they are called the *subtropical jet stream* and the *polar jet stream*.

The polar jet stream influences weather so much in the Northern Hemisphere that it is often referred to as *the* jet stream. Moisture in the warm tropical air meets cold polar air here and condenses, causing precipitation. The great temperature differences cause storm-producing spiral winds below the jet stream. The polar stream blows in a zigzag circle around the world that is often shown on weather maps because storms move along it.

In jet streams, wind blows in concentric tubes of air, with the highest wind speed, up to 200 miles per hour, in the center. The wind blows in pulses, much as water is released from a garden hose. The zigzags vary with the temperature differences between the poles and the equator, becoming larger and closer to the equator in winter.

In winter Asia is so cold and dry that air flows from high pressure over the land to low pressure over the warm Indian Ocean. Low pressure forming over the warm land as it is heated by the summer sun causes the winds to reverse direction. This rising air draws the cool, moist air from over the ocean across India, and together with the jet stream it causes the monsoon. During the monsoon, which occurs between June and September, India gets 150 to 300 inches of rain. That is why you don't want to plan to go on a Himalayan trek in summer.

CLIMATE

The monsoon is so important to the Himalayas that they are said to have a monsoon climate. As mentioned earlier, the term *climate* describes a region's long-term weather tendencies. Nearness to an ocean and the differences in solar radiation at varying latitudes determine climate.

Climate is also affected by *air masses*—large bodies of air with the same properties—that form when air stays over a uniform surface for several days or weeks. Air masses are named by kind, latitude, and location of formation. An example of an air mass is the Pacific High, which is maritime tropical. Climate zones are named for the air masses usually found there.

If you live on a coast you probably know that ocean currents affect coastal climates. Cold ocean currents along coasts cool the air so it can hold little water vapor. Thanks to a cold ocean current—and to its location in the rain shadow of the Andes and in the 30 degree south latitude desert belt—the Atacama Desert in Chile is one of the driest regions in the world.

Climate changes gradually over time. For the last 2.4 million years, the Northern Hemisphere has been experiencing an ice epoch with a number of different ice ages, or times when glaciers cover most temperate lands. During the present ice epoch the northern continents have been located near the North Pole.

What has caused the advances and retreats of ice within the present ice epoch? Most climatologists accept the astronomical theory proposed by Milan Milankovitch in the 1920s. This theory has three parts: a change in the earth's orbit from elliptical to nearly circular, with a cycle of 90,000 to 100,000 years; the change in the tilt of the earth's axis in relation to the sun, with a cycle of 41,000 years; and a change in the of the direction of the axis at the same tilt, called the wobble, with a cycle of 22,000 years. (To understand what the wobble is, grasp a pencil with your thumb and forefinger at its midpoint, then tilt the pencil. Now draw a circle by moving the pencil point but not your fingers. Note that while the tilt of the pencil stays the same throughout the circle, the direction does not.) These three changes affect the amount of solar radiation received by the earth.

The earth's axis tilts toward the sun less than it did 6000 years ago. Less tilt means that the distance of the northern and southern latitudes from the sun changes less in a year, so summers are cooler and winters warmer now than they were then. (To understand the effect of the tilt, which causes the seasons, take an apple, tilt it, and rotate it around a soccer or basketball, keeping the tilt the same. When the stem points away from the ball—the sun—it's winter in the northern hemisphere of the apple.) Owing to the tilt of the earth's axis, the equator receives two and one-half times more solar radiation than the poles do.

But have changes in the tilt, wobble, and shape of orbit been responsible for the whole ice epoch or just the ice ages within it? One theory explaining the cause of ice epochs is *continental drift*. Continental drift has two effects: It changes the location of the continents in relation to the poles and changes the circulation of the oceans. When continents are nearer to the poles they are colder. When straits form, allowing warm tropical water that evaporates readily to circulate farther north, snowfall increases. Increased snowfall in turn leads to the growth of glaciers.

FRONTAL STORMS

Because daily weather changes much faster than climate, you need to consider the weather before you plan a mountain trip. For example, spiral patterns of air called low-pressure areas bring frontal storms; spiral patterns called high-pressure areas bring good weather. You must also take into account mountain and valley winds discussed in Chapter 2 that cause thunderstorms.

Three things happen during a storm. Pressure becomes lower than that of the surrounding air. The air aloft rises, cooling and spreading out as it does so. Air on the surface flows toward the center of the low to replace the risen air. In the Northern Hemisphere, surface winds spiral counterclockwise (the same direction the earth is spinning), moving inward toward a low. Most of the curve of the path is caused by the frictional drag of the earth's surface on the air. In the Southern Hemisphere the spiral is clockwise.

In contrast, in a high-pressure area, which has pleasant weather, pressure rises above that of surrounding air. Air aloft converges, sinks, and warms as it descends. And air spreads outward along the surface from the center of the high.

You can imagine a high as a big doughnut of air: Air comes into the top of the doughnut hole, spirals counterclockwise (in the Northern Hemisphere) down the wall of the hole, and then continues in a spiral as it moves away from the hole at the bottom. In a low, air flows into the hole at the bottom, spirals up the sides, and exits at the top.

First proposed by a group of Norwegian researchers in 1918 to explain how storms operate, the *polar front theory* describes how fronts form where air masses meet. The group defined *fronts* as imaginary lines that separate air masses of different temperatures and densities that are moving in different directions.

According to the theory, the great differences between air masses keep them separate. When two air masses meet at a front, a storm system often forms, much as a wave forms on a lake or in the ocean. At first winds in each air mass blow parallel to each other, though in opposite directions. To understand how a storm begins, imagine that one of the air masses is a lake tipped up vertically and the other is the wind, blowing over

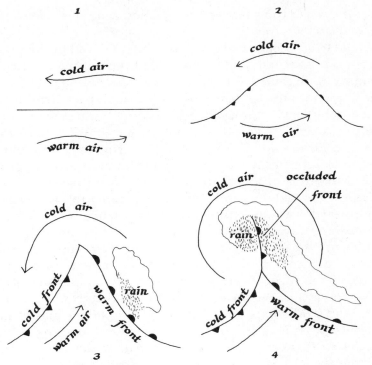

Figure 3.2. When cold air blows in a parallel but opposite direction to warm air, it pushes the warm air into a dimple that grows into a wave-shaped storm front.

it and making waves. The cold air pushes the warm air into a dimple that evolves into a large pointed wave (Figure 3.2).

Owing to the direction of wind flow, opposite sides of the wave have different characteristics: One side is the warm front, and the other is the cold front. At a warm front warm air rises over cold air that is moving away from it. At a cold front warm air rises over cold air that is moving toward it.

Theoretically, in a storm you see the warm front passing first, but this may not always happen. Here warm air overtakes and rides up over cold air at a low angle, then cools as it rises to higher altitudes, forms clouds, and loses its moisture as precipitation. As the front approaches, the wind shifts (winds in a warm front in the United States usually blow from the south). Precipitation is steady and gentle. As the warm front passes, the temperature rises and the wind direction again shifts. Air pressure along the front is lower than that of the surrounding air.

After the warm front passes, the weather sometimes clears until the cold front arrives.

A cold front occurs when cold air overtakes and pushes up the warm air at a steeper angle than that of the warm air rising at a warm front. Because of its steepness and speed—a cold front is much faster than a warm front—the cold front brings more violent weather than does the warm front, but it is over sooner. The wet, warm air ahead of a cold front contributes to thunderstorm formation. Air pressure falls during the front but rises as soon as it passes. Winds of a cold front are northwesterly in the Northern Hemisphere, but when the front passes, the temperature falls and the wind shifts. Fair weather follows, but may not appear for as much as 48 hours, depending on the location and the intensity and moisture content of the storm.

In Figure 3.2 notice that the cold front closes in on the warm front at the center of the storm wave. Here the cold front overtakes the warm front at ground level and pinches off the C-shaped crest of the wave. The warm air that was between the warm and cold fronts has disappeared, so the air masses meet and cause what is called an *occluded front*. Occluded fronts bring longer-lasting, more violent stormy weather than do warm or cold fronts.

The biggest weather problem you will usually encounter while hiking in mountains is thunderstorms. Whether they occur with frontal storms or independently, thunderstorms are common in summer. They evolve from small parcels of air that have been heated by the sun and are rising. For a thunderstorm to occur, the rising air parcels must be close enough together to avoid losing heat to the surrounding air. The moisture in the rising air condenses, forming clouds that continue to rise and become charged with electricity.

Thunderstorms develop in three stages. In the first stage moist air rises and condenses, forming cumulus clouds. As this air rises, it pulls in surface air, forming a strong updraft.

In the second stage the cloud has risen to 30,000 feet and its top has flattened out into an anvil shape as it reached a point of equilibrium in temperature with the surrounding air. When it begins to rain, a downdraft occurs, even though much of the air is still moving up. Turbulent winds and a sharp drop in temperature follow, often with hail, lightning, and thunder.

In the third stage the downdraft cools the surrounding air

and the updraft disappears. Then the rain lessens, the down-draft stops, and the clouds may disappear. Usually another thunderstorm cell has already formed to the side of the first storm by the time it has run its course. As the falling cool air spreads out it forces the warm air to the side of it upwards.

After the thunderstorm, sunlight shining through clouds can create rainbows. Rainbows form because raindrops act as prisms that split the light into colors. Each color of light in the water droplets travels at a different rate, so each is bent dif-ferently and thus separated. Because the drops are so small, an observer sees only one color from each drop.

LIGHTNING

Thunderstorms cause lightning, which is a danger in the mountains, both directly and as a cause of forest fires. Lightning may have a temperature five times that of the sun and a peak current of 35,000 amps. To produce lightning a cloud must be composed of ice crystals and rise high enough to gather strong positive and negative electric charges.

How do clouds become electrically charged? It may happen when the ice crystals form. According to this theory, water droplets freeze on the outside first. Before they freeze, the outsides gather positive charges, which migrate to colder water. The insides of the droplets retain the negative charges—the electrons. When the insides begin to freeze, the ice shells around each droplet burst, and the heavier, negatively charged water inside the droplets falls to the bases of the clouds.

Each lightning flash you see is really several separate strokes. That is why lightning appears to flicker. Each flash has two parts: a leader and one or more return strokes. In both, elec-trons move toward the ground. When the electrons first begin to flow they extend an electrically charged, or ionized, path, called the *step leader* from the cloud to the ground.

Then in the return stroke, electrons flow down each step of the path of the step leader, beginning with the step closest to the ground and working upward (Figure 3.3). However, most light-ning travels between clouds rather than between clouds and the ground. When clouds obscure the zigzag flash, you see sheet lightning.

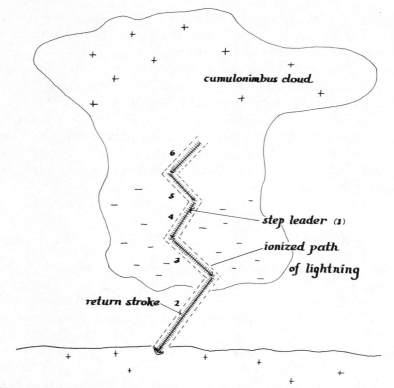

Figure 3.3.   In the return stroke of lightning, electrons flow down each step of the ionized path the step leader has made, beginning with the step closest to the ground and working upward.

The air suddenly expanding as it is heated by the lightning and compressing the air next to it makes the noise you hear as thunder. In five seconds return strokes of lightning travel 4800 miles and step leaders travel 240 miles, but the sound of thunder travels just one mile.

WHEN MOVING AIR MEETS A MOUNTAIN RANGE

Often when you drive along a highway near a mountain range you will see clouds and flashes of lightning on top of that range. That is because air is forced to rise over mountains, causing more clouds and precipitation than occurs in lowlands. As the air rises, its water vapor cools and condenses into clouds, which cool further as they continue rising. The moisture from the clouds then falls as rain or snow on top of the mountains. As the air, now dry, comes down again on the other side of the range, it is heated by the compression of the higher air pressure at lower altitudes.

Because the moisture has fallen on the side of the mountains toward the wind, a dry area called the *rain shadow* occurs on the lee side. Rain shadow causes many of the world's deserts, such as the Great Basin in North America. In contrast, the wettest places in the world are on the sides of coastal mountains that face the prevailing winds; here winds over the ocean pick up moisture from it. The windward side of one such mountain, Mount Waialeale in Hawaii, receives 486 inches of rain per year, the highest annual average in the world.

Warm moist air that blows against the mountains in winter, rising over them and becoming even warmer as it descends on the lee side, causes the warm wind called the *chinook* or *foehn*. Often the chinook displaces much colder air, creating a dramatic temperature rise in just a few minutes.

The effect of mountains on a particular parcel of air depends on several factors. One is the air parcel's stability. When a parcel of air keeps on rising by itself after something causes it to rise, it is considered unstable. If you have taken a ride in a hot-air balloon you have risen under a parcel of unstable air, which is unstable because it has been heated. Stability depends on the density of a mass of air compared with that of the surrounding air, and density depends on temperature. Unstable air is less dense (warmer) than the air around it, so it is lighter and rises. Stable air is denser (colder) than the air around it, so it sinks.

Air flows across mountains in two major wind patterns, known as *rotors* and *lee waves*. Rotors, eddies formed by the wind as it blows off the top of the mountains, create roll-shaped cumulus clouds near the top of the mountains. Lee waves, which are more common, may occur repeatedly on the lee side of the mountain for many miles, with each succeeding wave smaller than the preceding one.

Hikers often notice flattened, lens-shaped clouds, called *lenticular clouds*, above mountains. These clouds form at the tops of the lee waves when air rising over the mountain cools just enough to condense at the flattened bottom of the cloud. Lenticular clouds stay put even though the winds blow through them. The water vapor condenses, stays a cloud for a short distance, and then evaporates as the air rises higher. A lenticular cloud may form at the top of each of several successive lee waves. These clouds often signal that the air is becoming unstable and a storm will follow.

Storm winds and prevailing winds interact with the local daily air circulation of mountain and valley winds discussed in Chapter 2. When air at the bottom of a valley is colder than the air above, it keeps a general wind out of the valley. When the general wind blows in the same direction as a mountain or valley wind, the wind intensifies.

Mountain–valley winds and the rugged topography make wind in mountains so turbulent that in summer backcountry pilots fly only morning and evening, the least windy times. *Turbulence* is fluctuation in air speed or pressure caused when air flows past unevenly heated areas or a projecting object.

Two common types of turbulence are caused by air rising from unevenly heated slopes and by wind blowing through a channel, such as a mountain pass. Another type is downdraft, which is often caused by thunderstorms. Because downdrafts are common, mountain flying is dangerous except for experts. When downdrafts hit the ground they spread out in all directions in a phenomenon known as a *microburst*. As a result, a pilot flying through a downdraft may encounter a headwind one instant and a tailwind the next, a condition called wind shear. (There are other causes of wind shear, such as cold fronts.)

CLOUDS

Meteorologists use several measurements to help them predict weather. Among these tools are wind direction and speed, barometric pressure, and cloud type. To understand cloud types, you must first understand that clouds are collections of water droplets or ice crystals. They form because cool air holds less water vapor than does warm air, so as warm air rises and cools it becomes saturated with water vapor. In other words, the air holds as much water vapor as it is possible for it to hold. At saturation the vapor condenses on minute particles of dust into water droplets, creating clouds. If it is cold enough, the droplets condense as ice crystals, but if there are no particles to condense on, the droplets can stay liquid even below freezing.

Clouds are classified by height, appearance, and composition. But even when you have learned the types of clouds it is difficult to tell them apart.

The highest clouds, *cirrus, cirrocumulus*, and *cirrostratus*, found at elevations of from 16,500 to 45,000 feet, are usually made of ice crystals. Their presence often means that a storm is on its way (Figure 3.4).

When cirrus clouds form above 20,000 feet, they are wispy and filmy and may include plumes called mare's tails. One way cirrus clouds form is when there is an updraft, caused by a warm front, in the distance.

Cirrocumulus clouds may contain globular white patches or a pattern of waves or ripples. Rows of these clouds form the familiar mackerel sky, which may mean rain within 24 to 48 hours. Cirrocumulus clouds always appear with other high clouds but are the least common.

Cirrostratus clouds are closer to the front than cirrus clouds. They form halos around the sun and moon and a thin, filmy haze that may cover the entire sky. Because when this happens objects still cast shadows, these clouds resemble smog.

When an air mass lifts, two kinds of clouds, *altostratus* and *altocumulus*, form at midelevations (from 6500 to 20,000 feet).

Figure 3.4. Cirrus clouds, which form only above 16,500 feet and are made of ice crystals, often mean that a storm is on the way.

These clouds often bring light rain or snow just before a storm front, but they may also occur with thunderstorms. Altostratus clouds have blue or gray fibrous layers, and when they blanket the sky, the sun shines through only dimly. Over time they often darken, bringing rain or snow. These clouds precede a front, usually a warm one, but are closer to it than are cirrostratus clouds. Altocumulus clouds, which are usually larger than altostratus, may resemble rows of sheep or cotton balls.

Three kinds of low clouds, *stratocumulus, stratus*, and *nimbostratus*, extend from the surface to 6500 feet. Stratocumulus clouds gather in soft gray rolls or waves that may form groups, join together, or cover the sky. They bring light drizzle·or snow showers ahead of and behind fronts.

The rain or snow clouds called nimbostratus move along in the heart of frontal storms. They are ragged, thick, and dark and develop from altostratus clouds that descend.

Stratus clouds make a uniform layer that may be thousands of feet thick. They often form below a temperature inversion, producing drizzle or snow flurries. The sun usually evaporates stratus clouds, so they are a sign of fair weather (Figure 3.5). When they touch the ground, they are called fog. Fog can form in several ways. It can occur when the ground cools at night,

Figure 3.5.   After a storm in Grand Teton National Park, Wyoming, the sun is beginning to evaporate stratus clouds.

cooling the surrounding air enough for the water vapor to condense. Fog also occurs when moist air condenses as it moves up a mountain or blows over a cold surface, and when cold air condenses as it moves over warm water. When fog droplets hit the ground, they are called *fog drip*, which may exceed the rainfall. Finely divided surfaces like conifer needles rake out more drip from the fog than do smooth, unbroken surfaces.

A fourth type of cloud, *cumulus*, begins close to the ground and grows to great heights. Resembling handfuls of cotton with flat bases, cumulus clouds often turn into stratocumulus or altocumulus clouds in the late afternoon and then disappear at night. If you notice cumulus clouds growing tall in the morning, you can expect afternoon thunderstorms. These clouds form when parcels of air are warmed by the sun and rise to where it is cool enough to condense the water in them.

When cumulus clouds grow tall they become *cumulonimbus* clouds. These huge clouds have dark, ragged bases and flattened tops called anvils because they resemble the blacksmith's anvil. They bring thunderstorms with heavy rain or hail. These storms are more violent when cumulonimbus clouds occur ahead of a cold front than when they appear independently. The taller the cloud, the worse the storm.

It is hard to predict whether it will rain when you hike even if you know something about the principles of weather. That is because thundershowers form and dissipate within a few hours, so the day's weather depends on what the clouds do in the morning.

WEATHER FORECASTING

You can buy cardboard weather wheels to help you forecast weather from clouds and wind direction. Adding barometric readings converted for altitude will make your forecasts more accurate. Even today government forecasts of the weather for more than five days are no more accurate than they were in the past, but government forecasts for fewer than five days are up to 80 percent accurate.

You can generally tell if a frontal storm or thunderstorm is coming by observing clouds and weather indicators. If you see cirrus clouds in the west and if northerly or westerly winds stop, there will probably be a storm in 24 to 48 hours. Cirrocumulus or cirrostratus clouds, and in the Northern Hemisphere a shift to southerly or northeasterly winds, warn of a storm in 12 to 24 hours. A shift in wind direction, a steady fall in the barometer, and low, thick, and dark clouds coming from the south or southeast indicate immediate rain or snow. Towering cumulonimbus clouds warn of thunderstorms. In the Northern Hemisphere a wind shift north or west and a rising barometer mean it will clear up.

PRECIPITATION

You may wonder how clouds cause precipitation. *Raindrops* form in two ways. Sometimes ice crystals appear, grow heavy enough to fall, and turn into raindrops on their way down when they hit warmer air. Water droplets that are below 32°F but still liquid will freeze on contact with anything crystalline, so if the temperature is below 14°F ice crystals will form first. Other times raindrops form when water droplets collide and become large enough to fall.

Water vapor can condense or become liquid without forming clouds. Dew, for example, forms in much the same way as fog. Sometimes it forms when a cold surface causes water vapor in still air to condense on that surface the way water vapor given off by your body at night condenses on the walls of your tent. Dew also forms when water vapor in the soil migrates upward and then condenses.

Another form of condensation is *hoarfrost*. These needlelike crystals form in below-freezing temperatures, when water vapor in still air freezes onto a surface.

Still another form is *rime*. On mountain ridges, when it is below freezing and windy, supercooled water droplets freeze as rime onto objects on the side toward the wind. Rime has no real crystalline pattern. On the windward side of trees and cliff faces it makes coatings several inches thick. Rime and wind-driven snow often cover all sides of trees in exposed places. At high altitudes rime can be a major source of precipitation.

A form of frozen precipitation, but one that falls from clouds, is *hail*. Common during thunderstorms in mountains, hail forms only in cumulonimbus clouds, where repeated updrafts deposit layers of ice on ice crystals. Hailstones may reach 5 inches across, but they are usually less than one half inch.

Another type of precipitation, *freezing rain*, usually occurs only in winter. It falls when the ground and the air a few inches above it are below freezing but the air farther up is above freezing. This causes the raindrops to freeze when they hit the ground. Before they hit the ground, raindrops may freeze into hollow ice shells often called sleet, now officially termed ice pellets.

SNOW

Skiers will agree that the most important form of frozen precipitation in mountains is snow. Even where no one skis, snow brings life to mountains because it brings year-round moisture to places where there is little summer rain.

Snow forms when ice crystals that become heavy enough to fall meet with supercooled droplets on the way down. The droplets freeze onto the ice crystals, and if the air is cold enough they fall to the ground as snowflakes.

Because freezing water molecules release heat, snow often forms branching flakes; the branching separates and cools the molecules so more of them can freeze. Snowflakes come in many shapes: columns, the familiar stars, and more. All are hexagonal since the crystalline form of ice is a hexagon. As everyone knows, no two snowflakes are exactly the same shape.

Different types of snowflakes fall at different temperatures. Plates and stars form above 27°F, needles between 23° and 27°F, and hollow columns between 18° and 23°F. Below 18°F the snow is fernlike, columnar, or hexagonal. Newly fallen needle-shaped snowflakes are likely to avalanche. A thick layer of rime-covered snowflakes called *graupel* is more likely to avalanche, because the rounded grains of graupel don't stick together well.

Once snowflakes fall they gradually lose their branching arms and become rounded grains by a process called *metamorphism*. Metamorphism can be of three types.

The first type, *equi-temperature metamorphism*, occurs when the layers of snow are the same temperature. Squeezed by the pressure of adjoining flakes, water molecules move from one part of the crystal to another. This squeezing forms ice bridges between the snow grains. These bridges melt in spring during the daytime, loosening the snow grains into the skiers' corn snow.

When the layers of snow are different temperatures, the second type of metamorphism—*temperature-gradient metamorphism*—takes place. This time water vapor migrates from warm, moist snow to dry, cold snow and condenses on the nearest side of an adjacent cold crystal. On the far side of that crystal an equal amount of ice evaporates and then freezes to the next crystal. This process develops flattish crystals, called *depth hoar*, that are larger than snowflakes. Resembling a layer of sequins or flattened ball bearings, depth hoar is more slippery than other snow crystals, and it causes avalanches. When these crystals form on the snow surface they are called *surface hoar*.

The third type of metamorphism, which results from increasing pressure, occurs as succeeding layers of snow cover snowfields or glaciers. This process, called *firnification*, eliminates the air spaces in the snow, resulting first in compacted snow called *firn* and finally in *glacial* ice.

These air spaces scatter light differently than does the ice or snow alone, so they determine the colors seen in ice and snow. Snow and ice scatter all wavelengths of light equally, but they absorb red light, causing a bluish color. Because it has more air spaces, snow scatters light more than ice, so the blue color appears at shallower depths in snow than it does in ice.

AVALANCHES

Both metamorphosed snow and freshly fallen snow can avalanche and suffocate you in the backcountry. The danger of avalanche in old snow depends on the type of metamorphism taking place, the temperature patterns when the different layers of snow fell, and the temperatures after they fell (Figure 3.6).

The likelihood of an avalanche depends partly on the type of snow that has fallen. Dry snow contains so much air that it can avalanche with high speed and turbulence. Freshly fallen snow often slides in little sluffs during a storm; 80 percent of avalanches happen during or just after a storm. Fresh-snow avalanches are more likely when the snow is deep or wet, when it falls on surface hoar, or when wet snow follows prolonged cold weather. Snow containing a moderate amount of water sticks

Figure 3.6.   Avalanches are most likely when snow is fresh and very dry or very wet.
Courtesy of U.S. Forest Service, Intermountain Region.

together well, so avalanches are more likely when snow is very dry or very wet.

Avalanches that happen when the snow has stuck together through metamorphosis and then breaks loose as a unit are less frequent but more dangerous. Called *slab avalanches*, they occur more often when there are layers of depth hoar or ice within the snow.

Certain types of slopes have more avalanches than others: lee slopes (slopes that face away from the wind), convex slopes, or moderately steep slopes. Windward slopes or slopes steeper than 45° don't avalanche as often. Snow often begins to slide in bowls and gullies or at the edges of cornices, the overhanging snowbanks on the lee side of ridges.

Even with knowledge of the types of slopes and conditions that cause avalanches it is difficult to tell if a particular slope will avalanche. Therefore it is safest to stay out of the backcountry when the risk of an avalanche is high. Even at times of low risk, wear an avalanche radio device, always have someone with you, and use your route-finding skills and common sense.

After all this talk about snow you may wonder about how it affects mountains when it becomes a glacier. Because the work of a glacier depends partly on the kind of material it sculptures and how that rock was formed, the next two chapters give information about the geology of mountains.

FOUR

Mountain Building and Plate Tectonics

All mountains are one of four types: volcanic, folded, erosional, or fault block. All four are related to large-scale earth movements, which geologists explain in terms of *plate tectonics*. A revolution in the ideas of how mountains form occurred in the 1960s and 1970s when the theory of plate tectonics was proposed. What is this theory? It says that the earth's *lithosphere* (outside rigid layer) is divided into rigid sections, called *plates*, that move about over a plastic portion of the earth's mantle, called the *asthenosphere* (Figure 4.1). The earth's crust is divided into seven large plates: North American, South American,

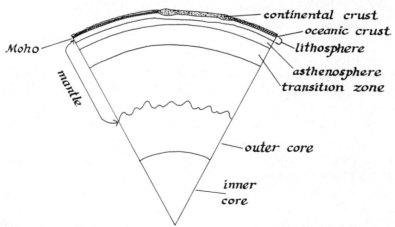

Figure 4.1. Continental and oceanic crust ride upon the rigid part of the mantle, called the lithosphere. The lithosphere and crust compose the plates.

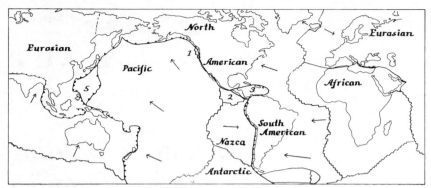

Figure 4.2.   The earth's crust is divided into large rigid plates that move about over a plastic layer called the asthenosphere.

Nazca, Antarctic, African, Eurasian and Indian-Australian as well as several smaller plates. The major plates are illustrated in Figure 4.2. Less tectonic activity occurs in the centers of plates, but at their borders, where plates collide, new rock is formed, plates grow, and mountains rise.

The theory says that plates may have three kinds of boundaries: *divergent, convergent* and *transcurrent*. At divergent boundaries plates move away from each, creating *spreading zones*, also called ocean ridges. At convergent boundaries they come together, forming *subduction zones*, also called ocean trenches. At transcurrent boundaries they slide past each other along *transform faults*. We will discuss each of these boundaries.

You can get an idea of the movement of plates if you examine a common "15 puzzle," a set of 15 square tiles in a single layer in a small box. These tiles can slide past each other, just as the plates do along transform faults. Imagine that the box is curved and that you can push a whole row of tiles under another row, much as one plate pushes below another at a subduction zone. Imagine also that as you push the tiles under, softened plastic comes up in the gap that has been left in the center of the box. This plastic solidifies into a new row of tiles, in much the same way that basalt rises and solidifies at a spreading zone.

The proponents of plate tectonics found several ways to prove that plate motion had occurred: paleomagnetism, the realization that earthquakes are more frequent along plate boundaries and the discovery of ocean ridges. Researchers who studied and mapped the ocean floors found these ridges, chains of high submarine mountains, in the Pacific and in the middle of the Atlantic Ocean. They observed basaltic lava being extruded from these ridges. As the researchers moved away from the ridges, they found thicker and older sediments on the ocean floor, indicating that new ocean floor was being formed at the ridge and gradually being carried away from it. This was evidence that plates were diverging and the sea floor spreading.

PALEOMAGNETISM

Other evidence for sea-floor spreading comes from research on the paleomagnetism of the ocean floors. *Paleomagnetism* in a rock is the direction in which its magnetic particles are aligned. When rocks solidify and when sediment is deposited the iron-bearing particles within them are lined up by the magnetism of the earth's poles. This lineup on the ocean floors shows where its rocks were formed.

Measuring paleomagnetism has shown that the direction of the north and south magnetic poles has reversed many times in the earth's history. A reversal occurs when the magnetic force within the earth weakens and then builds back up with polarity in the opposite direction.

Earth's magnetism has had hundreds of reversals in the last 3.5 billion years of the 4.6-billion-year history of the earth. These reversals have caused a pattern of magnetic stripes in the readings taken from the ocean floor, each stripe with magnetism in the opposite direction to the ones adjacent to it. (See Figure 4.3). When basalt erupts from a mid-ocean ridge it is injected into the narrow crack of the spreading zone and cools there. Then as the sea floor spreads farther apart, this basalt is split roughly down the middle, each half being carried away in opposite directions, so the magnetic patterns on a spreading sea floor mirror each other.

Why does the earth have magnetic poles? Geophysicists believe that the circulation of liquid iron within the earth's core generates electricity, which sets up a magnetic field. This field makes the earth act as though there were a big bar magnet along its axis.

Paleomagnetism also is evidence for *continental drift*, and continental drift shows that the plates have moved. In the early

1900s, geologists such as Alfred Wegener proposed that the continents had drifted, but no American geophysicists took him seriously because there was no proof. Wegener believed the continents were once all clustered together in a supercontinent he called *Pangaea.* If you look at a globe you can see how Africa and South America could have fitted together. As late as the 1950s textbooks described Wegener as mistaken. But today his ideas are accepted.

Researchers now believe that the southern continents and much of North America were the core of Pangaea with Europe and Asia in pieces at its edges. About 225 million years ago Pangaea began to drift apart.

Paleomagnetism can show continental drift has occurred because the magnetic particles are aligned both horizontally and vertically. The vertical magnetic inclination within a rock shows the latitude at which the rock formed and the direction of the magnetic poles at the time it formed. To understand this note that the needle of your compass points horizontally toward the magnetic north pole. If your compass needle could rotate vertically as well as horizontally it would point straight down at the poles, at an angle at 45° degrees latitude and horizontally at the equator because it follows the lines of magnetic force of the earth's magnetic field. These magnetic patterns, called fossil magnetism, make it appear that the poles of the earth have wandered, but instead geologists assume the continents have wandered.

Additional support for the theory that the continents have drifted comes from examining rock and fossil types, ancient glaciers, and the shapes of the continental shelves. For example, rock strata on the east coast of Brazil and west coast of Africa match in age and composition. In addition, scratches on rocks in the Sahara show that they were once near enough to one of the poles to have been abraded by glaciers. Also, coal found in Antarctica could have formed only in a warm climate.

PLATE MOTION

So, the plates have carried the continents around, but what makes them move? Geologists think the forces driving the plates are related to the structure of the earth (Figure 4.1). The plates are pieces of the earth's lithosphere, and the *oceanic crust* and the *continental crust* or continents ride on top of it. Below the lithosphere is the asthenosphere, or low-velocity zone, 120 miles of solid rock that is so hot (2500°F) it is plastic (not liquid). Its plasticity was discovered by studying the way earthquake waves travel through the earth and noting they travel at low velocity in this zone.

About 1800 miles below the asthenosphere the mantle is a solid layer. Heat from compression, radioactive decay, and residual heat from gravitational forces that formed the earth makes all layers of the *mantle* hot. Researchers have recently discovered that the core, which is below the mantle, has high peaks and deep valleys on its outer surface and is not a smooth sphere. The core is thought to be of nickel and iron; its outer 1350 miles are molten. (It would have to be molten in order to generate the earth's magnetic field.) Geologists think that it formed when gravitational heating caused the earth to heat up so much that the iron in it melted and sank to the center of the planet.

Several hypotheses as to what drives the plates have been advanced. According to the most accepted one today the plastic layer in the mantle circulates, rising at ocean ridges, spreading away from them, and sinking at subduction zones. This current drags the plates along. In another theory magma from an ocean ridge starts the plates on either side moving outward and the moving mantle underneath carries them along. In a third, gravity drives the plates. In this system subduction drives the plates because a subducting plate will sink of its own weight once it reaches the asthenosphere. Or the cause may be a combination of forces.

GAPS IN PLATE TECTONIC THEORY

The present theory of plate tectonics fails to explain all features of the plates. Precambrian rocks on the continents may have come from a different type of plate system than that operating today. They may have resulted from small platforms of granite solidifying and then joining quietly together. Groups of volcanic islands may then have joined the granite with little compression and folding. Some think that during the first two billion years no subduction occurred. At that time the mantle may have been so hot it melted plates as soon as they started to subduct, so the high pressure needed for mountain building didn't develop. Or maybe the colliding plates were too small to cause subduction.

The small granite platforms and volcanic islands collected together into the areas of ancient rock called *cratons*. These cratons appear to have been a mosaic of small plates formed by a long series of Precambrian-era collisions.

SPREADING CENTERS

But today we do have plates, which interact with each other at the three kinds of plate boundaries. At a midocean ridge or spreading center, two plates are moving apart. A ridge of mountains, shallow earthquakes, high heat flow, and upwelling basaltic lava mark a spreading center. This lava forms new oceanic crust at the center of the ridge. (See Figure 4.3.) When the emerging lava hits cold ocean water a crust forms, but the hot interior breaks through and squirts out, forming blobs of lava rock called *pillow lava*. Slower-moving ridges, like the mid-Atlantic, have a *rift valley* between the faults running along their centers.

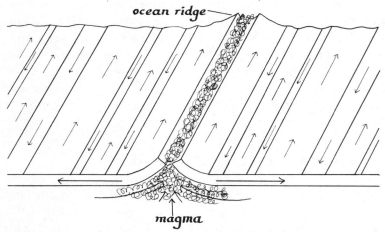

Figure 4.3. Lava upwelling at an ocean ridge spreads out on either side as the two plates move away from each other. Because the magnetic field of the earth has reversed many times, the direction of magnetism in the cooled lava forms a striped pattern that is identical on either side of the ridge.

Sections of an ocean ridge are offset and are connected by faults called transform faults. This makes the pattern of an ocean ridge on a map resemble stair steps. Along these faults, the plates slide past each other just as sliding doors pass each other.

Spreading centers can form within continents as well as in the ocean. When they form in a continent, they cause a new ocean to grow within it. The process is beginning in Africa's Great Rift Valley.

You may wonder how you can tell where a continent is developing a spreading center. The process is so slow that it is difficult to detect. Furthermore, rifting sometimes starts and then stops, as it did after the Oslo Rift formed in Norway. Rifting begins with uplifting of the mantle, which causes heating and stretching. Fault blocks tilt over a wide zone. After the cracks become faults, the block of rock between them sinks, forming a *graben* or depression in the earth. Next the crust ruptures and basaltic lava flows, as has already happened in Africa's Great Rift Valley. If the process continues, seawater floods the rift valley and a new ocean begins. The spreading center may extend itself gradually, opening like a zipper at either or both ends.

HOT SPOTS

Hot spots, places where columns of magma or molten rock a few hundred miles in diameter are upwelling from the mantle, also cause island chains, isolated continental volcanoes, and possibly, volcanoes along ocean ridges. A hot spot makes an island chain by creating a volcano as a plate moves over it. The moving plate, like a conveyor belt, carries the volcano away from the hot spot. As it does so a new volcano rises over the hot spot. There are more than 120 hot spots, of varying activity, in the world.

Researchers discovered that lava from hot spots has unusually high amounts of radioactive isotopes. They believe that hot spots bring heat from radioactive decay deep in the earth to the surface. In their theory, the asthenosphere, constantly cooled by the lithosphere above, keeps solidifying and sticking to the lithosphere. The heat from the hot spots keeps the asthenosphere plastic, allowing the plates to move.

Some think that a hot spot created the fault block mountains of the Great Basin, an area including Nevada and part of adjacent states, but there are several other ideas of the cause, such as that the area is a failed rift. Other geologists think that the Pacific plate stretched the area as it traveled northwest along the San Andreas fault, dragging the edge of the continent with it. In the Great Basin north-south fault block mountains alternate with narrow basins. The region has unusually high heat flow and an unusually thin crust. It also has many hot springs and earthquakes and two hot spots, the calderas of Yellowstone and Long Valley (near Mono Lake, California). Whatever the cause, the earth's crust in the Great Basin has been stretched from east to west to twice its former length. So far it has expanded 40 miles in 25 million years. The stretching moved the Sierra well west of where it formed.

SUBDUCTION ZONES

Most ocean ridges are several thousand miles from the second kind of plate boundary, the subduction zone or ocean trench. At subduction zones plates move toward each other and the edge of one plate subducts (slides under) the edge of another, similar to the way your shovel slides under the edge of a large rock in your garden as you get ready to pry it up and remove it (Figure 4.4). Subduction zones have deep earthquakes, abnormally low heat flow, and volcanoes that erupt lava.

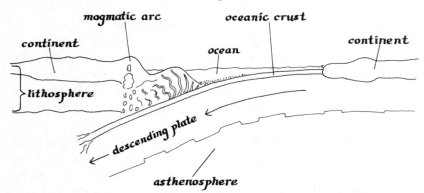

Figure 4.4. Water helps to melt some of a plate that has been heated by the friction of subducting under another plate. This magma rises into an arc of volcanoes or plutons on the overlying plate.

Evidence that subduction occurs comes from plotting the depth of earthquakes. Many earthquakes take place along the trenches in *Benioff zones*, zones that slant under the island arc or continent. In them the deepest earthquakes take place closest to the land. Most of the world's intermediate and deep earthquakes and andesitic volcanoes have arisen along trenches, especially around the Pacific Ocean in a zone nicknamed the Ring of Fire.

Volcanoes are one result of subduction. As the plate descends the subduction zone, it carries ocean water. The water helps some of the rock of the descending plate, which is heated by friction, to melt. This melted rock, or magma, rises and forms a chain of volcanoes on the overlying plate. In one type of subduction, a plate subducting under another plate in the ocean, the rising volcanoes create a chain of islands called an island arc. The lava of these volcanoes is stiff, either andesite or rhyolite, rather than the runny basalt squeezed out at midocean ridges. (When a plate subducts under a continent, it causes an arc of volcanoes on land.)

If the subduction zone is steep, the distance between it and the island arc or chain of volcanoes is short. If the zone is gently sloping the volcanoes are farther away or absent.

A second type of subduction occurs when one of the plates moving together carries a continent and that continent reaches the subduction zone of a plate that is not carrying a continent. The continent cannot be dragged down the subduction zone because it is of less dense (lighter) material, so instead the second plate will start subducting under the plate carrying the continent.

When a plate sinks under a continent, sediments washed from the continent collect in the ocean offshore and are dragged down the trench by the downgoing plate. In addition, the descending plate scrapes off sediment from the continent and carries it down the trench. Each new layer of sediment is "understuffed" below the previous one, forming a folded collection. This piled-up rock may form another set of islands, right along the trench.

The crust is thickened by the intrusion of magma and compression by opposing horizontal forces. The intruding magma may create volcanoes or it may stay below the surface and cool there into a *pluton* of granite or related rock. Plutons also occur in continental collision.

CONTINENTAL COLLISION

Collision begins when two plates carrying continents move together and the ocean between the continents lacks a spreading center but contains a subduction zone along the border of one continent. When continents collide they crumple up into a high mountain range. Ocean sediments, pillow lava, and pieces of the oceanic crust and the mantle are caught between the continents and uplifted into these mountains, marking the former subduction zone.

During the collision one continent will try to go down the subduction zone. As stated earlier, continental rocks are lighter than the mantle, too light to subduct, so the descending continent will stop moving. The attempted subduction will cause volcanoes and the upwelling of magma on the other continent.

An example of continental collision is the collision of Africa with Europe. Italy and the Matterhorn are part of the moving African plate. Before the ocean between the continents vanished, the Eurasian plate was being subducted, so the African plate is thrusting *over* the Eurasian. In contrast, the Indian plate, the moving plate under the Himalayas, began thrusting *under* the Eurasian plate 55 million years ago, perhaps because the Indian plate is thicker and harder than the Eurasian. India is still moving two inches a year under Asia.

When ocean-continent subduction and continent-continent collision cause the formation of mountain ranges it is called *orogeny*. For example, the Alpine orogeny also formed the Caucasus of the U.S.S.R. and the Pontic Mountains of Turkey.

Some think that the extreme thickness of the mountains that result from a continental collision occurs because the continent attempting to subduct scrapes pieces off the underside of the other continent's plate. These pieces sink into the plastic asthenosphere, which rises into the holes they left and melts some of the plate above into magma. The magma in turn rises and melts the base of the granite continental crust. Then this molten granite rises, leaving a hole for the edge of the continent on the downgoing plate to slide under the edge of the other continent. This double thickness makes the resulting mountain range very high.

MOUNTAIN RANGES AND BELTS

The high ranges formed by orogeny are often called *mountain belts*. Geologists define a *mountain range* as a long series of mountains that belong to the same geologic unit; mountain belts are collections of mountain ranges along the edges of continents. They have younger rocks than interior ranges do. The major mountain belts of the world, such as the Andes, the North American Cordillera, and the Himalayas, contain folded and faulted layers of sediments and old volcanic rocks as much as six miles thick. The most intense folding occurs at the centers of the belts where metamorphic rocks may contain thin layers that actually melted from the pressure. In broader terms, geologists think of mountain belts as *mobile belts* when they are along plate boundaries. The two principal ones are the Ring of Fire around the Pacific and the Eurasian-Indonesian belt, which includes the Alps and the Himalayas.

In orogeny while the folding and compression are going on magma rises to form plutons or volcanoes. At the same time uplift, erosion, and deposition are occurring. Uplift, rather than folding, causes the great increase in elevation. As subduction ends the crust on the continental side of the mountain belt may either be stretched or compressed. This uplifts fault block mountain ranges, which may be only tilted, like the Sierra, rather than raised straight up.

TRANSFORM FAULTS

Active mobile belts sometimes contain the third type of plate boundary, the *transform fault*. Sections of rock at a fault move relative to each other along a fracture. At a transform fault the moving sections of rock are plate edges. Their motion produces many shallow earthquakes.

The most famous transform fault in North America is the San Andreas in California, cause of the 1906 San Francisco earthquake. The San Andreas is actually a set of faults between the Pacific and the North American plates (Figure 4.5). The 1906 earthquake offset roads and fences along the fault by 21 feet. By

Figure 4.5. At the San Andreas transform fault, the Pacific and North American plates are sliding past each other.
Courtesy of R.E. Wallace, U.S. Geological Survey.

studying and dating the offsets of rock layers, a researcher determined that nine large quakes have taken place along the San Andreas in the last 1400 years.

Plates sliding past each other at a transform fault can also pull apart or squeeze together. Squeezing along a transform fault raised the New Zealand Alps and pulling along such a fault created the Dead Sea.

MICROPLATE TECTONICS

What happens if the colliding continents are only small islands? Evidence from paleomagnetism has led to a theory called *microplate tectonics*. This theory holds that continents have grown at the edges by the addition of large and small pieces of land that have been carried great distances by plates. As described earlier, paleomagnetism shows latitude, so it is possible to tell from how far north or south pieces of land have come. The edges of continents are jigsaw puzzles of these pieces from many different places. Known as *exotic terranes*, these blocks of crust have stuck to the ancient cores of continents. Sometimes these terranes are called microplates, but they are pieces of crust riding on plates, not separate plates. Exotic terranes differ from adjacent rocks in age, rock type, fossils, paleomagnetism, and place of origin. The fossils may even match those of a different hemisphere.

University of Oregon researchers have found Triassic fossils of a seagoing reptile, *Ichthyosaurus shastasaurus*, in the Wallowa Mountains of eastern Oregon (Figure 4.6). Subspecies of the same fossil occur in California and the South Pacific. Finds like this are evidence for exotic terranes.

The 200 million-year-old Wrangellia terrane, bits of which are found in Hells Canyon in eastern Oregon, on Vancouver and Queen Charlotte Islands, and in the Wrangell Mountains of

Figure 4.6. Fossils help show that small bits of land called exotic terranes have traveled to distant continents by continental drift. An example is this ichthyosaurus fossil found in the Wallowa Mountains, Oregon. The ichthyosaurus was native to the South Pacific.
Courtesy of William Orr, University of Oregon.

southern Alaska is an example of an exotic terrane. In the last 25 years researchers have discovered that half of Alaska is made up of over 50 different terranes from varied locations. In the Brooks Range in Alaska, the terranes are stacked up like pancakes, but elsewhere most terranes are side by side but elongated. At least 200 different terranes make up the western United States west of the edge of the original North American continent. This edge runs south from western Montana through eastern Idaho, the middle of Utah, the southern tip of Nevada and Southern California.

EFFECTS OF PLATE MOTION ON LIFE

From this brief summary, you can tell that the more geologists learn about plate tectonics, the more complicated it becomes. As you may guess, plate motion has had many effects on life. When continents moved to different latitudes, species died off because the climate changed. When continents stuck together, competition between species increased. When continents separated and islands formed, endemic species developed. Plate tectonics is only part of the story of how mountains form. Also important is the rock they are made of and its sculpture by weathering, streams, and glaciers. So the next chapter will cover rock formation and sculpture.

F I V E

Mountain Walls—
Forming, Changing,
and Disappearing

The rock of a mountain wall is like a cake, with the various minerals the flour, sugar, eggs, shortening, and baking powder. *Minerals* are defined as inorganic crystalline solids with specific properties; *crystalline* means that the molecules are arranged in a regular pattern. There are exceptions: Volcanic glass and hydrated minerals like opal have random grains. A mineral is composed of identical molecules that can only be taken apart by chemical action. A few minerals, such as gold, are elements, which have identical atoms. X-rays reveal that each mineral has an individual structural pattern as unique as a fingerprint.

Most of the 25 common rock-forming minerals are silicates, or compounds of silicon; calcite (calcium carbonate) is one of the few common minerals that is not a silicate. The main rock-forming minerals are quartz, feldspars, olivine, amphiboles, mica, calcite, dolomite, and pyroxenes.

Rock is defined as a compacted natural solid of particles of one or more minerals. Identifying the rocks and minerals on a mountain will help you determine how and when that mountain formed.

HOW TO IDENTIFY ROCKS AND MINERALS

The best way to learn to identify rocks and minerals is to compare the rocks you find with standard samples in a museum

87

or in a set of samples. Experts use other methods which may help you at times. If a mineral is in crystalline form mineralogists can use its shape to identify it. When the mineral forms, the molecules arrange themselves in a regular formation called a *crystal lattice*. Complete crystal shapes usually occur only when the crystal formed in a fluid. The symmetrical crystals of each mineral belong to one of six crystal systems. The simplest are cubes such as halite (salt). The most complex have 12 and 14 faces of various sizes. One of the most common is quartz, which has a six-sided pyramid at each end of a six-sided column, or two pyramids stuck together base to base. Some minerals, such as pyrite (fool's gold), take more than one crystal shape.

Minerals seldom occur in crystalline form, so you usually have to use other physical properties, such as as *hardness*, to identify them. Here is a hardness scale of ten minerals, ranging from softest to hardest:

1. talc
2. gypsum
3. calcite
4. fluorite
5. apatite
6. orthoclase feldspar
7. quartz
8. topaz
9. corundum
10. diamond

You can use common objects to determine hardness. For example, fingernails are 2.5, pennies are 3, and knife blades and glass are 5.5 on the scale.

Another useful property is *streak* color. To obtain the streak, rub the mineral across unglazed porcelain, such as the back of a ceramic tile. When the mineral is too hard for this method, crush a tiny bit of it with a hammer. Most minerals have white streaks, but for several a streak of a certain color is characteristic. Looking at the color of the mineral (called hand color) sometimes helps identify it, but often it comes in several colors owing to impurities.

Each mineral has a certain specific gravity, but most are close in value, so differences are difficult to determine in the field. *Specific gravity* is the ratio of the weight to an equal volume of water. A few minerals, such as cinnabar, an ore of mercury, are so much heavier than others that their weight helps you identify them.

Two other identifying properties, cleavage and fracture, refer to the way a mineral breaks. *Cleavage* is breaking along planes, often in more than one direction. It is described by its quality and by what geometric form its faces parallel. Fracture is the surface produced when the mineral has no cleavage planes and breaks or in rare cases breaks at an angle to its cleavage planes. Examples of fracture are *conchoidal* (small circular depressions) and *splintery*.

Another property is *luster*, or how a mineral looks in reflected light. Some examples of luster are metallic, greasy, pearly, or earthy.

You can identify a few minerals by their unique properties. Calcite, for example, bubbles when acid is put on it, even if the acid is only vinegar.

It's also helpful to know the type of rock formation where the mineral was found. A *rock formation* is a large or medium-size body of rock that has characteristics differing from rocks adjacent to it. You can identify rock through rock formation, grain size, and texture, as well as by some of the same criteria used to identify minerals. These will help you decide which of the three main categories of rock it belongs to: igneous, metamorphic, or sedimentary.

IGNEOUS ROCK

The first category, *igneous rock*, is molten rock, or magma, that has cooled. Some types, called *extrusive igneous rock*, poured or erupted from volcanoes. Others, called *intrusive igneous rock*, cooled from magma that welled up underground but never reached the surface. The differences in size of the mineral crystals can be used to help identify rock of these two types.

Magma is rock under the surface of the earth that is at high temperature and flows. It contains solids, liquids, and gases, including water vapor. Water and increasing heat help rock melt into magma. Minerals crystallize from magma in a certain order as it cools. In this way different types of minerals can crystallize from the same magma into various rocks.

The high silica rock that erupts from volcanoes is called *rhyolite*, and the high silica rock that cools underground is *granite*. The denser, high-iron rock that erupts from volcanoes is *basalt*, and the underground equivalent is called *gabbro*. Sometimes intrusive rocks called *ultramafic* occur in high mountains. Composed mainly of iron and magnesium high silicate minerals, they may have come from the earth's mantle. Basaltic lava is thin and runny, but rhyolite is so thick it hardly moves. One of the most interesting volcanic rocks you may find is *pumice*, a rock froth that forms when air is trapped in stiff lava. Pumice is so light that it floats.

Intrusive rocks make mountains when the rising magma pushes up and cools under rocks. Intrusive rock bodies, or *plutons*, are called *batholiths* if their exposed surface area is over 40 square miles; small ones are called *stocks*. Others, the plugged vents of old volcanoes exposed by erosion, are called *volcanic necks*. When magma squeezes horizontally between rock layers, it creates *sills*. When it is injected into vertical cracks, it forms *dikes*.

Granite, the commonest intrusive rock, makes up part of most mountain ranges. It need contain grains of only two minerals: quartz and a potassium feldspar, commonly orthoclase. Usually, granite is pink or white grainy rock with black dots of hornblende and biotite. It solidifies so slowly no one can make it in the laboratory. The reason you often see veins of quartz in granite is that silica-rich water escaping from almost-cooled magma coats the walls of cracks in the new rock with quartz.

VOLCANOES

Extrusive igneous rocks are made of lava. Lava varies in the way it comes to the surface: it can erupt from a volcano or flow from great fissures. Volcanoes usually have a central depression at the top with several small craters inside. There are four main types of volcanoes: shield, composite, cinder cone, and lava or plug dome. There are also related structures: calderas, spatter cones, and fissure flows.

Shield volcanoes, like those in Hawaii, quietly emit thin, hot basaltic lava from the top and from fissures and craters on gently sloping sides. When high-temperature lava cools, it forms a ropy texture called *pahoehoe basalt*, but when it cools slowly, hot lava flowing inside the cooling shell breaks it into a field of razor-sharp blocks called *aa*. Shield volcanoes occur commonly in the ocean, either along ocean ridges or at hot spots.

Occurring mostly in mountain belts on continents, *composite volcanoes* erupt stiff, cooler lava, usually andesite, sometimes rhyolite. They also blow out pieces of rock and volcanic ash called *tephra*. Composite volcanoes have alternating layers of lava and tephra. Their sides steepen from 5 degrees at the base to 30 degrees at the top. Eruptions are often explosive, as you may remember from the 1980 eruption of Mount St. Helens (Figure 5.1). This eruption blew away the top of the mountain and part of one side, depositing volcanic ash hundreds of miles away. Other volcanoes that blew themselves up were Tambora (1815) and Krakatoa (1883), both in Indonesia, and Mount Mazama (about 4600 B.C.), at the site of Crater Lake, Oregon.

Tephra ejected from a central vent forms *cinder cones*, which have 30-degree sides and, by definition, are less than 1000 feet high and .6 mile across. Cinder cones usually occur in groups like those in Mount Lassen National Park in California and Craters of the Moon National Monument in Idaho.

The fourth type, *lava* or *plug domes* such as Mono Craters in California, are made of sticky lava that solidified in or above a volcanic vent.

A *crater* is the depression at the top of a volcano. If the crater is more than one mile across it is called a *caldera*. Calderas form from the subsidence or collapse of underlying rocks and may be associated with volcanic explosion. A caldera is a large more or less circular depression or basin associated with a volcanic vent. Examples are Crater Lake in Oregon and the caldera in Yellowstone National Park. The center of the Yellowstone caldera has risen several feet in a century, so it is likely to erupt again.

Lava may flow from fissures rather than from a crater. When it does it may form flood basalts over one mile thick, such as the Columbia River basalts you see when driving across Washington and Oregon. One hypothesis states that these basalts flowed as the North American plate passed over a hot spot now under Yellowstone, but this is now a controversial theory as the North

Figure 5.1. The eruptions of composite volcanoes like Mount St.
Helens are often explosive. The 1980 eruption here blew away the
mountain's top and part of one side.
Courtesy of U.S. Geological Survey.

American plate is moving northwest and the supposed path of
the hot spot is east-west. Flood basalts often have lava-tube
tunnels, hexagonal columns, and changes in stream drainage.
When basalt continues to flow in the center where its outer part
has already cooled, it leaves a hollow lava tube. Hexagonal
basaltic columns, formed by shrinking (jointing) of the cooling
lava, may resemble a lumber pile on end. If you climb up on top
of basaltic columns, such as the Devils Postpile National Monument in California, you will see that the glacier-polished tops of
the columns resemble ceramic tiles.

Plateau basalts may change the course of rivers and streams.
The Big and Little Lost Rivers in Idaho disappear into the lava

and reappear at Thousand Springs on the wall of the Snake River canyon near Hagerman.

A different type of fissure flow occurs within a caldera when the volcano first collapses. Fissures emit gases, steam, pumice, and tephra that are so hot they fuse together as they fall, forming rock called *welded tuff.* Sheets of welded tuff cover Yellowstone.

SEDIMENTARY ROCK

The second type of rock, *sedimentary*, has three subdivisions: rock that was deposited by precipitation, such as that made by hot springs; rock, such as coal, that was formed of organic matter; and rock made of particles of minerals and other rocks cemented together, called *clastic rock*.

Minerals dissolved by water or compression, either from the weight of rocks above or from folding, may cement particles into clastic rocks. Some of these rocks you see often are limestone, sandstone, and shale.

METAMORPHIC ROCK

Physical and chemical changes caused by heat, pressure, and chemically active fluids create the third type of rock: *metamorphic*. Around plutons, where rocks were changed by the heat of magma concentric shells of different types of metamorphic rock form. This type of metamorphism formed ore bodies around the edges of the Idaho batholith.

A form of recrystallization occurs when rocks are bent under high pressure and temperature. This is often called *regional metamorphism* because it may extend over large areas. It often occurs in the cores of mountains and is the result of plate tectonics.

LANDFORMS

Weathering and erosion are constant processes, like the formation of rock and mountains. Weathering is the process by which rocks are broken down and decomposed without being moved. Erosion is the wearing away of the land by the action of rock debris transported by wind, gravity, ice, or water. It is more rapid on the steep slopes of mountains than it is on the gentle slopes of lowlands. The building and wearing-down of the land produce characteristically shaped features called *landforms*.

ROCK STRATA

Basic to landforms are the rock *strata*, or layers, within them. If you compared rock to Neapolitan ice cream, you would say the rock had strata of chocolate, strawberry, and vanilla. A stratum is a bed or layer of one kind of rock separated from the strata on either side of it by surfaces called *bedding planes*. A stratum is usually part of a rock formation, which is a thick body of rock different from the rock adjacent to it.

Geologists use the terms *strike* and *dip* to describe a stratum. *Strike* is the compass direction of a line formed by the intersection of the surface of the rock layer with an imaginary horizontal plane. *Dip* is the angle and direction the bed makes with this horizontal plane, measured perpendicular to the strike, as in Figure 5.2. If a shed roof of a house were a bed of rock, the strike would be the compass direction of the ridgepole, and the angle of dip would be the pitch of the roof.

When you see strata below and above a line dipping at different angles, the line is called an *unconformity*. It is a gap in the

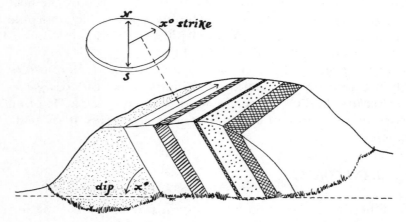

Figure 5.2.   The dip of a stratum or bed of rock is the angle and direction of its slope, and the strike is the compass direction in which the bed extends.

geologic record. Usually an unconformity shows a period of erosion when no deposition occurred. The beds above the unconformity are sometimes parallel to the ones below it. And sometimes the rock below the unconformity may be eroded igneous or metamorphic rock, rather than layered sedimentary rock.

The layers in strata may be fractured. Fractures in rock are either faults or joints. *Joints* are fractures where the rock hasn't moved parallel to the fracture surface; they are caused by expansion and shrinking. These size changes may come from drying, temperature change, or pressure reduction.

Figure 5.3. When overlying rock is eroded away or glaciers melt, the removal of pressure causes the rock to fracture in layers parallel to the surface. This is called sheet jointing.
Courtesy of N.K. Huber, U.S. Geological Survey.

Pressure reduction occurs when overlying layers are eroded away or glacial ice melts. It causes sheet jointing, which breaks rock layers loose parallel to the surface (Figure 5.3). When these layers break loose in curved, shell-shaped pieces, the jointing is called *exfoliation*. If the vertical joints are widely spaced, these pieces may be so large they form domes, like those in the Sierra.

The reason basalt often resembles logs on end is that when the rock cools it shrinks, so it cracks apart into columns. The commonest form of jointing is vertical. But usually the fractures are at right angles, forming four-sided columns, rather than the six-sided columns of basalt.

FOLDS

You may have noticed from observing road cuts that instead of lying flat, strata may be folded. There are three main types of *folds*. In a *monocline* the rock forms a steplike bend. In an *anticline* a fold bends up into a ridge, and in a *syncline* a fold bends down into a trough (Figure 5.4). In addition the folding may form domes and basins. These look as though a large ball had been

Figure 5.4.   Rocks will bend even without the benefit of heat if pushed slowly at high pressures. These bent rock layers form part of the Chinese Wall in the White Cloud Mountains, Idaho.

pushed up under the rock layers or pressed down on top of them. Folds are often asymmetric and may be overturned, which means flopped over beyond the vertical. If the overturning is complete, the fold will be *recumbent*, or lying on its side like a pleat in fabric.

Sometimes recumbent folds slide downhill or along a horizontal plane. These folds, called *nappes*, are often found in areas of continental collision such as the Alps. Pieces of nappes may be isolated by erosion into peaks called *klippes*.

The top side or limb of a recumbent fold may even break loose and with the help of water slide several miles down over the lower limb. The plane of this motion, called a *thrust fault*, is a type of fault. For example, the older rocks of the Blue Ridge in the southern Appalachians have been thrust west over the younger as much as 150 miles.

FAULTS

Faults are responsible for several landforms. A fault, you will recall, is a fracture in bedrock where the rock on one side of the fault has moved in relation to the rock on the other side. At the base of Idaho's Lost River Range you can trace the fault scarp from the earthquake of 1983 for 20 miles. Major faults have a zone of broken rock as much as 300 feet wide or a series of parallel faults with branches.

There are three main kinds of faults: dip-slip, strike-slip, and oblique slip. Most faults form an inclined plane. The *hanging wall* of the fault is the block that lies above the inclined plane; the block below it is the *foot wall*. In a *dip-slip fault* the rock on one side of the fault has moved up or down in relation to that on the other side.

A dip-slip fault can be a *normal fault* in which the hanging wall has moved down in relation to the foot wall. Or it can be a *reverse fault* in which the hanging wall has ascended in relation to the foot wall. A reverse fault leaves the top of the hanging wall as an overhang, but the overhang usually collapses. If a reverse fault forms a plane less than 45 degrees from the horizontal, the fault is called a thrust fault.

In the *strike-slip fault*, one side moves horizontally along the other side. This type can be right lateral, where the opposite side has moved to your right as you look at it from the side. Or it can be left lateral, where the opposite block has moved to your left. The special kind of strike-slip fault called a transform fault connects offset sections of midocean ridges. The third kind of fault, *oblique slip*, occurs when dip-slip and strike-slip motion combine. Faults are usually squeezed together at an angle and also undergo parallel stress in opposite directions.

Motion along faults can raise, lower, or tilt great blocks of land. A *horst* is an uplifted block, and a *graben* is a down-dropped block between faults. Lake Tahoe is an example of a lake in a graben. Horsts sometimes form mountains, but more often fault-block mountains are uplifted on only one side, forming a tilted fault block like the Sierra.

EARTHQUAKES

Rock slips slowly as well as rapidly along a fault. Slow slippage is called *fault creep*, and fast slippage is an *earthquake*. Earthquakes are one of the most important results of mountain-building processes. Some geologists favor the elastic rebound theory of earthquakes. This states that before the rock surface slips, stress from opposing forces accumulates in the rocks on either side of the fault. The accumulation causes them to bend, and the stress builds up at places where the fault is locked or undergoing no fault creep. When one of these locked places breaks, slipping of the rock spreads along the fault. After the earthquake releases the pressure, the rocks on either side of the fault return to the original position as though they were elastic, much as a bow returns to its original shape after the arrow is released. This theory is supported by studies of the San Andreas fault in which elastic strain has been measured.

When an earthquake occurs, special terms are used to report it. The *focus* is the point along the fault where the rock first slips. The *epicenter* is the point on the earth's surface directly above that focus. The *Richter scale* measures the magnitude (size) of the seismic waves of the earthquake. Each full step up has ten times the energy of the preceding step. The largest earthquake ever recorded had a magnitude of about 8.6.

Earthquakes cause two main kinds of seismic waves: *body waves* and *surface waves*. Both move outward from the earthquake focus. Body waves are of two types: *compressional*, or *P*, *waves*; and *shear*, or *S, waves*. Both travel through the earth's interior. P waves, the ones that get there first, alternately push and pull, S waves move up and down, much as a rope moves when shaken.

Surface waves move over the earth's surface from the epicenter like ripples on a pond, making each particle of rock go around in a tiny ellipse. Because of their slow movement, they cause more damage than do body waves.

Geologists use *seismographs* to measure these waves. If you went to look at a seismograph you would see a heavy pendulum hanging motionless within a framework installed underground, shielded from traffic vibrations, and attached to a pen. The instrument records earthquake waves with this pen, which moves over a paper drum. Three readings from different spots can locate an earthquake.

Those who experience an earthquake sometimes notice strange effects. For example, water-saturated sediments, when shaken, may become liquid and flow, tilting any buildings on them. Another example is the sand geysers that occur when shaking raises water pressure under sand so much that the wet sand erupts like a fountain.

Can anyone predict an earthquake? Researchers have discovered that certain events often occur before earthquakes, but how long before a quake they occur no one knows. In one of the events, called *dilatancy*, water moves into cracks in the rock and uplifts the ground. This water reduces friction along the fault faces, accelerating fault creep. Because it increases the amount of water in contact with rock, the emission of radioactive radon gas from wells near the fault increases.

If you live near a plate boundary you may feel many earthquakes. Earthquakes along ocean ridges and transform faults like the San Andreas are shallow. The deepest, most severe, and frequent earthquakes take place in subduction zones.

WEATHERING

As mentioned earlier, one process that breaks up rocks and wears down mountains is weathering. Wind, glacial action, temperature changes, organic matter, and water cause two kinds of weathering, mechanical and chemical, that wear down and break up rocks without moving them. Mechanical weathering exposes rock surface to air and water, and thus to chemical weathering, which occurs between mineral grains in rock as well as on the rock surfaces.

Weathering is a slow but powerful process: It is estimated that 20 vertical miles of rock have been eroded from the Alps in 30 million years. Hard rock weathers more slowly than soft, but a sundial carved in granite and exposed to mountain weather has been seen to disappear after 40 years. You probably have noticed that some rocks weather faster than others. Several factors help determine the speed of weathering.

If a mountain slope is steep, rock is more likely to roll off and expose new surfaces to weathering. In wet climates with plenty of water for chemical action, weathering is more rapid, especially in hot weather. It is also more rapid in cold climates, where freezing and thawing break the rock.

Some rocks weather faster than others because their minerals more readily decompose chemically. Rainwater combines with the carbon dioxide in the atmosphere to form weak carbonic acid, so it is a major agent in chemical weathering. The first minerals to solidify out of magma decompose first. Quartz solidifies and decomposes last, so granite, which has a large percentage of quartz, resists weathering. Because other minerals weather away first, sand, the product of extensive weathering, contains mostly quartz grains.

Rock with more joints weathers more rapidly. When rock breaks along joints, the corners of the blocks become rounded because they have three faces exposed to weathering. Chemical weathering of the minerals in the outer layer swells the rock: The feldspars are changed to clays and clays occupy a greater volume. So the outer layer of rock breaks off. Once rounded, rock weathers in shell-shaped pieces, a process called *spheroidal weathering*.

MASS WASTING

Once rock is broken by weathering it starts moving, carried by the agents of erosion: gravity, wind, water, or ice. Wind is a major agent only in deserts. Downhill motion from gravity alone is called *mass wasting*.

The three main types of mass wasting are *flow, slip,* and *fall.* In *creep*—the commonest kind of flow—rock, soil, and sediment flow up to several inches a year. Together with the pressure of snow, creep often curves the bases of tree trunks downhill into curves called *snow knees* (Figure 5.5). Creep also drags the tops of near-vertical beds of rock downhill so they bend over at the top.

Solifluction is faster creep in which saturated sediment flows downhill. It usually occurs above permafrost but can take place in any water-saturated soil.

In *earth,* or *debris, flow* the debris flows rapidly downhill like wet concrete. In contrast, *mudflows* are as thin as potato soup. They happen more often on bare slopes, in deserts, and in volcanic eruptions. In eruptions, hot ash melts ice and snow and mixes with them into a mudflow called a *lahar.* The lahar formed by the eruption of Nevado del Ruiz in Colombia in 1985 killed 25,000 people.

The second type of mass wasting, *slip,* includes rock or debris slide and slump. If you walk down a steep scree slope your footsteps may cause small debris slides. *Rock* or *debris slides* can be avalanches whose speed is so great (up to 200 miles an hour)

Figure 5.5.   The trunks of these trees in Olympic National Park, Washington, show the effects of pressure from winter snow and soil creep.

Figure 5.6. This view of Castle Peak in Idaho's White Cloud Mountains shows protalus ramparts and avalanche chutes. The protalus ramparts, small ridges at the base of the slope, have been formed by rocks sliding down snowbanks. The avalanche chutes have been gouged out along weak areas in the rock by rock and snow avalanches.

that the smaller particles ride on cushions of air (Figure 5.6). In the Zagros Mountains of Iran, a nine-mile-long rock avalanche sped 5000 feet down a mountain and over a 1600-foot hill in 1969. Debris and snow avalanches occur repeatedly in avalanche chutes on mountain walls. Following joints and faults, the chutes often form branching drainage systems.

Slumps occur when the rock or soil breaks away along curved surfaces. The tops of slumps move downward, but the bottoms move outward. To see how this works put a pancake in a bowl and tilt the bowl. The pancake slides down at the top but outward at the bottom.

In rock fall, pieces of bedrock fall off cliffs and ledges. They often form *talus*, a slope of rock fragments at the base of a cliff. The rocks themselves are called *sliderock* rather than talus. Rocks funneling through an avalanche chute make a cone. When rocks fall from cliffs and slide down snowbanks below, they form distinct ridges below the snowbanks. These ridges, called *protalus ramparts*, resemble glacial moraines, except that they follow the contour lines of the slope. In late summer, you can find large early-season snowbanks by noticing these ridges.

If snowbanks last long enough they can sculpture mountains. They don't have to be recrystallized into a glacier first. The action of snowbanks, a kind of mass wasting, is called *nivation*. Late-lying snowbanks on slopes of debris create nivation hollows. These are formed by meltwater underneath the snowbanks and frost action at their edges. On slopes steeper than ten degrees, the snow actually moves downhill, gently abrading and scooping the rock. The moving snow and the frost action around it create terraces with miniature headwalls at the upslope ends. By driving steel rods into snowbanks and watching the rods bend over time, researchers have proved that steep snowbanks move. They found that in some cases the stress on the rods is as great as that at the base of glaciers. However, to be a glacier, the moving mass must be ice rather than snow.

Between mass wasting and glaciers is a borderline form called a *rock glacier*, which is like a moraine with a core of ice that flows as a glacier does. If you see striped ice under loose rocks it may belong to a rock glacier. Rock glaciers have steep, lobed tongues and parallel curved wrinkles on their surfaces. Below the tongues are freshly overturned rocks, disturbed vegetation, and summertime streams. Rock glaciers are transitional between seasonal snow and glaciers, occurring where there are low temperatures but little snow.

The zone between the seasonal snow and the permanent snow is called the *snowline*. In this zone, permanent snow and glaciers cover the cold sections, but bare rock appears in summer in the warm ones. The snowline is highest in the Tibetan Highlands and the Puna de Atacama of the Andes, 19,800 to 21,500 feet.

GLACIERS

Glaciers, the final sculptors in many mountain ranges, are thick masses of ice that move under their own weight. The three main types of glaciers are *continental ice sheets, ice caps*, and *valley glaciers*. Most glacial features and landforms are common to all three types.

Snow turns to firn, and then to glacial ice, as the pressure of its own weight squeezes out the air bubbles and causes recrystallization. *Firn* is compacted snow that has lasted over at least one summer. Glacial ice takes a year to form in warm temperatures and up to ten years in cold ones. At the upper end of a glacier where the snow accumulates, new ice is forming. At the lower end, melting predominates. When a glacier's rate of melting exceeds its rate of advance, the glacier retreats.

The thickness the ice must be before it will move depends on the temperature and the angle of the slope, but generally it is about 60 feet. Glaciers move in two ways, by basal sliding and internal deformation. The speed depends on thickness, temperature, slope, and obstacles. *Basal sliding* glaciers, lubricated by meltwater beneath them, move as units over their bedrock. This occurs only when it is warm enough for water to be liquid. They actually slide downhill like a child on a waterslide. *Internal deformation* is similar to the shearing of rocks when they are deformed under pressure. The ice crystals line up parallel to each other and slide along planes. Thicker glaciers flow faster than thin ones, and glaciers flow faster along the surface than at their bases.

Occasionally glaciers speed up to as much as 15 feet per hour for short periods of time. *Surging glaciers* have shattered surfaces and loops and zigzags in their medial moraines. Studies of the Variegated Glacier in Alaska have shown that surges may occur when the water circulation under the glacier becomes blocked and the rising water pushes the glacier off its bed. The rise in the amount and pressure of the water melts cavities at the base of the glacier, reducing friction. When a glacier surges, a surge front, or thickening of the ice, passes along the glacier, the water pressure under the glacier rises, and the surface becomes a mass of ice needles.

Glaciers display several typical features, such as crevasses. Have you ever wondered why glaciers have these deep cracks?

The reason is that the ice at the top of glaciers is rigid because there is not enough pressure on it to make it plastic. So, from the surface to a depth of 100 to 200 feet, the flowing of the ice underneath cracks the upper ice into crevasses across the glacier. Glaciers also split in longitudinal crevasses because the ice in the middle moves much faster than that at the edges. On steep slopes where glaciers plunge down in ice falls, the two kinds of crevasses may intersect to form towers called *seracs*. At the heads of glaciers the ice pulling away from the rock causes a special type of crevasse called a *bergschrund*.

Another feature of glaciers is moraines. As the glacier moves down a valley, rocks fall onto its sides from the walls above and are carried along. By the time the glacier has flowed several miles, there are so many rocks they form a long narrow hill, called a lateral moraine. When two branches of a glacier join, these moraines form a line of rocks called a *medial moraine* down the center of the glacier. If several tributaries join a glacier, the medial moraines resemble a striped ribbon (Figure 5.7).

Figure 5.7.   The stripes here are medial moraines that formed when tributary glaciers carrying lateral moraines along their edges intersected with the main glacier.
Courtesy of A. Post, U.S. Geological Survey.

Mountains in the tropics and subtropics and even hills near the poles hold glaciers. The Ruwenzori Mountains, Mt. Kenya, and Kilimanjaro (all in East Africa), the Mexican volcanoes, the Snow Mountains of New Guinea, and Mount Ararat in Turkey all have glaciers.

GLACIAL SCULPTURE

Glaciers leave landforms of sediment and of sculptured rock. Rocks at the base of a glacier smooth and gouge the bedrock into glacial polish and grooves called *striations*. If the rock is steep and the polish shiny, you may even be able to slide down it. Large rocks leave semicircular grooves called *chatter marks* with the open end facing downhill.

Glaciers also pluck rocks or pull off pieces of bedrock. They can do this because pressure causes the ice upstream from a knob in the bedrock to melt and then refreeze below the knob. In this way the glacier sticks to the knob on the downstream side, pulls it off, and carries it along. The ice does this more easily where the rock is jointed.

Plucking and abrasion create hills of bedrock with smooth upstream sides and steep, broken-off downstream sides. These, called *sheep rocks*, surround many mountain lakes, with the cliff sides above the upper end of the lake and the rounded sides along the lower end.

Glacial lakes often form in strings along streams in mountains. Called *paternoster lakes*, they are found where glaciers scoop out a series of descending rock basins. Such a process occurred in the White Cloud Mountains of Idaho, where the 11 lakes of the Boulder Chain Lakes sit in a 3.5-mile-long row.

At the heads of glaciers, glacial erosion leaves semicircular hollows called *cirques*. Sometimes glaciers remove so much rock on both sides of a ridge as to form a knife-edged *arete*; sometimes they erode three or four sides and create a sharp peak known as a *horn*. Frost splits jointed rock on these aretes into saw-toothed ridges.

When you find a U-shaped canyon, you know it has been scoured out by a glacier. An end moraine or rock step may enclose a lake in the canyon. Yosemite Valley originally contained such a lake. Owing to the greater weight of main glaciers, any side canyons have slower erosion, resulting in side valleys called *hanging valleys* above cliffs on the canyon walls.

Fiords, steep-sided narrow bays carved by glaciers, can arise from two processes: The land may sink during or after the time that glaciers are sculpturing mountains that are above the water level, or the glaciers may sculpture underwater canyons, which are then exposed when the land rises or the sea level falls. Glaciers abrade rock under the sea to a depth of 800 feet.

GLACIAL DEPOSITION

Glaciers deposit the rocks they carry in several distinctive landforms. If you have been to mountains with active glaciers, such as the Canadian Rockies, you probably noticed the beautiful colors of the lakes, caused by *rock flour*. The passing of rock over rock makes this dust so fine it takes months to settle, and so colors glacial meltwater white or dirty gray. When rock flour reaches lakes or creeks, it makes them milky. The reflection of light on the water and rock particles makes the lakes and creeks appear an exceptionally brilliant turquoise, aqua, or green. Milkiness in lakes and streams is most noticeable in late summer when melting is at its height. When rock flour does settle, it forms two layers for each year, one consisting of fast-settling coarse sediment and the other a dark, slow-settling fine sediment. Geologists use each pair of layers, called a *varve*, to date glacial advances and retreats.

Melting glaciers drop rock debris as *till* or *ground moraine*. If you go to mountains where glaciers once were active but have melted you will see other glacial deposits. Sometimes glaciers leave huge boulders known as *glacial erratics* miles from where they originated. The melting of large blocks of ice that broke off glaciers leaves tiny lakes called *kettles* in outwash or in moraines.

When valley glaciers melt they leave ridges of rocks called lateral moraines, described earlier, which may be 1000 feet high or more. Glaciers also leave *end*, or *recessional*, *moraines*, which form when the glaciers stop for a time, thus allowing the rocks they were carrying to pile up. *Terminal moraines* are end moraines at the farthest points of glacial advance. Moraines often enclose lakes, such as Fallen Leaf Lake, which adjoins the south end of Lake Tahoe in California.

STREAMS

Stream erosion is the other major force shaping mountain valleys. When it rains or snow melts, runoff, called *overland flow*, runs in sheets and rills and causes erosion even before it reaches streams.

Streams are flowing bodies of water, including rivers, that run downhill through narrow, usually V-shaped, troughs. They wear away, dissolve, and carry bedrock and soil and deposit them at lower levels.

Mountain streams flow through rugged country whose areas differ greatly in elevation. How fast they flow varies with the terrain, but in most places they fall too sharply to have developed pools. In fact, their flow is turbulent and has many eddies, to the delight of white water rafters and kayakers. The amount of water in streams varies seasonally, and some streams flow only part of the year. Deep streams flow faster than shallow streams with the same *gradient*, or steepness. This is because in relation to their volume shallow streams have more surface area that comes in contact with the channel.

Steep streams have clear water, and they erode their channels rapidly. They have rapids, potholes, pools, falls, and lakes. Streams with gentle gradients erode slowly and have turbid water with bars, oxbows, and meanders.

The shape of the channel and the texture of the surface affect stream velocity, with the maximum speed occurring at the outside of curves. Although usually about 3 miles per hour, stream velocity can reach 15 miles per hour after heavy rain or spring snowmelt. The *discharge* of streams—the quantity of water passing a given point per unit of time—is greatest in late afternoon in early summer (usually June), when spring and daily snowmelt are both at their height.

Streams deposit material all along their channels. They carry two main loads, suspended load and bed load. The *suspended load* is rock dust that remains in the water indefinitely. The *bed load* is sediment that is dragged, rolled, or bounced along the stream bottom, then deposited as bars along the bank and in the center of the channel. The more sediment a stream carries, the more bars it deposits. If there is much sediment (more than the stream can carry) streams may become braided, that is, split up into a network of tiny streams that flow around many bars.

Streams sculpture their channels through the processes of abrasion, solution (the dissolving of rock by water), and hydraulic action. Hydraulic action is like moving dirt off a sidewalk with a garden hose. Abrasion by rocks is like the action of the grains in sandpaper. Some rocks of the bedload, trapped in eddies, scour potholes. If the scouring continues long enough, the trapped rocks become spherical, to the delight of children, who may think they are giant marbles. In areas of weak rock, the bed-load rocks abrade pools. The increased turbulence of the water falling into the pools deepens them. This causes abrupt drops in elevation of the stream between the pools, forming waterfalls. The turbulence of the falls erodes the cliffs, causing the falls to slowly retreat upstream.

MEANDERS AND TERRACES

Have you ever wondered why some streams have so many bends? Because the velocity of the water flowing on the insides of the curves in streams is low, sediment is deposited there. On the outsides of curves, where the velocity is high, streams erode their banks. Erosion of the outside downstream banks shifts the curves downstream and also enlarges them by moving them outward. When they form loops and wind across a meadow or valley, the curves are called *meanders*. Meanders may in time be so pronounced that the stream in flood cuts off the short distance across them. Then new stream channels, known as *meander cutoffs*, form. The old channels remain as curved loops of water, called *oxbow lakes*. *Incised meanders*, those within steep bedrock walls, occur when the land has risen or the sea level fallen after the meandering pattern was established.

Similar changes in cutting rate form paired alluvial terraces on either side of streams. When the streams change their courses as they simultaneously cut downward and sideways but maintain the same rate, they make unpaired terraces.

STREAM-DRAINAGE SYSTEMS

Does your city worry about preserving the watershed of the reservoirs in its water system? A *watershed* includes all the hillsides that slope toward streams and toward their tributaries. A *drainage system* is the watershed plus the stream and its tributaries. Stream-drainage systems have different patterns.

The most usual patterns resemble those of tree branches. If a stream flows through gaps between resistant rock layers, its tree and branches make right angles with each other. Radial patterns may extend outward from isolated mountains.

Streams can erode rapidly enough to keep up with rising mountains and maintain their original courses. The great rivers of the Himalayas, for example, have been able to keep up with the mountains and continue to flow south. As the Himalayas rose, they caught more monsoon moisture. This increased precipitation swelled the rivers and thus increased erosion.

Drainage systems may include temporary lakes. As we have seen, glacial scouring or deposition of moraines causes lakes. Other causes are lava flows, landslides, and stream deposition. The life cycle of lakes will be discussed in Chapter 6.

Stream drainage may be unusual. If you have been in a limestone cave like Carlsbad Caverns, you have seen *karst drainage*, which occurs in limestone rock in moist climates. The streams mostly flow underground because the carbonic acid in the rainwater that dissolves the limestone forms sinkholes, caves, and disappearing streams. The dissolved products may be deposited in caves as dripstone, flowstone, stalactites, or stalagmites. Over time intersecting sinkholes can lead to a landscape of dramatic needles. The landscapes in Kentucky, Tennessee, Yugoslavia, and Czechoslovakia show many karst features.

HOT SPRINGS

In areas where groundwater is heated by hot magma or hot rock underground it may emerge as hot springs. Because hot magma helps form mountains, hot springs are common in mountains, especially within old calderas and around active volcanoes. In some areas in the western U.S., you can plan backpacking trips to include backcountry hot springs.

When steam forces the water out of these springs, you see them erupt as *geysers*. The reason they erupt at intervals, as Old Faithful does, is that steam forms when the water at the base of the geysers boils. As water runs into crevices in the ground the weight of the overlying water increases the pressure, which raises the boiling point of the water underneath, so the water is superheated. As air bubbles escape from it, some water at the top overflows. This reduces the pressure enough so the super- heated water underneath flashes to steam and blows the water above out of the ground in a geyser. Then, more water must accumulate in the geyser and the process repeat itself before the spouting can occur again. Hot water can dissolve more minerals than cold, so hot springs dissolve and deposit large amounts of minerals.

Now that you are thinking about enjoying a soak in a back- country hot spring with your friends or family, it is time to think about the rest of the mountain environment. Rocks, glaciers, streams, and hot springs are physical factors in this environ- ment. You, and the algae in the hot spring, the yellow mimulus on the mossy bank above, the nearby chipmunk nibbling on fir cones, are part of the biology of this particular mountain en- vironment. These two aspects, physical and biological, are re- lated to each other in the organization biologists call an eco- system, the subject of the next chapter.

S I X

Living High: Mountain Ecosystems

Do you know what an *ecosystem* is? Biologists say it is the physical environment of an area plus the community of plants and animals that live there. A biological *community* may change membership seasonally, and species within the community may change activities seasonally. Each species has a set of relationships with the ecosystem that defines its *ecological niche*. A species is a type of plant or animal capable of freely interbreeding with others of its kind. Different species occupy different places, called *habitats*, within an ecosystem. An example of a habitat is the snowbed of the alpine tundra, the ground from which a late-lying snowbank has melted.

Imagine that a football stadium is an ecosystem. The quarterback occupies a niche, and the rest of the team, the cheerleaders, and band are one community. The food sellers and spectators are another. The playing field and the stands are the two habitats of this ecosystem.

PRODUCERS AND CONSUMERS

Because green plants produce food for ecosystems by photosynthesis, they are called *producers*. Producers in different ecosystems vary in how much they produce; those in alpine tundra, for example, produce very little. When animals eat plants and each other, they recycle the materials of their ecosystem by consuming them, so they are called *consumers*. Consumers include decomposers, the bacteria and tiny animals that feed on

112

decay, as well as nongreen plants called fungi, which act as parasites as well as decomposers.

As consumers, animals can alter their environments in a dramatic way. Beavers, for example, have more effect on their environments than most animals (Figure 6.1). Their dams flood the forest, kill trees, and create ponds. Their powerful jaws and sharp teeth enable them to cut a five-inch tree in less than five minutes. To construct a dam they poke cut logs into the bottom of the stream, plaster them with mud that they carry in their forepaws, and add more sticks and mud. The resulting pond, near the entrance to their lodge, allows a family of beavers to store food (unpeeled branches) for winter and to swim to get food in summer. Working only at night, the beavers use piled sticks to build their lodges, which have underwater entrances and aboveground rooms. They eat bark and twigs, as well as the leaves, buds, and fruit of woody plants. They are able to water-proof themselves by using the split toenails on their hind feet like combs to distribute oils from their oil glands throughout their fur.

Figure 6.1.   As consumers, a few animals, like the beaver, dramatically alter their environment.
Courtesy of National Park Service.

Dam-building behavior in beavers evolved along with their habit of eating aspen, willow, and alder trees. Like the beaver, each consumer has special adaptations to its food. Woodpeckers, for example, are able to peck hard and rapidly—sometimes at a rate of 100 pecks a minute—without hurting their beaks and heads. To reduce the shock to their brains, they have developed dense, spongy bone in the front of the skull and a very narrow space between the brain and its outer membrane.

Most animals eat more than one thing, so if you drew a diagram of who eats what, it would resemble a pyramid or web. At each of the levels the animals' metabolism consumes some of the energy, and at the top of the web sits the strongest predator. The arrangement of producers and consumers according to the order of predation in which each uses a lower member as a food source is called a *food chain*.

SUCCESSION

Over time, new producers and consumers replace those in a community in a process called *succession*. It occurs as the ecosystem's organisms, especially plants, respond to and modify their environment.

Succession starts after there has been a disturbance, such as a lava flow, glacier, logging, or a landslide, in the community and does not necessarily lead to the return of the original community. In the American West, for example, a large number of lodgepole forests arose after fire and cast so much shade that the original spruce and fir forests may never return.

The first stages of succession are much shorter than the later ones. The process begins with the development of communities of lichens and mosses and, almost immediately afterward, pioneer plants. Next come perennial herbs, then shrubs, and later, fast-growing trees—such as aspens and birches—take over. As these trees mature, the shrubs die from too much shade, so there is room for shade-loving trees to grow. The shade trees eventually dominate the forest and stay dominant unless the forest is disturbed. A species of plant or tree that is likely to become dominant likes shade and is larger than its neighbors, so it shades them and their seedlings and takes their nutrients and water. For example, a succession in the Rocky Mountains began with fireweed and other annuals; then huckleberry, currants, and other shrubs; followed by aspen or lodgepole and finally Engelmann spruce and subalpine fir.

Succession is affected by changes in climate, luck in seed dispersal, differences in growth rate, and reaction to stress. For example, if it is windy when the seeds ripen, the wind scatters the seeds widely.

Some biologists believe that only a certain community will eventually occur as the end point of succession in a particular climate. Called the *climax community*, it is theoretically stable and evolves over a long period of time. Because a climax community contains more varied species, it takes a large disaster to make much of a change in it. Others believe that communities last only a comparatively short time and that what grows in them depends on which plants, shrubs, and trees get there first and on how fast they grow. These biologists believe that seedlings are unable to grow into big trees if trees of another species are already using the space, light, and nutrients.

STRESS

Stress—shade, a shortage of nutrients, and a hostile climate—help determine where certain plants grow. For example, some plants, shrubs, and young trees grow well in shade, but many do not. In forests, stress produced by shade causes trees to lose branches at their bases. Shade-loving plants have large leaves and stomata that are more responsive to light, but they grow more slowly than sun-loving plants. Conifers are an exception. They have finely divided needles instead of large leaves, thus increasing their food-producing surface.

Where there is a lack of nutrients you will see plants with reduced growth, leathery leaves, longer leaf life, and creeping growth form. Some plants, such as bog plants, are adapted to nutrient lack; these insect-eating plants can nourish themselves by obtaining amino acids from the bugs they catch. The California pitcher plant, for example, produces nectar that attracts insects into a hole in the flower. Once inside, the bugs are unable to climb out over downward-pointing hairs and are dissolved by the liquid at the base of the flower.

Have you noticed how fast some plants come in after a disturbance such as fire or the construction of a road? In succession, these plants, called the *pioneer plants*, are annuals, often weeds, that usually are taller than they are wide, grow fast, flower early, and die soon. They produce many seeds, some of which stay dormant each year, so there are always some that will sprout when conditions are right.

Later in succession, *stress-tolerant plants* begin to take over. Usually evergreen with small leathery leaves, they live a long time and include mountain herbs, shrubs, and trees. Because they can spread by roots and rhizomes, they flower only now and then. Stress-tolerant plants such as tall trees and shrubs with a high, dense canopy and large leaves are called *competitive plants* because they are successful in competition.

Flowering plants often compete by taking advantage of conditions imposed by the dominant plants. For example, plants such as skunk cabbage can live in the shade of deciduous forests by flowering in the early spring light that falls through the bare branches onto the forest floor. And in the Rockies, steershead, which lives in dry meadows, blooms before the grass grows tall enough to shade it.

After a disturbance, succession begins again. New plants grow from seed or seedling banks or by vegetative reproduction, which is common on chaparral slopes, at timberline, and on alpine tundra. A plant species is said to bank seeds if some of the seeds of one summer sprout the next summer and some in following years. Some conifers, such as lodgepoles, release the seeds from some of their cones only after a fire and use these dormant cones as seed banks (Figure 6.2).

There are also seedling banks—groups of seedlings in the shaded floor of damp forests. They remain small for years until conditions change.

One change, for example, is the opening of a glade in the forest following the death of a tree. In snow country, once a glade is open, it grows; the trees surrounding it get more sun on the sides that face the glade, so the branches on that side grow longer. Eventually, those branches grow so long that snow on them tips the trees over, enlarging the glade. When the glade becomes large enough, wind blows through it so strongly that it blows the snow off these branches, so the glade stops growing.

If you go to the Great Smokies you will see rhododendron balds, which appear similar to glades but form differently. They are an example of changing conditions allowing new plants to

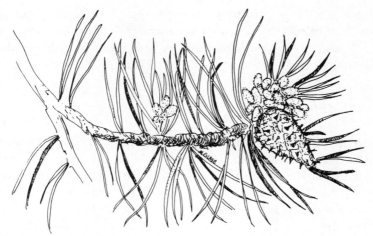

Figure 6.2. Lodgepole pine is a species that releases the seeds from some of its cones only after a fire. These dormant cones are its seed bank.
Courtesy of Marie Guise.

become dominant. Natural treeless areas that occur below timberline, the balds formed 4000 years ago when a change to a warmer and drier climate killed patches of spruces and firs. Beeches and maples filled in the spaces but died as it turned colder again, and grasses, alders, and rhododendrons invaded.

STRATIFICATION

Stresses are different in the vertical layers of a community. The forest floor, for example, has much more shade stress than the tree canopy. Scientists call the differences between these layers *stratification*. The layers in a forest include lichens and mosses, plants, shrubs, and trees.

Ferns love shade, so you often find them on forest floors; the fern fronds grow from rooted rhizomes under the ground. Each frond uncoils from a little roll, or fiddlehead. To reproduce, ferns grow spores underneath the fronds. A spore sprouts into a prothallus, a quarter-inch plant with one set of chromosomes and both an egg and sperm. To start a new fern frond, the egg and sperm must unite within water, which is why ferns live only in wet places.

Also common in the shade of the forest floor, where they live on decomposed leaves, are mushrooms, toadstools, and puff-balls. These fungi produce billions of spores in gills on their undersides that drift out or shoot out with sudden breaking.

SYMBIOSIS

Many fungi are parasites. Parasitism is a kind of symbiosis (or way that different species live intimately together) in which one organism exploits the other, sometimes hurting it (Figure 6.3). For example, the dwarf mistletoe, which lives on conifers, causes burls, resin dripping, and an overgrowth of twigs in one part of the tree. Insect galls are another product of parasites that you may notice. Plants and trees form galls by growing extra tissue

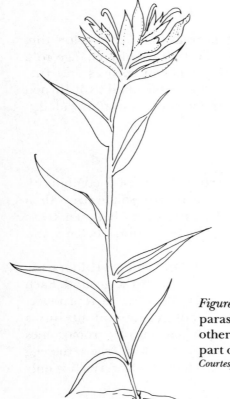

Figure 6.3. Indian paintbrush is a partial parasite. The roots grow into the roots of other plants, such as sagebrush, and steal part of their food.
Courtesy of Marie Guise.

to shut off insect parasites, usually midges or wasps. The extra tissue provides food for the insects' larvae.

Another kind of symbiosis, called *mutualism*, occurs when the relationship is necessary if both species are to thrive. For example, in order to grow, most conifers must have fungi called *mycorrhizae* on their roots. These threadlike soil fungi coat the root tips to get their food from the trees and absorb nutrients from the soil faster than the trees' root hairs can. The mycorrhizae stimulate growth, root branching, and reproduction in the host plants. Mycorrhizae are most common where nutrients are scarce, such as on the podzolic soils where conifers grow. Some mycorrhizae grow on only one species, others on several. Some mushrooms are the fruiting bodies of mycorrhizae.

Epiphytes demonstrate a kind of symbiosis called *protocooperation* in which both species gain from the interconnection, but it is not essential for either. If you have ever seen moss growing on a tree, you have seen an *epiphyte*. Obtaining nutrients from air and rainwater, epiphytes such as mosses, lichens, ferns, and orchids grow without roots on other plants. Most grow in temperate and tropical rain forests, where they often cover the trees with immense mats. Using climbing equipment, a researcher discovered that the trees grow aboveground roots into the mats to catch nutrients, which are scarce in rain forests because they are washed away by the heavy rain.

Another type of symbiosis is *allelopathy*. Allelopathy occurs when a plant or animal poisons its competitors. For example, the roots of the creosote bush produce toxins that kill competing plants. Many chaparral shrubs also secrete poisons. Still another type of symbiosis is *predation*, the eating of one animal by another.

Just as you may find yourself adopting a western drawl if you move to the west, some plants, even if they are not in symbiosis, change or develop characteristics according to the activities of plants or animals they depend on. Researchers found that at high elevations in some areas the small, trumpet-shaped flowers of scarlet gilia change color halfway through the summer to attract a different pollinator (Figure 6.4 and Figure 6.5). At first the flowers are red to attract hummingbirds. Then, after hummingbirds go south in late August, the new blossoms are pink or white, to attract hawkmoths (white and pastels are more visible at night when hawkmoths are out).

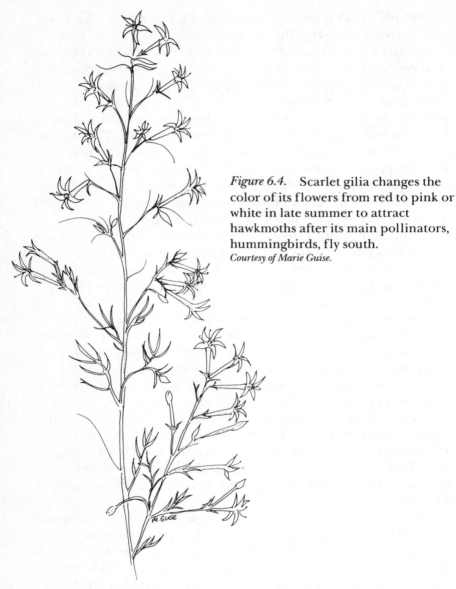

Figure 6.4. Scarlet gilia changes the color of its flowers from red to pink or white in late summer to attract hawkmoths after its main pollinators, hummingbirds, fly south.
Courtesy of Marie Guise.

The sky pilot, or *Polemonium*, has developed characteristics to foil those that eat it. This plant has small, double-ranked leaflets and light blue, funnellike flowers. Sky pilots produce either a sweet or a skunky odor depending upon whether attracting pollinators or repelling pests is more important where they live. At timberline and on tundra they are twice as likely to be sweet-

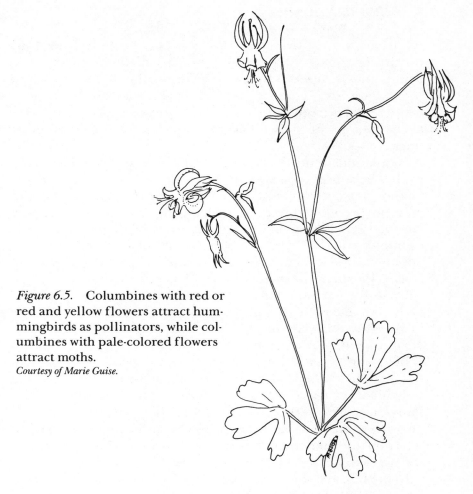

Figure 6.5. Columbines with red or red and yellow flowers attract hummingbirds as pollinators, while columbines with pale-colored flowers attract moths.
Courtesy of Marie Guise.

smelling, so they can attract bumblebees, as they are lower down. At lower elevations, where there are many ants to damage the plants, most of the flowers smell skunky, to repel the ants.

Conifers in the Pacific Northwest fight pine squirrels eating their cones by shedding their seeds before the young squirrels are old enough to eat them. In addition, every so often all the trees in a certain area produce no cones at all.

Another example is the two kinds of crossbills that live in the northern coniferous forests throughout North America and Eurasia. They have evolved crossed beak tips. The crossed beaks make it easier to pry apart the scales of the pine and fir cones these birds depend on.

POPULATIONS

Various ways of living together also occur within *populations*, which are groups of plants or animals of the same species. Populations originate by reproduction and by moving from somewhere else. Lack of food or space controls population increase. Any community has a limit, called the *carrying capacity*, to the number of individuals it can have in each of its populations.

Populations tend to increase and decrease in cycles. Many studies have been done on this tendency, but the cause remains unknown. Some biologists believe that a new population cycle may be brought about by a change in precipitation, over-crowded conditions, or new interactions with predators. For example, every few years the California tortoiseshell butterfly population will increase so much that there is a great migration. During the migration you often see flocks on mountaintops.

Less-suited populations tend to become extinct when their cycles become too extreme. Extinction can result from a change in heredity, such as the development of a lethal gene, or in environment, such as a long-term drought.

Behavior affects the arrangement of individuals in a population. Animals often have home *ranges*, areas occupied by one individual, or *territories*, areas occupied and defended by an individual. The territorial system helps isolate local groups, favoring inbreeding and the development of new species. The selection of a territory depends on the food supply and may change seasonally.

In the forested areas of mountains in Canada and the western United States, wolverines, large, dark brown weasels with a yellowish band on their coats, have territories of up to 100 square miles. These solitary creatures eat carrion, small animals, fish, and berries, and even though they are only the size of bear cubs they are so ferocious they can drive cougars and bears from kills (Figure 6.6). To keep away other animals, they mark their food caches with bad-smelling musk.

Like the wolverine, most animals mark their territories, either with their scent glands or with urine. Some use other methods. For example, black rhinoceroses stomp in their own dung to leave scent trails for other rhinos to follow. These rhinos, which

Figure 6.6.   Wolverines are so aggressive that they can drive bears and cougars away from kills.
Courtesy of New York Zoological Society.

live at elevations as high as 11,500 feet in Africa, are five feet high at the shoulder and weigh up to 3000 pounds. They are dark gray and have two 4.5-foot-long horns made of keratin, the hair protein. Because they have poor eyesight, black rhinos charge when they hear unfamiliar sounds or encounter unknown smells.

BEHAVIOR

Population density is regulated by aggressive behavior because it affects mating and the defense of territories. For example, during the rut, male elk, deer, and bighorn sheep fight to mate with the females. Because only the largest and strongest males can mate, the females bear sturdy offspring.

Reproductive behavior usually has rituals, such as behavioral *displays*. Many human activities could be considered displays—from playing football to wearing the latest fashion. Displays may be to discourage rivals, such as the baring of fangs in wolves, or to attract females, such as the drumming call of the sage grouse which it makes by inflating the sacs on its neck and expelling some of the air sharply. In spring the males congregate in certain open areas, called their *leks*, to parade up and down, sacs inflated and drumming.

Another bird that displays on the ground is the red-gold cock-of-the-rock which lives in the Andean and Guianan cloud forests. It is known for its mating dance, which it performs for the brown female in a three-foot space it clears on the forest floor.

Some animals grow special structures, such as antlers or extra feathers, to use in their displays. For example, courting male birds of paradise, which live at elevations of 9000 feet in Australia and New Guinea, display capelike plumes and ribbonlike tail feathers in forest clearings. Species of these birds are varying combinations of these colors—electric blue, dark blue, bright green, gold, and scarlet.

In addition to courtship and mating, reproductive behavior includes care of offspring. The greater the care given, the lower the egg and sperm production needs to be. Warm-blooded animals give the most care. In birds both sexes care for the young, but in mammals the mother provides most of the care. Both parents are needed to supply enough food for the young, so birds are usually monogamous.

The mountain environment affects reproduction because the short growing season reduces breeding. For example, Olympic marmots in Washington's Olympic Mountains, where timberline is low and the growing season short, breed less often than yellow-bellied marmots in the Rockies, usually only every other year. The young of the Olympic marmots also stay with their parents longer and mature more slowly.

Behavior of similar species may also differ with the habitat. Even-toed ungulates (hoofed mammals) that live in the open, such as antelopes, tend to be large runners with horns and distinctive markings; they usually graze in herds. Those that live in forests, such as deer, tend to be small camouflaged browsers that avoid running and live alone or in small groups. Predators mostly attack only those at the edges, so herds, flocks, and schools protect individuals in the groups.

STREAMS

Like grassland, fresh water is an open habitat unless it is clogged by vegetation. Life in moving water varies with the speed of the water, just as we find swimmers in still water and rafters and kayakers in white water. In fast streams, riffles provide food and pools provide shelter. The fast sections of mountain streams contain much oxygen but few fish and water plants and no plankton (miniature animals and plants). The current carries silt and sand along, leaving only rocks on the bottom. The diatoms, moss, and algae keep getting washed downstream, so they have developed a type of cement or other ways to stick to the rocks. For example, blackfly larvae attach themselves to rocks with a circle of hooks on their rears.

Living on the similar stonefly larvae is the torrent duck, which is found at elevations of 5000 to 18,000 feet in the Andes. This black, white, and gray duck has such large webbed feet that it can stay motionless, swim upstream, run across the surface of the water, or hide behind waterfalls. Using stiff tail feathers for balance, it can climb cliffs but seldom flies.

Silt and organic matter accumulate on the bottom of pools, where decay produces carbon dioxide. Other kinds of animals, including plankton, mollusks, and fish, live in pools screened by the marsh grass along the shore.

STANDING WATER

Lakes, large pools of standing water, are stratified into layers by temperature. The top layer of a lake is the warmest in summer and the coldest in winter. In the temperate region the warmest and coldest layers change places seasonally in processes called the spring and fall *overturns*. The overturns occur because water is densest at 40°F, so both warm and cold water will float on it. In tropical mountains, where daily temperature changes are great, overturns occur every day. In temperate mountains, life in lakes continues even when the upper layers of water are frozen.

Owing to variations in light, lakes and ponds have zones of life at different depths. *Ponds* are small lakes so shallow that rooted plants can grow on the bottom. Plankton and some fish live in the *limnetic zone* at the top of the water. The *littoral zone* is near shore, where light reaches the bottom, and so contains the most life. Typical pond plants are sedges, reeds, and pond lilies, which have air sacs to help their stems and leaves float. Little

light reaches the *profundal zone*, which is just above the bottom of
the lake, so few plants and animals live there. The bottom of the
lake, the *benthic zone*, is home to many decomposers.

Marshes, bogs, and swamps are distinguished from lakes by
the kinds of plants that live in them. *Bogs* are common in
mountain forests, where the ground is saturated year-round.
Semifloating masses of vegetation, such as heaths and sphagnum moss, encircle the edges of bogs; air cells in these mats
make them float. Peat is dead sphagnum moss that has not
decayed due to lack of oxygen. Bog water is so acid that it keeps
out plants from the surrounding forest. Boggy areas occur
around lake edges, on the sites of former lakes and ponds, and
in areas with poor drainage. Occasionally a mat of bog vegetation around the edges of a lake breaks loose during a sudden
rise in water level and becomes a floating island. Many lake
borders are *marshes* where sedges, reeds, and grasses grow. A bog
or marsh with trees in it is known as a *swamp*.

FRESHWATER LIFE

Many kinds of plants and animals live in and near fresh water.
Some have one cell, such as bacteria, molds, protozoa, and
algae; these are included in the category *plankton*. Plankton also
includes microscopic multicellular animals, such as rotifers,
ostracods, and water fleas. Larger freshwater animals include
insect larvae, fish, bank animals, water birds, snails, hydras,
flatworms, water beetles, worms, shrimps, mussels, and sponges.
Other animals, such as water striders, stonefly larvae, and
crayfish, live in the moving water of streams and rivers. Some
bank animals are muskrats, otters, beavers, frogs, and salamanders. Water birds include ducks, loons, terns, ospreys, and
the dippers of the alpine tundra.

An unusual freshwater animal found along mountain streams
and lakes in the United States is the water shrew, a six-inch black
insectivore. Water shrews live among boulders and spaghnum
moss and eat small animals. So much air is trapped in their fur
that they have to keep swimming to stay under water. Air-filled
fringes of hair on their back feet enable them to run across the
surface of the water.

Freshwater fish have adapted their bodies for maneuvering,

accelerating, or cruising long distances. Most fish you see in mountains migrate upstream to spawn, so they have the cruising type of body: thin and streamlined with strong lateral muscles. An example is the salmon, which migrates up to 1500 miles. Salmon swim from the ocean upstream to spawn and then die, and the young migrate back downstream to the ocean. Did you know that they return to the same stream they hatched in? Researchers discovered that salmon with their noses blocked lose their way, and that the odor memory comes from what the baby salmon eat in their first weeks.

Two more examples of mountain fish with bodies adapted for cruising are cutthroat and golden trout. Cutthroat trout, endemic to western North America, may reach 40 pounds in the Rockies. They are named for the red markings on their lower jaws. Originally found only in the Kern River drainage in California, golden trout have been transplanted to many high-elevation lakes and streams throughout the West. If reared at a high altitude, they are colorful, with yellow bellies, red stripes, and orange dorsal fin tips.

LAKES BECOME FORESTS

Lakes go through stages, starting out as *oligotrophic* lakes. These deep, geologically young lakes have a high amount of dissolved oxygen and few plants, animals, or nutrients. On a sunny day their water is clear blue and often colder than 40°F. Most alpine and subalpine lakes are oligotropic.

As lakes age they begin to fill in, and their water is less clear. They become *eutrophic*: shallow and warm, with a muddy bottom and many organisms. In summer so much decomposition occurs on the bottom of these lakes that it lowers the dissolved oxygen. The many nutrients that result from this decomposition make productivity high. If pollution adds excess nutrients, the algae will "bloom" or overgrow and use up the oxygen, killing the animal life. Nutrients are often high because soft rocks, from which water can easily dissolve minerals, surround the lakes.

Sediment and organic matter gradually fill in eutrophic lakes. Growth of each type of plant begins at the edges of the lake and moves toward the center. In the first stage rooted but submerged plants like pondweed cover the bottom of the lake.

Later, pond lilies and other plants with floating leaves grow. Still later, plants that project above the water appear, followed by shrubs and finally trees, as the lake gradually fills with organic matter and dries up.

Have you ever noticed small conifers in mountains advancing into flat meadows? These meadows were once lakes. Clumps of large trees on areas of higher ground in the middle of these

Figure 6.7.   The oldest bristlecone pines have only a tiny strip of living material. This one grows in the White Mountains, Inyo National Forest, California.
Courtesy of U.S. Forest Service, Pacific Southwest Region.

meadows once grew on islands. If conditions are right, eutrophic mountain lakes may change from mostly open water to mostly grass in as little as 50 years. Eventually forest takes over. Bogs, marshes, and swamps also become forests when accumulating organic matter raises the levels enough to dry them up.

Forests need certain conditions: a moist climate at all seasons, subsoil with a water reserve, few grazing animals or fires, and precipitation (rain in the growing season and enough snow to melt and provide water in summer).

The most widespread mountain forests are coniferous. One of the most remarkably adapted conifers is the bristlecone pine, which grows at elevations of 9500 to 11,000 feet. The oldest bristlecone, located near Wheeler Peak in Nevada, is 4900 years old, but the pines grow to an unusual age only on the dolomite soil found in the driest places. Those in sheltered places with plenty of nutrients and moisture die of heart rot at a much younger age. Dolomite holds more moisture than the surrounding sandstone and granite. It contains fewer nutrients but more easily releases those it has. Only a tiny strip of living tissue runs up the dead trunks of the oldest trees to nourish a few needles on single branches (Figure 6.7). The trunks grow only one-quarter inch in diameter in 60 years. Plenty of resin plus close-together growth rings make the wood decay resistant. You can see bristlecone pines in Nevada's White Mountain Wilderness, east of Bishop, California.

Examples of types of conifer forests and other ecosystems will be given in the next chapter, which discusses the distribution of plants and animals and ways of classifying this distribution.

SEVEN

Distribution of Mountain Plants and Animals

If you climb from California's Central Valley to the summit of the Sierra, you will notice a great change in plant life. On the first hills, oaks are scattered among the grasses. Farther up, scraggly digger pines grow with oaks and shrubs such as chamise and ceanothus. Beyond the foothill towns, forest begins with ponderosa (yellow) pine, Douglas fir, white fir, black cottonwood, incense cedar, and sugar pine. The shrubs now include madrone, with its red bark and shiny leaves. At 7000 feet the forest contains Western white, lodgepole, and Jeffrey pine, Sierra juniper, quaking aspen, and red fir, together with shrubs such as manzanita and huckleberry oak. Climbing a peak or riding a ski lift brings you to mountain hemlock and whitebark pine. The animals change, too, with elevation—the brush rabbit and gray fox of the digger pines give way to the pika and rosy finch of the whitebark pines.

In the Rockies, trees change from pinyon pine and juniper to whitebark and limber pines. In the eastern Himalayas trees progress from tropical silk cotton, through magnolia, tree ferns, and oaks, to rhododendron forests and then dwarf rhododendrons and junipers. On every mountain range the species change with elevation.

CLASSIFYING DISTRIBUTION

Biologists have found similar changes in going from the tropics to the poles and from moist forests to deserts. They noticed that climate controls the distribution of plants more than that of animals. In 1847, Friedrich Von Humboldt became the first to propose that the types of plants depend on soil and climate. Biologists tried to classify the differences between plants and animals in different areas, but they have never agreed on how to do this or even if it should be done. Some say life varies so much throughout the world that it is impossible to create comparable, accurate categories, but many have tried.

One problem is that each scientific specialty devised its own system. Faunal realms and floristic or floral regions—systems created by biogeographers—are classified according to the species in each region and the appearance of the vegetation. The life-zone system, first invented by a U.S. forester, uses only the appearance of the vegetation, as does the more recent biome system, originated by ecologists.

BIOGEOGRAPHICAL SYSTEMS

Biogeographers—those who study the distribution of plants and animals—divide the world into faunal realms (based on the higher animals) and floristic or floral regions (based on plant life). The *faunal realms system* was first used by P. L. Sclater in 1858 and Alfred Russell Wallace in 1876.

The system divides the world into three main realms: the Eurasian-African-North American, the South American, and the Australian. One subdivision, the Arctic-Temperate Region, including parts of North America, Europe, and Asia, shows that the basis for this classification system is that many of the same animals occur in different places.

The wolf, for example, ranges over Canada, Alaska, and Asia, in isolated areas of Europe, and in the extreme northern United States. Wolves are larger and have longer, larger noses than coyotes. Through cooperative effort in packs, wolves hunt several hoofed animals but also eat smaller animals like field mice (Figure 7.1). They concentrate on old, very young, sick, or in-

Figure 7.1.   Through cooperative effort wolves can successfully hunt large animals like moose.
Courtesy of New York Zoological Society.

jured animals; a particular pack usually hunts one type of animal. They cooperate in feeding and babysitting the young. Only once has a wolf attacked a human in North America, and the wolf was rabid. Accounts of European wolf attacks are exaggerated. Wolves do follow people traveling over snow but only so they won't have to break their own trail. Only the dominant male and female of the pack mate each year. During copulation the base of the penis swells and can't be withdrawn for a half hour. Wolves howl at any time, with a sound more likely than that of coyotes to be of constant pitch.

The second biogeographical system, that of *floristic regions*, has divisions that differ in area from the faunal realms. Its main divisions are *Boreal* (North America, Europe, and Asia); *Pa-*

leotropical (Africa, India, Southeast Asia, and Polynesia); *Neotropical* (South America); *South African*, or *Cape* (the southern tip of Africa); *Australian*; and *Antarctic* (Patagonia, New Zealand, and the South Atlantic islands). The Cape region of South Africa has many unique plants, such as proteas, that put it in a separate category. Proteas are shrubs or small trees that are pollinated by birds, but at high elevations some proteas, which have flowers hidden in the foliage, are pollinated by rodents. Proteas attract the rodents with nectar that is 40 percent sugar.

DISTRIBUTION TYPES

Besides dividing the world into sections, biogeographers have classified each species by a distribution type: cosmopolitan, endemic, or disjunct (discontinuous).

Genera found throughout the world in the same climate are called *cosmopolitan*. (A genus is the next-higher classification above species.) Cosmopolitan distribution is one of three types: *Arctic-alpine, temperate*, and *pantropical*. An example of a cosmopolitan genus is *Senecio*, an Arctic-alpine plant. Plant genera adapted to the year-round growth, seasonal variations in rainfall, and the lack of large storm systems in the tropics are called pantropical. Genera occurring in the moister parts of the Northern Hemisphere and in northern Southern Hemisphere mountains are called temperate.

Most species of mountain plants differ from those found on other mountains. For instance, if you look at Labrador tea, which grows in mountains of both the eastern and western United States, you will notice that the eastern plant has rust-colored wool underneath leaves with curled edges, but the western plant has only a thin coating of white hairs on flatter leaves (Figure 7.2). How closely related plants are depends on the distance and barriers between them. The two varieties of Labrador tea are endemic to their regions.

Endemics live in only one region or in only one tiny area. Their habitat may be unique, but usually isolation has made them distinctive. Mountain endemics are unable to migrate downhill because their respiration and photosynthesis rates are too high for lower elevations and warmer conditions. The farther south you go the more endemics there are. Most species of the region you live in are broad endemics like ponderosa pine.

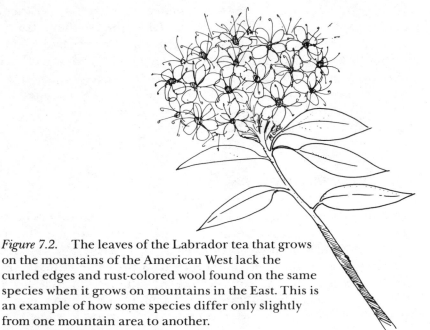

Figure 7.2. The leaves of the Labrador tea that grows on the mountains of the American West lack the curled edges and rust-colored wool found on the same species when it grows on mountains in the East. This is an example of how some species differ only slightly from one mountain area to another.
Courtesy of Marie Guise.

An example of a broad endemic is the snow leopard of Asia. Paler and smaller than true leopards, it lives in the Himalayas and Central Asia at elevations above 8000 feet. It has pale, gray-brown fur about two inches thick and round black spots on the head and faded rosettes on the body. The leopard's huge feet help it walk on snow, and its tail is fluffy for warmth. In summer it lives in a cave above timberline, but in winter it descends to forests as low as 3000 feet. Snow leopards can leap 50 feet in a single bound.

But other endemics called narrow endemics are restricted to a few square miles or acres. A few, like the giant sequoia, are remnants; others just haven't migrated yet. Some may never migrate because the barriers that isolate them will last longer than the life of the species. Giant *Sequoia* trees, the world's largest living organisms, weighing 1400 tons and standing 250 feet tall, live as long as 3200 years. They grow in scattered groves in the Sierra, at elevations from 5000 to 7000 feet. Fire-resistant dark red bark, up to two feet thick, covers the trunks; scalelike, quarter-inch-long needles cover the twigs.

Some endemics on mountain slopes evolved from lowland species. Most come from species that migrated from other mountains when the climate was cooler.

Mountain habitats resemble those on islands in the ocean, but mountaintops have more species. On mountains, zones of equal elevation form concentric rings, so the highest elevation has the smallest area and the fewest species. Still fewer species live on the more remote and smaller mountaintops. Some oceanic islands have endemic oversize woody plants on their mountains similar to the giant lobelias and groundsels of the African mountains. An example is the silverswords of the Hawaiian volcanoes (Figure 7.3). The Haleakala silversword, the best known of these plants, has long, thick silver leaves in a basal rosette covered with short, silky hairs. Every 20 to 200 years, the plants put up flower stalks with small wine-colored daisies. Instead of the usual air spaces between cells in their leaves, silverswords have a gel that can store water between rains. They are related to the tarweed found in California.

In the Great Basin of the American West each mountain range has its own, less-spectacular endemics. They evolved from species that lived on all the ranges when the climate was cooler. The coniferous forests at the summits of these ranges are remnants from 12,000 years ago, when the area was cooler and wetter than it is now.

When many miles separate populations of a species, the species is *disjunct*. Disjunction, frequent in mountains, occurs because the species disappeared in part of its range or migrated. Climate change, migration, mountain uplift, and continental drift can cause disjunction. When a species is disjunct, how do biogeographers know where it lived first?

The plant with the smallest number of chromosomes is the most primitive, so botanists have been able to trace the centers of origin of many plants by counting chromosomes. For most tropical species that is the Orient. All temperate families probably evolved from tropical ones.

MERRIAM'S LIFE-ZONE SYSTEM

In 1892, as the result of an 1889 study he led for the U.S. Department of Agriculture, C. Hart Merriam proposed that

Figure 7.3.   The silversword of Hawaii is a giant alpine plant endemic to Haleakala.
Courtesy of Haleakala National Park, Hawaii.

zones of vegetation be classified according to altitude and latitude. Merriam divided the zones by temperature and equated zones of latitude with zones of altitude.

Merriam's system has three regions: *Boreal, Austral,* and *Tropical.* Within the Boreal region, in order of decreasing latitude and altitude, are the *Arctic-alpine, Hudsonian, Canadian,* and *Transition Zones.* The Boreal Region includes the *tundra, taiga,* and *northern coniferous forests.* Within this region, the Arctic-alpine zone is treeless land. The Hudsonian Zone includes the taiga of

Canada and the upper regions of the subalpine forests. *Taiga* is the area of stunted trees between forest and tundra in the Arctic.

In the Hudsonian Zone in the Rockies, you may see foot-long Clark's nutcrackers, which are light gray with black tails, white bellies, and black wings. These birds build stick nests in junipers, larches, and pines near the tree line. They carry pine nuts in pouches under their tongues and hide them in inch-deep underground caches.

The Canadian Zone comprises the northern coniferous forests in Canada and the lower part of the subalpine forests. The coastal and montane forests in the West and the deciduous and coniferous forests in the East overlap in the Transition Zone. Below the Transition Zone in the West are the *Upper and Lower Sonoran Zones*.

One problem with Merriam's system is that the sequence of plants and animals on one mountain range differs from that on another range and from one side of the same range to the other. Furthermore, changes in elevation and latitude do not cause equivalent changes in life; Arctic species are subject to the midnight sun and long, dark winters, and mountain species are not. Biologists no longer use Merriam's system, but you may still find references to it. Local adaptations of his idea, such as a similar system for the northern Rockies, are still used.

OTHER ALTITUDE-ZONE SYSTEMS

In 1967, L. R. Holdridge attempted to revive the life-zone system by making it two-dimensional, with the altitude zones subdivided into types according to moisture.

A 1969 study found that altitude zones can never be true zones because plants appear and disappear independently of each other with elevation. For example, if you walk in the mountains of the western United States, you will see that different stands of Douglas fir have different understory plants, from grasses to huckleberries, at the same elevation. Moreover, the range of many species includes more than one altitude zone.

In 1973, Heinrich Walter divided the world into *zonobiomes*, divisions based on climate differences, and subdivided these into altitude zones he called *orobiomes*, or zones unique to the mountains of a particular zonobiome. Walter set up this system to account for his observation that the succession of altitude belts on mountains in different zonobiomes has little similarity and that those on one side of a range differ from those on the other because of the rain shadow. For example, the dry steppe or desert of the western Himalayas has some cedars, spruces, Himalayan fir, and birches. In the more humid eastern Himalayas, plants change from tropical to alpine in five vertical miles; silk-cotton trees give way to alpine tundra plants like *Saussureas*. These jug-shaped plants are found on limestone in the Himalayas at elevations between 16,000 and 17,000 feet. Their narrow, curly leaves are covered with thick pink or yellow wool. The warmth inside the holes in the tops of the plants attracts bumblebees, which pollinate the flowers.

BIOME SYSTEM

Ecologists have divided the world into types of ecosystems they call biomes. By the term *biome* they mean a large, recognizable set of biological communities, produced by a combination of climate, plants, animals, rocks, and soil. We have already discussed one of the major biomes, the alpine tundra. The biome system, originated by Frederic Clements in 1939, is the most accepted system today, but other ecologists divide and name the biomes differently. The system considers the whole community and its ecology as well as the kinds of plants and animals that live in it. Each biome has its own climate, day length, stages in succession, plants, and animals. The species in the same biome in different parts of the world are usually unrelated but often look similar. We have previously noted that all tropical alpine tundra contains giant plants.

Mountains contain several biomes—from alpine tundra to steppe, grassland, or forest. Climate prescribes the precipitation and its yearly distribution in a biome. Except on mountains, each biome generally covers hundreds of square miles. Biome boundaries correlate with latitude and altitude. Except for a few generalists, plants and animals in each biome are specially adapted to it. One of the generalists is the cougar. Cougars formerly lived throughout North and South America in a wide variety of habitats but now are found mainly in mountains and other wild areas. They prefer to stay away from people and will escape if possible rather than attack. Even though cougars prefer deer, they occasionally eat livestock, so settlers killed them off and often received bounties for doing so. Now they are protected in many areas. Adult cougars live alone except for the two-week breeding season, which is most commonly in winter and spring. The two to six cubs live with their mother about two years. Cougars respect each other's territories, which are marked with heaps of urine-scented brush or pine needles. The territories of adult males may be as broad as 150 square miles.

Within mountains plants and animals are adapted to differences in dryness caused by rain shadow. Both red and Douglas squirrels in the Pacific Northwest prefer fir cones, but when fir cones are scarce they will eat others. The red squirrels have stronger jaws than the Douglas squirrels. These jaws help them eat the hard cones of lodgepole pines, which are plentiful east of the Cascades. The smaller, dark-colored Douglas squirrels blend into the dark coastal forests and can easily reach the cones of the coastal hemlock, which grow at the ends of small branches. Thus more red squirrels live on the east side of the Cascades and more Douglas squirrels on the west.

TEMPERATE BIOMES

Temperate biomes include alpine tundra, rain forest, deciduous forest, chaparral, grassland, and two kinds of coniferous forest, *montane* and *Northern*. We have already discussed the alpine tundra in detail.

Northern Coniferous Forest

Spruces, firs, and pines distinguish the northern coniferous forest biome, which grows all across northern Asia and North America. Its northern boundary is the taiga, a zone of stunted trees at the edge of the Arctic tundra. The northern coniferous forest has less snow but a colder winter than the subalpine coniferous forest, which is the extension of the northern coniferous forest southward along the ranges. The soils of the northern forest are podzolic and usually thaw in summer when most of the precipitation falls. Ice-age glaciers changed the river-drainage patterns, so drainage is poor, with many tea-colored lakes and bogs. Spruces dominate, accompanied by firs, birches, and species of *Populus*.

The *Populus* of western North America, *Populus tremuloides*, is called the quaking aspen. These aspens often take over after fires because their seeds need bare soil and because they have advantages in this environment. Their bark can photosynthesize before the leaves come out and after they fall, and they mostly reproduce by suckers, forming clumps. They are called quaking

Figure 7.4. The grizzly bear, now restricted to a few isolated mountain ranges of North America, is more aggressive and unpredictable than the brown bear of Eurasia, even though the brown bear is so closely related to the grizzly that it is considered a subspecies.
Courtesy of Yellowstone National Park.

Figure 7.5.   A mother black bear with cubs can be as dangerous to humans as a grizzly bear.
Courtesy of Yellowstone National Park.

aspens because their leaf stalks are flattened next to the leaves
and turned 90 degrees to the leaf surface; this thin attachment
makes the leaves tremble in a breeze.

Shrubs and plants associated with the trees of the northern
coniferous forest are heaths, alders, ferns, huckleberries, members of the orchid family, and, in bogs, sphagnum moss. In
Europe the species differ, but the genera are the same. Typical
animals are beavers, moose, elk, weasels, wolves, bears, deer,
snowshoe hares, wolverines, lemmings, woodpeckers, and owls.

The grizzly bear (*Ursus arctos*), of the northern North American mountains, now rare, is more aggressive and unpredictable
than a subspecies, the brown bear, of Eurasia. Grizzlies avoid
humans except in areas where they become addicted to garbage
or picnic coolers. They are omnivorous, but their meat is usually
small animals and carrion. They have six-inch-long claws and
frosted-looking fur and shoulder humps. Their rumps are lower
than their shoulders, and their brow-to-nose line has a dent in it
instead of being straight like the black bear's (Figures 7.4 and

7.5). They may be brown, black, or pale beige. In winter they hibernate in excavated dens below timberline, but the rest of the year they prefer open areas. Advancing civilization has driven this once-widespread animal back into mountains. The bears in Alaska and western British Columbia make up an enormous subspecies, the Alaskan brown bear. Weighing up to 1700 pounds, Alaskan brown bears are heavier than polar bears.

Montane Coniferous Forest

The montane coniferous forest biome occurs only in the Northern Hemisphere. If you love mountains and live in this hemisphere, this may be your favorite forest. Firs, spruces, or pines dominate. The greatest number of species in any coniferous forest occurs in the American West. Understory plants differ greatly in the moist western and dry eastern sides of mountains in this biome; the western side supports lush forest plants such as rhododendron, and the eastern desert supports plants like rabbit brush and mountain mahogany.

Taking advantage of the moisture in forests on the west slope of the Sierra is a saprophyte, the snow plant. Found at elevations of 4000 to 8000 feet, this plant lives on decayed organic matter, flowering as soon as the snow melts. The entire plant is bright red, with an inch-wide stem and tiny scales for leaves.

Temperate Rain Forest

The coastal forests along the western edge of the United States are a temperate rain forest biome owing to their high rainfall; the heaviest rainfall in the continental United States (250 inches per year) falls on Olympic National Park on the coast of Washington. The major trees in this biome are western hemlock, western red cedar, Douglas fir, and Sitka spruce. Only a few epiphytes, mainly mosses, grow here, not the profusion found in tropical rain forests. Here there are several understory shrubs such as the devil's club, which has enormous maplelike leaves and long spines that cover all the branches and twigs. There is no dry season, but it is cold in winter. The frequent fog contributes 50 inches of the precipitation. Frogs, salamanders, and slugs love this wet forest, but the little forage allows few large animals. Blacktailed deer and Roosevelt elk are two major species. Berries, ferns, horsetails, and foliose lichens are typical. Other places in the world where temperate rain forests grow are southern Chile, Tasmania, southeastern Australia, and New Zealand.

In a rain forest in Chile and Argentina southern beech and *Araucaria araucana*, the monkey puzzle tree, dominate the lower mountain slopes in a narrow zone 200 miles long. The monkey puzzle has two-inch, sharp-pointed, overlapping leaves that cover its branches. Its ten-inch cones, borne only by the female trees, contain about 200 edible seeds, each about one and one-half inches long, called *pinones*.

Temperate Deciduous Forest

The temperate deciduous forest biome has deciduous hardwood trees, a definite winter season with snow, and precipitation of 30 to 50 inches evenly distributed throughout the year. So if you hike or backpack here, prepare for rain. These forests are often called *hardwood forests*, but some conifers have harder wood than the trees found here. The growing season lasts at least 120 days with no droughts.

In the United States, deciduous forests occur in the East and in the Midwest as far south as Texas. The warmth needed for broad-leaved trees is present in Japan and eastern North America because the Kuroshio and Gulf Streams bring warm ocean water north from the tropics. Elsewhere, deciduous forests grow in northeastern China, southeastern Siberia, Europe, western Russia, and the southern tip of South America.

Annual leaf shedding creates thick humus, rich in nutrients and earthworms. Because of all the rain, this humus and leaf litter are wet and support many salamanders. In the Appalachians, especially in the Smokies, each major ridge has its own species. One, the hellbender, is two and a half feet long. Salamanders manage to live at ground level here only by secreting smelly substances to repel the shrews that would otherwise eat them.

Many woodpeckers, squirrels, tree frogs, and other tree-dwelling animals also live here. Other common animals are weasels, bobcats, hawks, owls, raccoons, foxes, opossums, deer, black bears, and wild turkeys. Maples and beeches occur where it is moist; oaks and hickories where it is drier. Other trees are walnuts, tulip trees, and hornbeams. Cottonwoods, elms, willows, and sycamores grow along streams. Conifers like eastern hemlock, eastern red cedar, and eastern white pine are found in the United States together with understory plants like blackberries, raspberries, and sassafras. In western and central Europe oak woods occur. In the Southern Hemisphere southern beeches, members of the genus *Nothofagus*, dominate deciduous forests. Southern beech is similar to other beeches except trunks may be buttressed and some species are evergreen. The cove forests of the southern Appalachians, which occur at the lower ends of swift mountain streams where the ground levels out, have the most species of any deciduous forest.

Chaparral

The chaparral biome depends on frequent fires for its maintenance. Most plants here could be called brush. Leaves are evergreen, tough and leathery like those of oaks. Poison oak, snowbush, mountain mahogany, chamise, and manzanita are common shrubs in the western United States. Precipitation occurs mostly in winter as rain. The growing season lasts only two to three months between winter cold and summer dryness.

The pinyon-juniper woodland of lowland areas in the Great Basin and Rockies is an example of the chaparral biome and the mesquite of the Southwest is a chaparral shrub. Chaparral is also found in Mexico, the central and southern California coasts, central Chile, the Cape region in South Africa, southwestern Australia, and the Mediterranean.

North slopes of California chaparral may have California laurel, live oak, and shrubs, but south slopes have only grasses. Typical of the few animals are deer, elk, ground squirrels, and cougars. Chaparral here varies from a tangle of shrubs and small trees to open grassy woodland that would be called *savanna* in the tropics. Some ecologists place this woodland in a separate biome.

An animal endemic to the chaparral-covered California Coast Range is the California condor, which is black with a yellow head and red neck. With a nine-foot wingspan, this vulture is the largest North American bird. One reason it is nearly extinct is that it doesn't breed until it is ten years old and then only every other summer, when the female lays a single egg. All wild California condors have been captured in order to breed them to save them from extinction.

Temperate Grassland

The temperate grassland biome is divided by the height of the grasses. In the United States the grass gets shorter as you go from east to west, from tall-grass prairies through short-grass prairies to the cold semideserts of the Great Basin. Short-grass prairies and semideserts occur on lower mountain slopes throughout the world; the short-grass prairie that occurs in Eurasia from the Black Sea to Manchuria is called *steppe*. The 12 genera of grasses have more species than any other family except composites and orchids. Most grassland mammals are rodents or hoofed mammals that chew their cuds. Ants, as well as earthworms, mix the soil.

Grasslands have hot summers and cold winters, and they get most of their precipitation in summer. The tall-grass prairies of the U.S. Great Plains had summer precipitation and formed thick sod (a mixture of roots, soil, and grass rhizomes). This prairie rose into the low hills of the Midwest, but today trees and cultivation have taken it over.

Short-grass prairies have a dry hot summer, a severe winter, and bunchgrasses. In the United States buffalo grass, feather-grasses, needlegrass, and blue grama were commonly found on these prairies, but today cheatgrass (*Bromus*), an annual grass, has mostly taken over owing to overgrazing. Herbs include locoweeds, lupines, and balsam roots. Along streams grow willows, cottonwoods, and the nonnative Russian olive. Birds include warblers, magpies, blackbirds, and waterfowl, and among the small animals are prairie dogs, gophers, and ground squirrels. Larger animals include coyotes, pronghorn antelopes, and badgers. Once 13 million American bison roamed the tall- and short-grass prairies.

Original plants of the steppes in Asia were feathergrasses, blue sage, and peonies; some animals were horses, bison, and saiga, but cultivation and overgrazing have eliminated most of them. On the mountain slopes and in high valleys between the ranges of the Andes are the *punas*, areas of thin grasses inhabited by vicunas, chinchillas, guinea pigs, and mountain viscachas.

Red-brown or golden vicunas, which live on the punas, eat tola plants and grasses. Like llamas, an entire band of vicunas deposit their feces in the same mound to mark the territory they defend. Their large hearts, lungs, and large number of red corpuscles enable vicunas to run 30 miles an hour for several miles at an elevation of 15,000 feet. The larger, dark brown and white guanacos graze up to 17,000 feet, and like llamas, they spit at each other when angry.

In the southern Andes live a few chinchillas, rodents similar to pikas, that have been pushed to the edge of extinction by trapping. The hairs of their blue-gray fur grow so closely that lice and fleas can't enter.

The mountain viscacha is larger than the chinchilla—up to 15 pounds—and molts in patches all year, so its fur is less valuable. Viscachas live in crevices under rocks and whistle like marmots. They are like fat, gray rabbits, with short ears and long tails with brown tufts at the ends. Bristles under their noses resemble black mustaches.

DESERTS

Several mountain ranges have a desert biome on their lower slopes. In both temperate and tropical regions, evaporation exceeds rainfall. When rain does fall it often falls in deluges, causing flash floods. The rain often evaporates before it reaches the ground, so dew is a major source of water. The soil and rock absorb most of the solar radiation they receive by day, then radiate almost all of it back by night, so day and night temperatures differ greatly. Winters are mild. Major deserts are found in Arabia, Iran, Turkestan, western India, Africa (the Sahara), China, the Southwest, and South America.

Deserts usually have scattered thorny plants, succulents, and small annual plants called *ephemerals* that arise only after rains. The seeds of the ephemerals contain growth inhibitors, which wash away only when it rains enough. Because their roots compete for soil moisture, shrubs are widely spaced. Creosote bushes or cacti dominate the hot deserts of the United States.

Other plants are mesquite, acacia, agave, yucca, ocotillo, iron-wood, and palo verde. The small trees, such as mesquite and acacia, are often legumes. Roots grow down as far as 100 feet or spread wide at shallow depths.

You find severe winters in cool deserts. Sagebrush dominates the cool deserts in the United States, accompanied by bur sage, shadscale, greasewood, saltbush, and winterfat. There are also cold deserts: glacial ice, snow fields, and mountain fellfields.

Desert animals avoid drought by being dormant most of the year or, like rattlesnakes, by being active only at night. Sub-species of the western rattlesnake are found as far east as Texas and south into Mexico at elevations as high as 9000 feet. Dark blotches on muted ground colors pattern the skins of this five-foot-long snake. The markings are larger and more diamond-shaped than those of gopher snakes, and their heads are much wider than their bodies. They have heat-sensing pits on the sides of their heads to help them find prey. The pits can sense 3°F temperature differences.

Some desert animals, like kangaroo rats, make the water they need chemically from the food they eat. Their urine is crystal-lized, and feces are dry. Other desert animals show unique adaptations. Some snakes and lizards have special valves to shut their nostrils so they can dive through the sand. Some animals, like the desert foxes, or fennecs, of North Africa, have large ears to radiate heat. Other desert animals include the collared pec-cary, pocket mouse, jackrabbit, pronghorn antelope, roadrun-ner, cactus wren, doves, sage grouse, and sage sparrow.

TROPICAL BIOMES

Biomes of the tropics include savanna, thorn forest, monsoon forest, and tropical rain forest. Containing both tall grass and scattered thorn trees, *savannas* are intermediate between forest and grassland. Shrubs and trees overtake savannas if fires don't occur often. Savannas resemble the open chaparral of the Northern Hemisphere. They have frequent fires and seasonal rain but no winter. In the Southern Hemisphere, savannas bor-der most of the major grasslands and some desert areas. The typical pictures you see of Africa—with lions and giraffes—were taken in the African savannas, which have the largest number of species of grazing mammals in the world. Similar to the savannas are the *thorn forests*, also called *scrublands*, which have small twisted thorny trees, thorny brush, succulents, and annuals.

Many savannas have areas of rock outcrops where animals adapted to rocks are found. These animals also live high in the mountains on similar rocks, especially in Africa.

For example, rock hyraxes are found in rocky areas, and tree hyraxes occur in trees throughout Africa and the Middle East. Underneath their front paws, suction cups, moistened by a special gland, help these animals climb trees or rocks. These 18-inch vegetarian rodents show their relationship to elephants: The females have teats in both the front and the rear, as elephants do. Hyraxes have a patch of erectile yellow or white hairs on their backs, which cover glands used for marking the rocks around their homes.

Another example of a savanna animal is the 20-inch-tall klipspringer antelope, which leaps up and down steep cliffs in Africa. Male and female klipspringers take turns guarding their territory, which they have marked using the glands under their eyes. They both guard the territory, a practice unusual in mammals, because they are so small they have many predators.

In the tropical deciduous forest biome, often called the *monsoon forest*, rain falls mostly during the summer monsoon. Winters are dry and cool, and bamboos are common. These forests are found in Thailand, Burma, Indonesia, northeast India, and the southern approaches to the Himalayas, which are known for their colorful birds like pheasants and sunbirds. The Himalayan monal (Impeyan pheasant), for example, is iridescent blue, with touches of green, purple, and copper. In summer it ranges into the alpine zone. Tragopans (horned pheasants) are red with blue legs and neck pouches. Except for red splotches on a gray-green breast, the blood pheasant resembles a partridge but whistles like a marmot. Sunbirds take the place of hummingbirds here, with bright metallic plumage and long slender bills for drinking nectar. An example is the fire-tailed sunbird, which is yellow and red with a bright red tail.

A similar biome is the broad-leaved *evergreen subtropical forest biome*, which occurs where summer and winter vary only slightly in temperature and rainfall is high. Trees are mostly evergreen. Travelers will see this biome in Japan, Hawaii, southeastern

Australia, Taiwan, the Sudan, Brazil, Paraguay, southern China, the southern United States, and on the lower slopes of the Himalayas and the eastern slopes of the Andes.

Tropical rain forests, which have existed for millions of years, have more plant species than any other biome. Rainfall and temperatures are high and uniform. The forest is mostly ever-green, with epiphytes such as orchids, treetop animals, and vines called *lianas* growing in the little sunlight. The forest trees lock up most of the soil nutrients, and the heavy rains leach the rest of them, so undergrowth is sparse. Many of the trees are buttressed, meaning that the roots branch from the trunk aboveground. Usually there are several major trees in an area. Leaves are large, leathery, and simple (not lobed). Reptiles reach immense sizes here. Tropical rain forest is found primarily in Southeast Asia, West Africa, and the Amazon Basin. Slash and burn agriculture and firewood cutting are causing the rapid disappearance of this forest. As you go up tropical mountains the trees shrink, and the forest becomes montane rain forest, then cloud forest, and finally elfin woodland.

In the lower montane rain forests in South America, rainfall is heavy but of short duration and falls every two or three days all year. Most of the species are endemics. The trees are but-tressed and have aerial roots descending from the branches; palms, tree ferns, tree bamboos, and epiphytes are common. Flowers may grow right out of the trunks, a characteristic called *cauliflory*, because they resemble heads of cauliflower.

As you go up, the leaves decrease in size, bark is thicker, and there is less buttressing, cauliflory, and variety in tree sizes. Lianas, flowering plants, and the number of species decrease while lichens, mosses, epiphytes, and bamboos increase. Some temperate trees and plants occur above 1000 meters (3300 feet).

Between 3300 and 10,000 feet are *cloud forests*, consisting of stunted and twisted trees less than 20 feet tall. Mosses and liverworts cover the entire tree.

Central American and Andean cloud forests are brightened by a red, white, and emerald green species of the *Trogon* genus called the quetzal. These pigeon-size birds, which bear three-foot long trains of green feathers, were sacred to the Aztecs and Incas.

Above the cloud forests on windswept ridges in the *elfin*

woodland lives the gnarled quenua, or *Polylepis* tree. In Bolivia and Chile one species grows up to 15,570 feet, the highest elevation of any wild tree in the world.

Now that you have learned something about the natural history of mountains, you will want to get out in the mountains and see for yourself some of the things you have read about. But you first need to be prepared, so next is a how-to chapter on the basic methods of mountain travel, hiking, and backpacking.

E I G H T

On Foot In the Mountains: How to Hike and Backpack

Only hiking and mountain climbing pit you personally against the mountain environment. In some countries hiking has a different name: trekking, tramping, hill walking, or bush walking. You can usually ride a bus or drive to within a few days' walk of your destination. But to be able to travel safely and enjoyably on foot in mountains, you must prepare. This chapter gives you basic information on planning, safety, equipment, food, and wilderness ethics for hiking and backpacking. You will find out what information, skills, and equipment you need before setting out. Safe mountain climbing requires field instruction so is not covered here.

Mountain weather is unpredictable and can lead to fatal hypothermia, so every person who walks even a short distance in mountains needs information on equipment and safety. Getting information from local people in advance will help you plan. Conditioning, learning the skills, and advance planning of food, equipment, and route are the keys to a successful backpacking trip. Also important is maintaining a positive attitude when things become difficult, such as when it rains or snows. Thorough preparation will make trips more enjoyable.

PREPARING FOR A HIKING TRIP

The most important preparation is getting in shape so you will be fit enough to enjoy the trip. To strengthen the heart and

151

lungs, run, swim, bicycle, or take brisk walks for several weeks. To avoid injury, start this exercise program slowly. The jolting of running stresses the feet, knees, and back, so always run on a soft surface such as a golf course or dirt road. Choose a road with little traffic, wear white or light-colored clothing, and watch for traffic. Start by walking and work up to running. If you have a problem knee, back, or ankle, choose an alternative activity.

You also must be sure your boots are in shape by wearing them around town. Pressure points from new boots can cause blisters if not pressed out gradually by the feet. Check old boots to be sure the linings are not so worn that they will cause

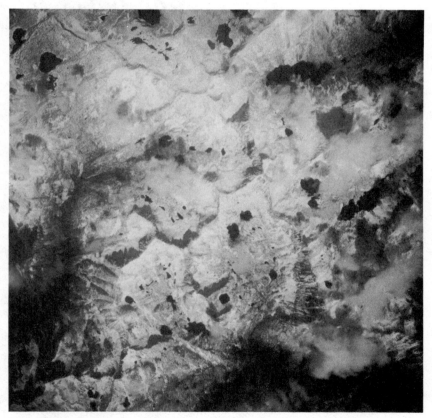

Figure 8.1.   To measure elevation differences, the makers of topographic maps merge two aerial photographs, taken from slightly different spots, into a three-dimensional image.
Courtesy of Stan Magryta.

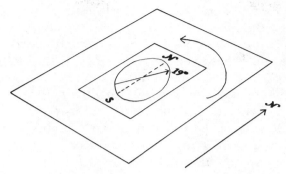

Figure 8.2. To use a compass with a topographic map, you must allow for the angle of declination, the difference in direction between magnetic north and geographic north.

blisters. Then take some day hikes in your boots and trip clothing.

Trips with an organized group will give you practice in backpacking and confidence in your hiking ability. Groups like the Sierra Club in the United States offer organized trips nationally and with local chapters. Another way to learn is to take a course in backpacking and then go on some day hikes and an overnight backpacking trip before attempting longer trips.

To help you plan your trip get topographic maps of the area you are visiting (Figure 8.1). Only topographic maps give enough details to be helpful when you encounter uncertain turns in the trail. Contour lines on these maps show the steepness of the terrain. On a topographic map the closer together these lines are, the steeper the slope. You can obtain topographic maps for the United States from Branch of Distribution, U.S. Geological Survey, Box 25286, Federal Center, Denver, Colorado 80225. Information on obtaining similar maps for other countries is given in the Appendix.

In order not to get lost, you should always figure out your location on the map at the beginning of a hike and continue to check your location as you proceed. To do this you must first orient the map using a compass as follows: (1) set the compass on a flat surface and turn it so its needle points north (N); (2) lift the compass up without turning it and put the map under it so that the needle points to the top of the map and is parallel with its sides (Figure 8.2); and (3) turn the map with the compass on it until the needle points to the number of degrees in the angle of declination east or west of north. North on the compass dial is now north on the map and in your surroundings. The angle of declination is the difference between magnetic north and true north at the spot where you are. For example, in the Sawtooth Mountains of Idaho the angle of declination is 19 degrees east of north. For that declination you will turn the map with compass on it counterclockwise until the needle points to 19 degrees.

While following trails, you can practice taking bearings on landmarks to learn to travel cross-country. A book on using maps and a compass will be helpful.

TRIP PLANNING

When you plan a trip, consider the terrain, trail, and possible emergencies. Choose an area and trail suitable for the physical condition and experience of all members of your party. If some members are inexperienced, begin with a well-marked trail that has a good access road. At first avoid trails with a steep climb or descent over a short distance. You can work up to remote areas, cross-country routes, poor access roads, and unsigned or poorly marked trails.

If the trail head is 5000 feet or more above where you live, plan to spend one to three days there to avoid altitude sickness. If a trip requires climbing several thousand feet at the start, allow two or three days for this part of the trip, so that the first day or two will be easy. At altitudes of over 12,000 feet limit your ascent to 1000 feet per day for the first week or so. You can climb more than that on side trips as long as you sleep only 1000 feet higher each night than you did the night before. Deliberately increasing breathing and fluid intake will also help prevent altitude sickness.

If your party includes beginners, choose a destination less than five miles from the trail head with a climb of less than 1200 feet. Once camp is set up, the energetic can take a side trip. Trying to hike too far and too fast leads to fatigue, which can cause accidents, altitude sickness, or even a heart attack. If the trip is easy and fun your companions will want to go again. At moderate altitudes average experienced hikers in good condition can do seven or eight miles and a 2000-foot climb while carrying a reasonable amount of weight: less than 35 pounds for women and less than 50 pounds for men. After three weeks of hiking at high elevations you can hike longer distances with comfort.

Before planning a trip get current information on trail and access road conditions in the area. For national forests of the United States, contact the district ranger's office for the district you will be hiking in. You can get that address from the forest supervisor's office. For national parks or land under jurisdiction of the Bureau of Land Management, contact the office of the particular park or the BLM office nearest the area. If you are going abroad, call the tourist offices for the countries you'll be visiting to find the best sources of information. Many countries require permission and a guide for some or all regions. Countries with political problems may close their mountains to hikers and climbers, and even if they haven't it may be dangerous to attempt a trip until the political situation is stable.

You must also find out if the access road will be open and if snow will still cover the trail by the time you take your trip. Ask about the condition of the trail or route. Are there temporary obstacles such as avalanche areas, washouts, burned areas, or high water? If it is too snowy, ice axes and experience in using them will be necessary. In that case, postponing the trip to later in the summer may be wise.

When you plan your trip allow yourself plenty of time to cover the distance in daylight so you can hike at a comfortable speed. The Sierra Club estimates one hour for every two miles of hiking, plus one additional hour for each 1000 feet of vertical climb when carrying a pack. You may be slower, so find out first by going on a practice hike. To avoid fatigue, keep from getting out of breath. Rest five minutes every 20 to 30 minutes. To save time and effort, don't bother taking your pack off while you're resting, but instead prop it on a log, rock, or hillside. If your companions begin to complain of fatigue, distract them with conversation, word games, jokes, or stories.

HIKING WITH CHILDREN

Distractions such as those just mentioned are especially useful when children are along. When hiking with children plan shorter hikes at a slower pace. For helpful hints on how to hike with children you may want to read the Sierra Club's *Starting Small in the Wilderness*. Backpacking with toddlers is so much trouble that you should consider limiting yourself to day hikes or hiring a babysitter. Infants and children over three years of age are easier to take along. Whatever their age, children need to be watched carefully.

If they are eighteen months or older, encourage your children to walk at least part of the time on a day hike, although many types of baby carriers are available. At four, our youngest went on a five-day trip, hiking about half the time and riding a horse with one of his parents during the rest. At seven, as an experienced hiker, he carried his own sleeping bag out from a base camp and went on adult-length day hikes.

When hiking with children, keep in mind that they prefer water, snow, and dirt to scenery. Take toys, games, and books to keep them occupied. Small children enjoy carrying a toy, their jacket or blanket, and some snacks in a little pack.

To make a trip with young children easier, hire a horse packer, who can inexpensively spot-pack your family and gear into a base camp. Then you can take day hikes from the base camp. In some areas you can rent mules, burros, or llamas.

Teenagers prefer to go on independent expeditions, but first they need some experience with family or organized group trips. When teenagers go on a trip with friends, it is wise to help them make an equipment checklist and have the trip members meet the night before to check their equipment and be sure no one is planning to carry too much. And, whether teen or adult, if you have the right equipment you will have a safer trip.

PLAN FOR SAFETY

You need to plan your trip for safety. Always leave your exact itinerary and expected return date in writing at home or at a ranger station. Remember to check back with the ranger station after the trip. In some areas permits are required in advance. Always allow extra time and food for an emergency. When you leave word with the ranger or someone at home add an extra day to your itinerary. That way if someone has a stomach ache or you miscalculated the difficulty, you can take your time.

Take two or three people with you, so someone can stay with the injured while another goes for help. Three is the minimum for remote areas, except for experts. When experts go alone they carry extra food, water, first-aid equipment, and a signaling method. On day hikes experts will take equipment to stay overnight.

Be equipped for unusual weather. If you're wearing rain gear, you can keep walking in the rain, except in a cloudburst or when lightning is striking nearby. It is all right to hike when snow is falling if you can keep warm and find the trail, but use caution to avoid slipping. It may be safer to camp until the snow melts. In a thunderstorm get off peaks and away from isolated trees, the crest or base of cliffs, and large open areas. The safest place is in a valley or forest, but avoid standing under large trees.

HYPOTHERMIA

Storms can bring hypothermia, the biggest danger in the outdoors, which can be fatal. Hypothermia occurs when exposure to cold and wetness lowers body temperature to dangerous levels. In many mountain ranges it can snow any day of the summer. If your clothes get wet, you can get hypothermia at 40° or 50°F. So take a shelter, warm clothing, and rain gear even on day hikes. Use several light layers of clothing, rather than one or two heavy layers, for more warmth and flexibility. Put on warm clothes, including a wool hat and gloves, when it first seems cold. Avoid getting your clothes wet with sweat by putting them on and taking them off as needed. Check your rain gear for leaks. Clothing must stay warm when wet, or you must include a tested method of keeping it dry. Carry your sleeping bag in a plastic bag inside a waterproof stuff sack so that there are two layers of waterproof material around it. Wool, some synthetics, and polyester or nylon pile or fleece keep you warm even if wet. Wet down and cotton chill the body.

Wind adds to the chilling of cold temperatures, as shown in the table on the next page. If someone in your party develops persistent shivering, he or she is in the first stage of hypothermia, so make camp and put dry clothes and a warm sleeping bag on the victim. Then give a hot drink and a snack. If hypothermia has progressed to the second stage, the person will act confused, stumble, and may be semiconscious. At this stage avoid hot drinks because they worsen the condition. Very gently, put the

WIND CHILL FACTORS

		Effective Temperature in Fahrenheit						
	0 mph	50	40	30	20	10	0	−10
Wind Speed in	*10 mph*	40	30	15	5	−10	−20	−35
Miles Per Hour	*20 mph*	32	20	5	−10	−25	−35	−50
	30 mph	23	10	0	−20	−30	−50	−65
	40 mph	16	10	−5	−20	−35	−55	−70

victim into a sleeping bag, stripped, with another stripped person. Rough handling or a too-rapid rewarming of the victim could be fatal, as could any exertion by the victim. Hot drinks and a snack are helpful only when the victim begins to recover. Afterward, full recovery takes eight hours. Checking equipment before a trip and seeing that rain gear is put on when rain first starts can often prevent hypothermia. Overexercise, tobacco, alcohol, dehydration, fever, or injury increase the risk.

CROSSING STREAMS

When planning your trip always consider stream crossings, another major danger. Detour or turn back rather than trying to ford a dangerously high stream. Logs floating down a creek mean danger. You can wade a swift stream safely only if it is less than 12 inches deep and a moderate stream only if it is less than knee-deep, but you can wade a deeper stream if it is slow. In murky water probe ahead with a stick. Never tie into a rope to cross a stream because it can hold you under water. Your group leader might rig a hand line, then the rest of the group can cross on the downstream side of the line to avoid being entangled in it should someone fall.

Wet or moss-covered logs are treacherous. Sometimes you can cross an uncertain log on hands and knees or by hitching along while sitting down. It's safest to wade across on gravel in the wide part of the stream. If the stream is swift, sand is treacherous. Rounded rocks under water are very slippery. Keep your boots on, but tie them loosely so they can be removed easily if you fall. Wet socks cause blisters, so change to dry socks as soon as you reach the other side. Or you might take off your socks and wear the boots alone to wade the stream, then replace the socks once you've reached the other side. Tennis or running shoes lack the ankle support vital in stream crossing. If there are many fords, wear plastic bags over your socks and let the socks get partially wet. The smooth surface of the plastic helps prevent the blisters the wet socks would otherwise cause.

Before crossing a stream unfasten the hip belt of your pack so it won't hold you under water in a fall. Face upstream and move sideways diagonally upstream. Use a stick and hold it upstream from your feet. Then move only one of your three "legs" at a time. Three hikers can form a tight circle with arms on each other's shoulders and then cross with one person moving at a time. Stronger hikers may wish to carry others' packs across.

CROSSING SNOWBANKS

Another danger is crossing snowbanks. The easiest time of day to cross is in midafternoon when the snow is soft and steps can be kicked. But large, steep snow slopes can avalanche on warm afternoons, so cross steep ones in the morning. If you will need to cut steps or wear crampons, carry an ice ax and know how to use it. This type of snow travel requires previous training and practice in the use of an ice ax. Glacier travel requires mountaineering training and ropes. Plan your route to avoid snow and glacier travel, or take the training in advance of the trip. Unexpected large areas of snow call for a change in route.

ACCESS ROADS

Another source of problems can be the access road, so take it into account when you plan your trip. Access roads vary in quality and times during which they are open. Some of those that are drawn on the map with two broken lines are much worse than others and are not suitable for passenger cars. Ask when the road will be open, if it is rocky or muddy, and what type of vehicle can travel it. Take your car to the garage for a checkup before the trip and carry a jack, lug wrench, and in the fall carry chains. Two-wheel-drive cars may not be able to travel some roads in bad weather, and even four-wheel-drive trucks can get stuck.

LEAVING NO TRACE

The shortness of the growing season on mountains means that the damage hikers do to them can last for hundreds of years. To avoid hurting the environment, follow suggestions for no-trace or low-impact camping. Plan your trip so that you will leave no trace of your presence in the mountain environment.

You can minimize damage by staying on the trail if there is one. Besides causing erosion, taking steep shortcuts can be dangerous, especially with a pack. Do not cut across switchbacks; it is illegal to do so in U.S. national forests and parks. When hiking in a meadow keep to the most worn path. Cross snow on the trail, rather than taking a detour around it, if it is safe to do so. In remote areas you may leave a cairn of rocks to mark places where hikers might otherwise lose the trail. Elsewhere use only temporary markers, if any, and remove them on the return. Finally, before leaving rest sites or camps, pick up litter.

SELECTING A CAMPSITE

In selecting a campsite, first consider the environment. Camp at least 100 feet from a lake or stream and 100 feet from a trail. Use sites that have been used before but not overused. Camp on conifer needles, on leaves, or sand but not on grass. If grassy sites are all there are, move the tents every night.

Second, consider your comfort and safety. Select camp sites with good drainage. If they are too level, water will puddle when it rains. Instead of digging trenches, put a plastic sheet inside the tent to keep things dry, and use a foam or air mattress instead of boughs. Place extra clothing under sleeping bags and pads to add warmth. Keep tents out of gullies and from under dead trees or limbs, very large trees, and boulder fields. Choose campsites with morning sun and afternoon shade, unless you will be up and gone before sunrise. If so, you might prefer late-afternoon sun. Meadows, lake shores, and stream bottoms are cold and have mosquitoes, so camp on knolls if possible. Since wind blows upslope during the day and down at night, pitch tents so trees shelter them from the night wind.

Third, consider the enjoyment of other campers. Select sites away from other parties and try to be quiet. Use unobtrusive dull colors for tents and equipment. However, for maximum visibility during hunting season hunters and hikers should use brightly colored equipment and wear blaze orange.

STOVES AND FIRES

Use backpacking stoves and preserve wood supplies at camp-sites for warming fires or emergencies. Stoves save time, especially in rain. Avoid using picturesque dead trees or logs for firewood because they may be the homes of animals or birds. Build only warming fires, and build them only when there is plenty of wood and little wind. Use existing fire rings or bare ground. A ring isn't needed for a warming fire. Due to the lack of wood, do not build fires at or near timberline. Burn only wood that is on the ground and can be broken by hand; axes are hazardous and leave unnatural scars. Be sure the fire is away from anything that will burn, especially dead logs. Any time you leave camp, water the fire until it's cool.

If camping at an unused site, avoid building fires on humus or pine needles or next to a big rock. Fires scar rock. Put the fire in a small trench dug down to mineral soil. Refill the trench after the fire is drowned and cool.

SANITATION

To keep the wilderness clean, carry out trash that will not burn. Do not throw it in backcountry or campground toilets. Do not bury it—animals dig up and scatter buried garbage. Burn or carry out fish guts, leftover food, diapers, tampons, and sanitary napkins. Foil food envelopes will not burn, and the aluminum oxide that is formed by attempting to burn them will prevent plants from growing. Carry out any trash you find; unless you do so, most of it will stay there forever.

Try to prevent the spread of disease by water pollution. If there are backcountry toilets, use them. Otherwise, go 200 feet from water and campsites and dig holes six to eight inches deep and refill them after use. Bacteria in that layer of soil decompose waste faster than if it is buried deeper or left on the surface, but that is not very fast in the human time scale, so be careful where you dig. Burn toilet paper carefully on the site, or put it in a plastic bag to burn in the fire. When conditions are dry, carry the toilet paper out with you. Toilet paper decomposes slowly, and animals will dig it up and scatter it. Consider using moss or leaves instead.

Remember to also bury your dog's waste. If you can't make your dog mind, leave it home. Keep dogs out of the water by having them drink from a dish. Keep them from bothering other hikers or wildlife. Dogs attract bears, so you may prefer to hire someone to care for your dog at home. In some areas dogs are not allowed; in others they must be leashed.

Keep lakes and streams clean by washing and dishwashing at a distance from them and dumping the wash water on the ground. Before swimming, wash and rinse first, away from any lake or stream. Use small amounts of biodegradable soap, sold in tubes or bottles at backpacking stores.

GIARDIA

If everyone were careful with sanitation, intestinal diseases like *giardia* would be rare. Giardia is a protozoa-caused diarrhea that has become widespread in mountains in the United States and other countries. Wild animals can get giardia, so once humans bring it into an area it will stay. No matter how clear, all mountain water is suspect. Giardia causes severe diarrhea, gas, and stomach cramps six days to four weeks after exposure. It varies from annoying to incapacitating and if not treated recurs. Twenty percent of the population are symptomless carriers.

Either boil water for three to five minutes at a full rolling boil or use a filter. Boil it 20 minutes if you are concerned about bacteria and other organisms. Giardia cysts are about 5 by 9 microns, so any commercial filter with 0.2 to 0.4 micron filtration should work if the filtration is as advertised. Just be sure to change the filter unit as often as the directions say. Water from small side streams and springs with good drainage will be the cleanest untreated water, but it cannot be trusted. In some areas you can catch other intestinal diseases from water, if giardia alone isn't enough to persuade you to boil or filter it.

SAFETY

Wildernesses are less dangerous than highways, but you still need to take some precautions for safety on a hiking trip. You can be a danger to yourself outdoors. For example, you can fall by tripping over tent cords, by looking at the view while walking, by loading the pack so the weight is centered too high, and by climbing cliffs with inadequate training. You can also fall or pull a muscle because your pack is too heavy. You can have an accident with a knife, ax, or gun. Be careful on steep grassy or needle-covered slopes. Follow stove directions carefully. Be careful with fires. Swim in toward shore and only in calm water that isn't ice cold. Watch out for old, unmarked mine shafts. Panic caused by fear of the dark can lead to an accident. The biggest danger in that scary dark is you.

Try to resolve any problems as soon as they arise. Turn back or make camp in bad weather or at once when someone is ill. Put moleskin on sore spots on feet right away; don't wait for blisters. When cold, don't wait for hypothermia to develop before stopping for a hot drink and snack. Exhaustion makes accidents and hypothermia more likely, so make camp as soon as you become tired. If the trail is in bad condition, or seems more difficult for some of your party than anticipated, turn back or shorten your goal. If you encounter thick fog, make camp and wait until it clears. Caution your party to avoid kicking loose any rocks that might fall on other hikers. Keep the party together or check on everyone often by having faster members stop and wait at agreed-on check points. Someone experienced should hike with the slower members of the party.

ALTITUDE SICKNESS

The first symptoms of altitude sickness are headache, nausea, sleeplessness, dizziness, mild shortness of breath, and mild swelling of hands, face, or ankles. Headaches may occur with exertion if you are 5000 feet or more above where you live. Altitude sickness happens even to the physically fit. A difficult hike and heavy pack make it more likely, as does ascending to 10,000 feet or higher too rapidly. It occurs more often in children and in acclimatized people who spend several weeks at a lower elevation and then return to the mountains. Full adaptation to high altitude takes several weeks.

Altitude sickness can develop into life-threatening pulmonary and cerebral edemas, but usually only at altitudes well over 9000 feet. Cerebral edema causes violent headaches, loss of coordination, and extreme weakness. The symptoms of pulmonary edema resemble those of pneumonia. Symptoms warning of a possible threat to life are continued vomiting or headache, a heart rate of over 100 after resting, blueness of lips or face, and great shortness of breath. If suffering from any of these, descend immediately in order to avoid sudden death.

HEAT ILLNESSES

Learn to recognize problems caused by heat. The symptoms of heat stroke are hot and dry skin, a lack of sweat, confusion, a temperature of over 105°F, and possible loss of consciousness. Immerse victims in cold water, or cover them with cool, wet cloths. Rest alone will not bring down the high fever. Prevent heat stroke by drinking enough water, eating salty food, wearing a hat, dampening the hat and your clothing, and resting often in the shade. In hot weather, travel only in the morning and evening. The condition can recur and be fatal, so take victims to the doctor as soon as possible.

Heat exhaustion is less serious. The symptoms are pale, moist, cool skin; a low temperature; and fainting and nausea. Have victims lie down in the shade and drink salted water. They can hike again but must be more careful.

Dehydration occurs in winter as well as in summer. Symptoms include reduced urine output, thirst, slow motion, lack of appetite, drowsiness, and high temperature. Dehydrated people can become delirious and wander off. To prevent dehydration, drink two quarts of liquids per day in moderate weather and a gallon in hot weather.

The air is thinner in the mountains, so there is more ultraviolet radiation to cause sunburn. Use sunburn cream and keep untanned skin covered most of the day. Children are more susceptible to ultraviolet than adults. Creams containing PABA are the most effective.

PLANT AND ANIMAL HAZARDS

Animals and plants can be a hazard, so find out about the local ones before you go. Common hazards in the United States are insects, spiders, snakes, bears, poison oak and ivy, and diseases carried by rodents. To prevent insect bites wear a long-sleeved shirt, a hat, and a head net, and use an insect repellent containing N,N, diethyl-metatoluamide. In areas where ticks are common in spring and early summer, examine yourself once or twice a day for ticks. Ticks usually walk around several hours before burrowing, and only embedded ones cause disease. In addition, only a few are infected. Ticks carry Rocky Mountain spotted fever and tularemia in the western United States and Lyme disease in the East. These diseases can be treated with antibiotics. Insect repellent or white gas may encourage a tick to back out, or it can be pulled out with tweezers. If you find ticks embedded in your skin consult a doctor after the trip. To pull out a tick with tweezers, pull slowly to encourage the tick to relax its grip and to avoid breaking off its head.

Those allergic to bee stings should bring their medicine along and keep it handy. An injection of adrenalin (epinephrine) is necessary to save someone with a severe allergy. Black widow spider bites usually cause only redness, swelling, and stomach cramps; these spiders live under rocks and logs. Brown recluse or "violin" spiders can cause large, boillike infections that must be treated with antibiotics. Scorpions live in tropical and desert areas, and some are poisonous, but few bites are fatal. Scorpions in the U.S. Great Basin have a bite similar to a bee sting and can be treated similarly.

Rattlesnakes are found all over the United States, usually only at elevations below 5000 feet. Many mountains are too high, and thus too cold, for rattlesnakes. Other poisonous snakes in the United States are the coral snake and copperhead. Treat a bite only with bed rest and a constricting band, not a tourniquet. Keep the bite lower than the level of the heart. In half the cases of snake bite, little or no venom is injected. Ice and cut-and-suck methods cause more damage than the bite itself. Consider the cut-and-suck method only in severe cases where medical help is more than five hours away. To prevent snakebite always *look* before placing your hands and feet. In high grass or brush in snake country, swish a long lightweight stick ahead of you to prevent surprising a snake. In other parts of the world consult local authorities about poisonous snakes and the treatment of snake bite.

Bubonic plague is endemic in rodents, so never feed or handle any. Plague-carrying fleas can infest the burrows as well as the animals, so avoid pitching a tent near rodent burrows.

Rats, skunks, and raccoons may be rabid. If bitten, try to catch and kill the animal and keep the head. Refrigerate it if possible. See a doctor immediately, so preventive treatment can be started if needed, because rabies is fatal. In some areas so many bats are rabid that you should avoid sleeping outdoors without a tent.

BEARS

Proper food storage, personal hygiene, and cooking and sleeping locations will help avoid unpleasant encounters with bears. Most bears in the United States (except for Alaska) are black bears, but a few grizzlies live in Glacier and Yellowstone parks and in remote areas nearby. Grizzlies are common in Canada. Few bears in remote areas will come near humans or campsites. But where bears see people often, there are problems.

Black bears are only about 25 percent as dangerous as grizzlies, but following the same precautions will prevent problems with either bear. In remote areas problems usually occur only in drought years. When hiking through brush make a loud noise, as by blowing a whistle. If you meet a bear, talk softly to it while backing slowly away. If it charges you try to distract it by dropping a pack or camera. Automobile or pencil flares will often scare bears away without the dangers caused by firearms. In bear country avoid camping near signs of bear activity, hang food in a tree at night, and keep food and cooking downwind and at least 200 yards from tents. Don't sleep out without a tent.

A good method for hanging food is to put it in a plastic bag inside a coated nylon stuff sack at least twelve feet from the

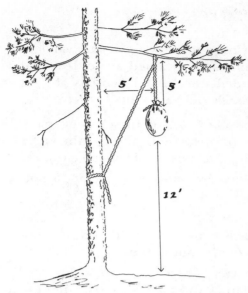

Figure 8.3.   In bear country, hang your food in a tree at least 12 feet above the ground and at least five feet from the trunk and from any branches.

ground, five feet from the trunk, and five feet below any branches (Figure 8.3). To do this, tie a nylon cord to a small rock and throw the rock over a tree limb. It is difficult to raise more than 15 pounds on one cord, so you may need to split up the food and hang each bag separately. Hang any unburned garbage with the food, downwind from your camp. If you climb trees well you can make a bear-proof cache by stringing a line between two trees and hanging the bag from the line. Keep food out of tents, and keep sleeping bags and the clothing you wear to bed clean. Do not sleep in the same clothes you cooked or ate in. Keep the campsite clean and the garbage burned, but make sure it burns completely. Plastic garbage bags over packs at night will keep dew off and will keep animals like porcupines from chewing the sweat-salty straps.

Women should not plan to go into grizzly bear country during their periods. If you are in grizzly country during a period in spite of planning, use tampons and wash several times a day. Burn the tampons thoroughly if fires are allowed. Otherwise wrap them in several layers of plastic and carry them out.

THE TWELVE ESSENTIALS

You usually need to know about survival only for a short-term emergency such as a sprained ankle. For an emergency, carry the items termed the "Ten Essentials" by the Seattle Mountaineers, although there are actually twelve.

1. Extra clothes (all of these): long pants, sweater, pile, fleece, or insulated jacket, rain jacket and pants or poncho and chaps, wool hat and gloves, extra wool socks.
2. Extra food beyond needs of trip; a pot or metal cup is optional.
3. Pocket knife.
4. Waterproof matches, with scratch plate from box if needed, or butane lighter.
5. Fire starter. There are four kinds: stick, paraffin and cardboard, jelly in a tube, and conifer pitch.
6. First-aid kit, including prescription pain medication to treat shock.
7. Flashlight with extra bulb and batteries.
8. Topographic map.
9. Compass.
10. Sunglasses. If it snows, sunlight on snow can cause temporary but painful snow blindness.
11. Shelter. On a backpack trip you have a tent, but on a day hike carry a space blanket, tarp, or tube tent with cord to put it up.
12. Full water bottle or method for filtering or boiling water.

FIRST-AID KIT

The contents of a first-aid kit vary with the length and remoteness of the trip. Some suggested items are:

1. Prescription pain medication (essential for treating shock)
2. Prescription antibiotic for wounds
3. Prescription diarrhea medication such as Lomotil

4. Prescriptions for recurring medical problems or illnesses
5. Aspirin, Tylenol, or anti-inflammatory pain killer
6. Antibiotic ointment such as Polysporin
7. Band-aids
8. Telfa or gauze squares with adhesive edges
9. Adhesive tape
10. Moleskin and nail scissors to cut it
11. Nail clippers
12. Lip balm
13. Sunburn cream containing PABA
14. Antihistamine-decongestant such as Chlortrimeton
15. Tweezers
16. Needles
17. Butterfly bandages
18. Snakebite kit (only for remote snake country)
19. Cortisone ointment for insect bites or poison ivy
20. Ace bandage, 4 inches
21. Milk of magnesia for laxative and upset stomach
22. Infant diarrhea formula such as Infalyte for shock
23. Insect repellent
24. First-aid book

WHAT TO DO IF LOST

Avoid getting lost by using a map and compass, and backtrack immediately if you lose the trail. If you get lost anyway, sit down and orient the map and compass with landmarks. Panic is what kills, so stay still, keep calm, and plan what to do. If separated from the rest of your party, shout, whistle or signal with a mirror. Try marking a spot and then walking a search grid pattern. While doing this, be sure to carry your pack so you won't lose your essential equipment. If this tour is unsuccessful, stay put and make camp. Let others find you.

Set up a shelter near water, and build a fire if needed. You can set up a tarp as a lean-to facing the fire. Green branches on the fire will create a smoke signal. Three separate small fires mean

SOS. Put plastic bags over your socks, wear all your clothing, and pad the ground under you with dry leaves, grass, or pine needles to help you keep warm. You can survive a month or so without food, but water and warmth are vital. Insects and their larvae are the most convenient and safe survival food. Field guides to wildflowers often list edible plants, but avoid any plants that might be confused with poisonous ones, especially members of the parsley family.

GIVING FIRST AID

A Red Cross first-aid course will give you confidence in an emergency, and a class in cardiopulmonary resuscitation will teach you that life-saving technique if you haven't time for the full Red Cross course. If you haven't taken a class, read a Red Cross or mountaineering first-aid book, and take it along on the trip.

When an accident happens, follow Red Cross procedures. Check first for breathing and heartbeat and give cardiopulmonary resuscitation if needed. Then control bleeding and treat for shock. Do not move a victim unless his or her life is in danger. Nonprescription formula powder for treating the chemistry imbalance of infant diarrhea is helpful for shock. If giving antibiotics for a wound be sure the person is not allergic to that antibiotic, and if giving an aspirin-containing pain killer check that the person is not allergic to aspirin. Avoid giving the new anti-inflammatory pain killers to anyone with asthma or an aspirin allergy. The Red Cross book describes procedures for treating many problems.

Blisters are the commonest problem on a hike. Moleskin is both prevention and treatment. Apply moleskin at the first feeling of a sore spot. If a blister breaks, cut a small telfa pad to fit it and cover with a large piece of moleskin. To take pressure off the blister, cut a second piece of moleskin into a doughnut shape with the cutout the size of the blister. Place it over the first. Extra layers of moleskin seem to stick better than molefoam. Another remedy for blisters is the jellylike Second Skin®.

Before the trip learn how to send for rescue in the area. Always send for help in cases of suspected neck or back injuries. You can walk on a mildly sprained ankle in 48 hours with the aid of an ace bandage, stick, and someone to lean on. But never walk if there is a chance the ankle is broken. If you have a large group and a small victim, you can make a stretcher using two poles and a sleeping bag by ripping out the stitching in the foot of the bag and inserting the poles.

If in doubt, send a written message for help with the exact location, names of the victim and those still at the scene, the type of injury and when it happened. When more than two are in the party, leave one person with the victim while you go for help. Be sure the message gets to the right authorities. Stay around so you can lead the rescuers to the site if needed. Helicopters are available in most areas in the United States, but they are expensive and may not be covered by your insurance.

CHOOSING EQUIPMENT

If your equipment is adequate you will be able to deal with most problems and emergencies. Choose backpacking equipment by weight as well as purpose. Use what you have, and buy new items gradually to avoid gimmicks. To go light you will need to limit the hobby equipment (cameras and fishing gear) that you take. Someone who backpacks only once or twice a year can get by with less durable equipment than a person who backpacks often. Some stores rent tents, packs, and stoves. Renting before buying will give you a better idea of your preferences. Buying boots or a pack from a catalog sometimes costs less than buying them from a store, but to be sure of the size try on some at a local store before ordering.

Minimum equipment includes the following items:

1. The "Twelve Essentials," including first-aid kit
2. Tent
3. Pack
4. Boots
5. Extra clothes, including long pants
6. Mirror and whistle for signaling if you're lost
7. Food
8. Sleeping bag inside plastic bag and waterproof stuff sack
9. Sleeping pad

10. Stove and fuel

11. Cooking pots, cups, and utensils

12. At least 25 feet of nylon cord

13. Toilet paper

14. Assorted plastic bags

15. Extra socks

16. Sun hat

17. Water bottle

18. Toothbrush and toilet articles

Boots

Of all the equipment on the list, boots are the most important. The best boots are lightweight all-leather ones. Mountaineering boots weigh too much, and most partly fabric boots
do not give enough ankle support for backpacking. Good boots
are expensive, but cheap leather boots dry into wrinkles after
they get wet. Heavy people need heavy boots. For those with foot
problems such as heel spurs, the comfort of a fabric boot may
outweigh the lack of support. Test boots for support by bending
the boot top to the side. Stitching around the outside top of the
boot soles shows that the boots can be resoled. A few boots are
stitched on the inside, but most that have no visible sole stitching are cemented and cannot be resoled. Vibram soles give the
best traction but do more environmental damage. Women
should buy women's boots because they will fit better.

Try boots on at the end of the day so your feet will be at their
largest. Use both layers of your hiking socks. When the boots are
unlaced and the feet slid forward, one finger should fit behind
each heel. Also, when the boots are laced up and tied and the
feet are slid forward on a slope, the toes should not touch the
ends of the boots. To break in boots, wear them around the
house for a week, and return them if they don't fit. After that,
wear them around town and on several short day hikes before
wearing them backpacking.

To make boots comfortable wear two layers of socks—an
outer sock of rag wool or wool with a curly layer inside, and an
inner sock of any light material except cotton. The most comfortable liners are polypropylene. Socks with cotton in them

cause blisters; cotton is abrasive when damp. If allergic to wool, use a synthetic, not cotton. At bedtime dry socks keep your feet warmer than sweaty ones.

Clothing

All mountains have much colder, wetter weather than lowlands, so take clothing that protects you from cold weather and rain. Mountaineering expeditions and high-altitude treks will require expedition-weight clothing and sleeping bags. For moderate climates and altitudes the equipment described here will be sufficient and in warm areas can be lighter.

People who tend to stay warm can substitute a vest for the insulated jacket. Take a down jacket only if you are sure you can keep it dry. Three light layers are better than two heavy ones. Those with a tendency to be cold may also wish to take along polypropylene or wool long underwear. Polypropylene wicks moisture away from the body and stays warm when wet. Buy clothing and sleeping bags with a vapor barrier layer only if you will mostly be using them *below* 32°F; above 32°F vapor barriers feel wet and clammy. Take wool pants as your extra pair of pants, perhaps a pair from a thrift shop. Pile or fleece pants are fine if kept out of stickers, which can ruin loosely woven, fuzzy pants. Avoid jeans—they are heavy, cold if wet, and dry slowly. Poplin is good for the other pair of pants because it is lightweight and dries fast. Take waterproof, micropore, or coated nylon rain gear with both body and leg protection. Plastic tears too easily. To keep out water, micropore fabric must be kept clean according to directions. All micropore fabric lets a little moisture through and allows some condensation. It is more comfortable than waterproof fabric but loses water resistance under heavy use.

Sleeping Bags and Pads

Sleeping bags have either down or synthetic fill. Down weighs less and has a smaller volume while providing the same warmth. Synthetics are cheaper and less durable, but they stay warm if wet, which down does not. Loft (thickness) or "Good to *x* degrees" describes sleeping-bag warmth. "Good for −10°F" bags may feel cold at 20°F but too hot at 60°F. Companies vary in the loft and amount of fill they say will be warm enough at a certain temperature. Construction also affects warmth: Close-fitting bags are warmer than roomy ones.

Three-season bags, the best weight for summer mountain backpacking, should contain at least two pounds of down or three and a half pounds of synthetic fill. Construction methods will make the bag weigh from four to seven pounds. People who more readily feel cold will want a winter weight, but not expedition, bag. The best construction for down is slant or overlapping tube. The best synthetics have offset seams with a double thickness of insulation quilted separately. Nylon toothed zippers wear better than metal or nylon coil zippers. If you are cold in your sleeping bag consider buying a micropore fabric cover or a lightweight shell or liner bag to add warmth without the expense of a new bag. Even an old lightweight blanket, folded and sewed up the side and across one end, can serve as a liner.

You can machine wash most sleeping bags on gentle cycle once a year. Some must be hand washed, so be sure to read the label. Dry them in the dryer with a clean tennis shoe to fluff the down. A special down soap is available. Sleeping bags can be dry cleaned, but a special solvent is required for down. Afterward, air the bags thoroughly for two or three days because the fumes can be *fatal*.

Sleeping pads insulate you from the cold ground. Closed-cell foam will stay dry but is less comfortable than open cell. Air mattresses without foam filling are comfortable but give no insulation. Self-inflating air mattresses filled with foam are heavier but more comfortable than either type of pad.

Tents

Buy a backpacking tent that keeps out insects and has a breathable shell and separate coated rain fly. A tarp or tube tent is inadequate except in emergency, because water vapor condenses on the inside of a coated tent, just as it does in a shower. A breathable nylon tent with separate rain fly is warmer than a micropore fabric tent. Micropore tents are lighter but expensive, and some moisture does condense. Avoid tents with guy lines in front of the door; you might trip on them. The most practical size is a two-person tent that weighs less than seven pounds. To clean a tent, set it up and wipe out the inside with a damp rag. Reseal the seams every year with seam sealer.

Stoves

There are two main types of stoves, white gas and butane. To start a white-gas stove you first prime it by burning a little white gas to heat the burner. These stoves often will flare up when you prime them. They burn unleaded gasoline or camp stove and lantern fuel. White-gas stoves heat water much faster than butane, but only a couple of brands have models that will simmer.

Butane stoves operate so poorly if it's below freezing that they must be kept warm in your sleeping bag at night. They are easy to operate; you need only to turn on the gas and light. Be sure to check the cartridges for tightness before each lighting. Cartridges can be changed only when they are empty. The heat output drops as they empty, so the last meal on each one will take a long time to cook. Cartridges must be carried out, and the strong smell of butane will permeate food carried with them. Butane stoves do simmer, but they go out if turned too low.

Other Useful Equipment

Aluminum pots are lighter than steel ones and spread heat better. For a party of three or four, take only two pots unless you plan to boil water for drinking. If so, take an extra pot that holds at least two quarts. Plastic cups and nylon utensils save weight and avoid burning your lips with hot metal. You don't need plates. Pot grippers or gloves are helpful for cooking. Nylon-filament pot scrubbers make fine dishcloths. Also take a metal pot scrubber if you plan to cook fish or eggs. Use a metal spoon with a flat bowl as a spatula, or buy a tiny spatula at a gourmet food store. Plastic tubes with screw lids and roll-up ends are handy for margarine, jam, and peanut butter. So are small Nalgene plastic jars you can buy at backpacking stores. Those made of other kinds of plastic usually leak.

Put together a repair kit containing such things as dental floss, large needle, clevis pins and rings for pack repair, repair patches for tents and air mattresses, stove-maintenance kit, duct tape, safety pins, small piece of wire, and a glasses screwdriver.

Bandannas or cloth diapers make lightweight towels and washcloths. Those whose boots are heavy will find tennis shoes or insulated booties a welcome luxury for evenings. Paperback books and decks of cards or miniature games are fun for rainy evenings. Try to keep personal items like toothpaste to a minimum by sharing some things.

Packs

Padded shoulder straps and a full padded waistband are essential for a comfortable backpack. To be comfortable, the padded waistband must *completely* encircle the waist separately from the pack.

External frame packs are best for loads over 25 pounds because almost all the weight rests on the hip bones, but they can catch on things or sway. Climbers, cross-country skiers, and those going off trail usually prefer internal-frame packs because the weight stays close to the body and is evenly distributed between hips and shoulders. The weight will pull on your shoulders and rest on the small of the back, making you lean forward. In hot weather internal-frame packs make the back sweat. So try on both kinds with more weight than you normally carry to see which you prefer. A good store will have weights. To ensure quality, buy a well-known brand of pack. To save weight and expense avoid extra straps and large capacity. A long-waisted person will take a larger-frame size than normal. The top of the waistband should rest on the top of the hip bones.

Men are most comfortable with a total pack weight of less than 45 pounds and women with a total pack weight of less than 35 pounds. The weights for longer trips will probably have to be more than that, but try to carry less than 30 percent of body weight. You can arrange food "drops" for longer trips by having food flown to an airstrip at a guard station or ranch, by having a packer meet you at a prearranged place with food, or by hiking out to a vehicle or a post office partway along.

FOOD

One of the most important preparations you will make for your trip is for its fuel: the food. A diet high in carbohydrates and moderate in protein, fats, and sugars provides the best nutrition and the most energy. Freeze-dried food saves weight but is expensive, so many backpackers try to use little of it. Using freeze-dried meats with grocery-store casseroles avoids the need for canned meats. For the first night's dinner you can take solidly frozen hamburger or steak and it will thaw by dinner time. Some food ideas are given in the list that begins below.

Buy only this year's freeze-dried food, and make sure there are no punctures in the envelope. Punctures allow water vapor to enter and spoil the flavor, so pack the food carefully.

Make a menu for each meal of each day, then figure the quantities. Better digestion and nutrition will result from eating several small meals instead of three large ones. Make a table listing the items, how many each package serves, the number of

---

Backpacking Store Foods

Breakfast

freeze-dried eggs and omelets	bacon bars

Lunch

pilot biscuits	freeze-dried fruit
dehydrated cheese	freeze-dried ice cream
dehydrated peanut butter	freeze-dried sandwich spread

Dinner

freeze-dried dinners	specialty desserts
freeze-dried casseroles, meats, and vegetables	

Beverages

egg nog mix

Grocery Store Foods
Breakfast

instant oatmeal
granola
pancake mix
fresh eggs for the first day
    or two carried in a
    plastic box

canned chopped ham
hash browns
fresh or canned bacon
English muffins
granola bars
toaster pastries

Lunch

unsliced bread
English muffins
sourdough rolls
crackers
cookies
cheese (especially Gouda
    or Edam cheese in
    paraffin)
squeeze-tube cheese
dry salami
peanut butter, jam, or
    honey

margarine
raisins
dried fruits
fruit leather
banana chips
nuts
granola bars
any candy that won't melt
beef jerky
trail mix (fruits, nuts, and
    candies)

Dinner

packaged casseroles
canned tuna, chicken, or
    roast beef
Chinese noodle soup
    mixes
packaged sauces with
    noodles or rice
dried scalloped potatoes

dehydrated and freeze-
    dried soups
instant and cooked
    pudding and desserts
cooked dehydrated
    apples
cookies

Beverages

dehydrated fruit drinks
powdered milk
coffee

tea
instant cocoa

meals at which it will be served, the number of servings needed, and the number of packages to buy. For example, instant oatmeal comes in a box that serves ten so for four breakfasts for two people you will need to buy one package. On long trips you can probably carry only one pound of food per person per day, due to weight considerations, and thus you will probably lose weight during the course of your trip.

Take the food out of boxes and put it in plastic bags, being sure to include directions cut from the boxes. Leave freeze-dried food in its envelopes or cans; once open, they keep only for a day or two. Put each meal for each day in a separate bag, labeled with a permanent marker ("Dinner #1, Breakfast #2," and so on). Group these bags in larger plastic bags, marked for breakfasts, lunches, and dinners or with day numbers. Put condiments such as cocoa and margarine in small bags within a large separate bag.

PACKING YOUR PACK

To pack a backpack, put the heaviest items toward the top nearest the back, with frequently used things in pockets. On an external-frame pack attach the sleeping bag underneath the pack bag. Tie it on the pack with straps, not stretchy nylon or rubber cords. You can alleviate hip soreness by padding the hips with a sweater or jacket around the waist.

Now that you have read about how to prepare for backpacking trips, you are ready to take an armchair trip to the mountains of the world in the next chapter.

N I N E

Ranges and Peaks of the World

To give you ideas of new places to backpack, this chapter takes you on a tour of the mountain ranges of the world. Orient yourself by looking at the maps as you read. Along the way are tips for travelers and descriptions of what it is like to be in a particular range. The tour begins at the Coast Range of western North America and goes east around the globe, moving from north to south in each region. The more prominent ranges are identified on the regional maps. Note that spellings and place names, especially for Asia, can vary significantly from one source to another. Thus the names or spellings you see here may differ from those you've seen before.

NORTH AMERICA (MAPS 9.1–9.5)

The **Rockies, Sierra Nevada, Cascade,** and **Coast** ranges form north-south barriers in North America from Alaska to Mexico. **Mount Logan,** the highest peak in Canada (5951 meters; 19,519 feet), rises over 16,000 feet above its base, and other mountains have cliff faces as tall as the 7000-foot ones of the **Tetons,** so all these western ranges are rugged. Some of the mountains glitter with immense glaciers, while drier ranges hold ice under moraines in rock glaciers. The climate varies from Arctic to hot desert. The best weather is in July and August, although in a few desert ranges it is more pleasant in September and October. In season the wildflowers sprinkle multicolored dots over the grassy slopes and meadows. An example of the colorful mountain flowers in these ranges is the alpine laurel (*Kalmia microphylla*), which lives in meadows and bogs. The anthers of these tiny, pink bell-shaped flowers are tucked into pockets in the petals, which form swellings on the outside. Insects entering the flowers dislodge the anthers, which spring up and cover them with pollen.

A double mountain chain hugs the coast of the western United States and Canada from Alaska to southern California. Along the coast in the Yukon River watershed stand the **Saint Elias Mountains**, with Mount Saint Elias (5402 meters; 18,008 feet), and inland from them is the **Kluane Range**. A favorite hike in Yukon Territory is to retrace part of the famous **Chilkoot Trail** of the Klondike gold rush from Dyea to Bennett, British Columbia.

In Alaska you see the Coast Range as a backdrop from Juneau, Wrangell, or Ketchikan. **Kates Needle** (3055 meters; 10,020 feet), and the **Devils Thumb** (2767 meters; 9077 feet) are two of the highest peaks here. Farther north, as the range turns west, the name changes to the **Fairweather Range**. Northwest of the Saint Elias Mountains the **Wrangell Mountains** in Alaska include the 4949-meter (16,237-foot) Mount Sanford near Valdez. West of the Saint Elias Mountains along the Alaskan coast lie the **Chugach Mountains**, with **Mount Marcus Baker**, near Anchorage, the highest peak at 4016 meters (13,176 feet). The Fairweather Range contains **Mount Fairweather** (4663 meters; 15,300 feet), and **Glacier Bay National Monument**. These mountains of the Alaska panhandle, the highest coastal ranges in the world, have such severe weather that they look as if they had been carved out of ice rather than rock. The **Alaska Range**, which includes **Mount McKinley** (6194 meters; 20,320 feet), the highest mountain in North America, forms an immense arc north of the Chugach and Wrangell mountains. You can drive from Anchorage or Fairbanks to Denali (formerly Mount McKinley) National Park on the Denali Highway, but you must ride a bus to tour the park. The Alaska Range continues southwest into the **Aleutian Range** along the **Aleutian Islands**. The highest of the Aleutian volcanoes is **Mount Torbert** (3479 meters; 11,413 feet) in Katmai National Park. The **Brooks Range** extends east and west across northern Alaska in hilly Arctic

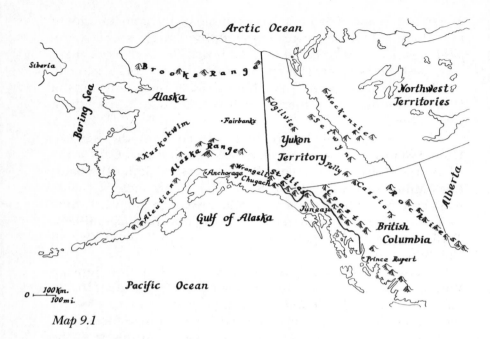

Map 9.1

tundra with a few rock towers. Access is from airstrips at Wiseman and Anaktuvik. The highest peak is **Mount Michels** (2816 meters; 9239 feet).

In British Columbia the west section of the Coast Range sinks into the ocean as mountainous islands: Vancouver and Queen Charlotte. These continue into southern Alaska, where the best known are **Baranof** and **Admiralty**. The tallest peak on Vancouver Island is the **Golden Hinde** (2200 meters; 7216 feet). On the mainland, the eastern chain, simply called the Coast Range, contains glacier-covered **Mount Waddington** (4016 meters; 13,177 feet).

The next named section of the Coast Range is the **Olympic Mountains** of Washington with 2428-meter (7965-foot) **Mount Olympus** in Olympic National Park. Because these mountains are so near to the ocean, they receive up to 200 feet of snow each winter and have timberline at only 4500 feet. Even on a sunny summer day you may see wisps of mist drifting up from the Pacific and swirling around the peaks. Here you first walk through the green shadows of a rain forest of western hemlock, Sitka spruce, and Douglas fir where moss covers tree branches. On the moss of every fallen log grows a row of little evergreens.

If it weren't for these nurse logs, the seedlings would drown. Higher up, among the mountain hemlocks and subalpine firs, salal and blackberry-like salmonberry bushes overgrow the trail. On grassy hillsides clumps of purple lupine and red mountain heath grow much taller than normal.

North of San Francisco the coastal section is just called the Coast Range. The interior range from north to south contains the **Trinity Alps** and the **Klamath**, **Yolla Bolly**, and **Mendocino** mountains. The Klamaths rise to **Mount Eddy** (2754 meters; 9038 feet), near **Mount Shasta**. In California chaparral cloaks many of these ranges. Farther north they reach the full mossy splendor of the temperate rain forest.

Along the outer part of this chain in southern California run the **San Gabriel**, **San Bernardino**, **San Jacinto**, **Santa Ynez**, and **Santa Lucia** ranges. Inland about 20 miles is the **Diablo Range**, which runs from San Luis Obispo north to **Mount Diablo** near San Francisco Bay.

The Cascades stretch from **Mount Lassen** in northern California to southern British Columbia. They are famous for their volcanoes, such as Mount Lassen (3187 meters; 10,457 feet) and Mount Shasta (4317 meters; 14,162 feet) in California; **Mount**

Map 9.2

Map 9.3

Hood (3427 meters; 11,235 feet) in Oregon; and **Mount Rainier** (4392 meters; 14,410 feet), **Mount St. Helens** (2550 meters; 8364 feet), and **Mount Baker** (3285 meters; 10,778 feet) in Washington. The **North Cascades** contain nonvolcanic mountains with saw-toothed peaks, widespread glaciers, and a precipitation difference between the western and eastern slopes of as much as 75 inches. White avalanche lilies fill the meadows near the melting snow here.

You can take the **Pacific Crest Trail** along the crest of the Cascades from **Mount Baker** in northern Washington through northern California to join the 250-mile-long **John Muir Trail**, which stretches from Yosemite to **Mount Whitney** along the summit of the Sierra. Because of crowds, hiking the Muir Trail requires a permit.

The **Sierra Nevada**, bordering California on the east, is a tilted fault-block range containing Mount Whitney (4418 meters; 14,494 feet). Even though you can climb this peak by trail, it is the highest peak in the United States south of Alaska. Glaciers in the Sierra have sculptured white granite into aretes, horns, domes, ridges, and miles of pavement. **Lake Tahoe**, a 23-mile-long sapphire blue lake, stretches between two uplifted fault blocks. Three-thousand-foot granite walls, famous for excellent rock climbing, enclose **Yosemite Valley**. A string of wildernesses and national parks follow the crest of the range.

In the **Desolation Wilderness** west of Lake Tahoe you see acres of cobalt blue lakes—**Ropi, Aloha**, and others—lapping against acres of white granite. Mountain hemlocks with bent tops and needles carried in whorls crouch in meadows between the granite benches next to the bells of white mountain heath. A pale brown chipmunk striped with black and white may try to steal your sandwich.

The **Great Basin** extends from the Sierra to the **Wasatch Mountains** in Utah and north to Idaho. One geologist described the many short fault-block ranges as a bunch of caterpillars crawling north to the Snake River. Here in the **White Mountain Wilderness** stands the highest Basin and Range peak, **White Mountain** (4316 meters; 14,246 feet), sprinkled with bristlecone pines on the upper slopes. Other ranges include the **Trinity**, **Toiyabe**, **Monitor**, **Pancake**, **Snake**, **Egan**, **Santa Rosa**, **Independence**, **Ruby**, and **Jarbridge**. In the Jarbridge Mountains near the Idaho border, the **Matterhorn** reaches 3304 meters (10,022 feet), and the **Ruby Mountains** east of Elko contain **Ruby Dome** (3471 meters; 11,387 feet). In these desert ranges, which have only 4 to 11 inches of annual precipitation, the vegetation may change directly from sagebrush to spruce-fir forest as you climb.

The **Rockies** form the backbone for North America for 450 miles from Mexico to northern Canada. In Idaho and Colorado, the Rockies widen into several ranges up to 900 miles across. Streams on the west flank of the Continental Divide drain into the Pacific, and those on the east into the Atlantic or Gulf of Mexico.

The **Selwyn Mountains** barricade Canada's Yukon Territory from the Northwest Territories. The **Big Salmon**, **Pelly**, and

Dawson ranges in the south and the **Richardson, Ogilvie,** and **Wernecke Mountains** in the north slant across the center of the territory. The highest peak in these ranges is **Keel Peak** (2972 meters; 9748 feet) in the Selwyn Mountains. In the Northwest Territories the **Mackenzie Mountains,** with **Mount Sir James McBrien** (2758 meters; 9049 feet), face the Yukon.

There are many glaciers and the **Columbia Icefield** along the Alberta-British Columbia border near Banff and Jasper. Most lakes here contain enough rock flour to tint them a milky turquoise or aquamarine. The highest peak in the Canadian Rockies is **Mount Robson** (3954 meters; 12,972 feet), just west of Jasper in British Columbia.

Typical of the Canadian Rockies are **Lake Edith Cavell** and **Angel Glacier** in **Jasper National Park.** The milky aquamarine lake sits below the dark face of **Mount Edith Cavell,** which is striped at an angle with snow on rock ledges. The two arms of the glacier rest on a ledge, while the body spills down the wall in a narrow ice fall. Ponds in the moraine contain so much rock flour that they resemble pea soup. Gray-and-white Clark's nutcrackers sing noisy background music as they beg for handouts.

If you were flying over southern British Columbia, you would see west of the Rockies a network of ranges, including the **Monashees, Cariboos, Selkirks,** and **Purcells.** The highest in the Purcells is **Mount Garnham** (3468 meters; 11,378 feet) of the **Bugaboo** group. **Mount Dawson** (3390 meters; 11,123 feet) is the highest in the Selkirks. The highest in the Cariboos is **Mount Titan** (3581 meters; 11,750 feet), and in the Monashees it is **Mount Monashee** (3246 meters; 10,650 feet). The trees in these mountains in the Northwest and southern Canada are a mix of Rocky Mountain and coastal species, because the moisture-bearing winds from the sea reach inland. Between the Rockies and the Coast Range in the north are other short ranges: the **Cassiar, Three Sisters, Ominec,** and **Skeena.** The highest mountain is **Edziza Peak** (2787 meters; 9143 feet) in the Skeena Mountains.

In the middle of Wyoming the Continental Divide outlines both sides of the Wyoming basin. This break in the chain of the Rockies divides the range into northern and southern sections. The Northern Rockies in Montana, Idaho, and Wyoming include several ranges and subranges.

Among those in Montana are the **Cabinet** and **Salish Mountains** in the northwest; the **Sapphire Mountains** east of the Bitterroots and south of Missoula; the **Purcell Mountains**, which are shared with British Columbia; the **Mission Mountains**, southeast of Flathead Lake; the **Big and Little Belt Mountains**, east of Helena; and the **Absaroka Mountains**, which run northwest from the east part of Yellowstone. The highest peak in the **Bitterroots**, a range shared with Idaho, is **Trapper Peak** (3094 meters; 10,150 feet), at the southern end of the range. The highest peak in Montana is **Granite Peak** (3901 meters; 12,799 feet) in the **Beartooth Mountains** at the north end of the Absarokas. The most well known mountains in Montana are the pinnacles and walls of layered sedimentary rock in Glacier National Park. If you hike from **Many Glacier** on **Lake Sherburne** to **Grinnell Glacier** you pass milky turquoise lakes, waterfalls, and wildflowers as you approach a battlement of the Continental Divide called the **Garden Wall**.

If you travel in Idaho you find many ranges of the Rockies within the state, including the Bitterroot, Selkirk, **Clearwater**, and **Coeur d'Alene Mountains** north of the Salmon River; the **Seven Devils Mountains** east of Hells Canyon; the **Salmon River Mountains**, a great block of ranges formed by the Idaho batholith in the center of the state; the **Sawtooth Range** and its associated minor ranges; and the **Lost River** and **Lemhi** ranges between **Mount Borah** and the Montana border. Mount Borah (3859 meters; 12,665 feet) is the highest peak in Idaho. Idaho has solid rock or talus domes, rolling wooded ridges, granite needles and saw-toothed ridges, and mountains of black lava, white limestone and twisted multicolored stripes. The deepest gorge in North America, Hells Canyon, divides southern Idaho from Oregon.

In eastern Oregon two ranges, the **Wallowa** and **Blue** mountains, fringe the Rockies. Highest in the Wallowas is the 3050-meter (10,006-foot) **Matterhorn**. Most trails gain 3000 feet in four to six miles here, so you find many visitors using horses and llamas.

In Wyoming, the jagged, triangular peaks of the Tetons rise out of a valley of woods, lakes, and the young Snake River. These are some of the most spectacular mountains in the United States. The **Grand Teton** is 4197 meters (13,769 feet). The highest peak in Wyoming is **Gannett Peak** (4201 meters; 13,785 feet) in the **Wind River Mountains**, between Pinedale and Lander.

If you climb to the Continental Divide from Big Sandy in the Wind Rivers, you will face the dark gray, 900-meter (3000-foot) walls of the **Cirque of the Towers**. The alpine flowers on the divide include ground-hugging alpine tundra plants: pink moss campion and blue alpine forget-me-not with their hundreds of tiny blossoms.

East of the Wind Rivers the **Wyoming Range** holds 3471-meter (11,388-foot) **Wyoming Peak**. The summit of the Absarokas, **Francs Peak** (4005 meters; 13,140 feet) is in Wyoming. Other high points are the **Bighorn Mountains** with **Cloud Peak** (4013 meters; 13,165 feet), east of Worland; the **Gros Ventre Range**, between there and the Tetons; the **Laramie**, with **Laramie Peak** (3131 meters; 10,274 feet); and the **Medicine Bow**, with **Medicine Bow Mountain**, (3659 meters; 12,005 feet), south of Casper and west of Cheyenne.

In Utah the **Uintas** run east and west north of Vernal. Their highest peak is 4114-meter (13,528-foot) **Kings Peak**. The **Wasatch Range**, just east of Salt Lake City, contains **Mount Nebo** (3621 meters; 11,880 feet).

It would take you years to climb all the mountains over 14,000 feet in Colorado. There are 53 of them. Because of the sheer wall called the Diamond in the center of its east face, **Longs Peak** (4345 meters; 14,255 feet), in Rocky Mountain National Park near Denver, is the most famous fourteen-thousander. Southwest of there, west of Colorado Springs, the **Sawatch Range** holds the highest peak in the state, **Mount Elbert** (4399 meters; 14,433 feet). Just west of Colorado Springs is **Pikes Peak** (4301 meters; 14,110 feet); an auto road and cog railway go to the top. The **Elk Range**, west of the Sawatch near Aspen, includes the **Maroon Bells** (4314 meters; 14,156 feet), with their brownish maroon layered cliffs. Southwest of that, near Durango, rise the **San Juans**, with **Uncompahgre Peak** (4361 meters; 14,309 feet). The San Juans are of multicolored limestone and sandstone with a wonderful display of wildflowers, such as blue harebells and the large blue-and-white columbine that is the state flower of Colorado. Southeast of the Sawatch, near Pueblo, is the **Sangre de Cristo Range**, with **Blanca Peak** (4373 meters; 14,346 feet).

The highest peak in Arizona is **Humphreys Peak** (3850 meters; 12,633 feet) in the **San Francisco Peaks** near Flagstaff. Arizona's **Grand Canyon** encloses red-and-white peaks such as the **Vishnu Temple**.

The **Sangre de Cristo Range** in New Mexico reaches 4011 meters (13,161 feet) in **Wheeler Peak**, northeast of Taos. **Sandia Peak**, near Albuquerque, is 3254 meters (10,678 feet).

In western Texas the highest peak in the **Guadalupe Mountains** is **Guadalupe Peak** (2667 meters; 8751 feet), and the highest in the **Chisos Mountains** is 2388-meter (7835-foot) **Emory Peak**.

The Rockies also run south through Mexico to Guatemala, with the chain dividing into two main ranges, the **Sierra Madre Occidental** and the **Sierra Madre Oriental**. The highest peak in the Sierra Madre Occidental is **Nevado de Colima** (4340 meters; 14,240 feet), near Tecalitlan, and in the Sierra Madre Oriental the highest is **Cerro Potosi** (3713 meters; 12,182 feet), near San Luis Potosi. At mid-elevations on the east slope of the Sierra Madre Oriental is a cloud forest where tropical species like palms grow beside trees from New England such as sugar maple, sweet gum, and hickory. South of Mexico City the **Sierra Madre del Sur** runs along the seacoast.

Map 9.4

Volcanoes independent of these ranges stand on the plateau of the **Mexican Highlands**, near Mexico City. The best known are **Pico de Orizaba**, (5747 meters; 18,965 feet), the highest mountain in Mexico and the third highest in North America. **Popocatepetl** (5452 meters; 17,887 feet) and **Ixtaccihuatl** (5286 meters; 17,343 feet) overlook Mexico City.

Mountain ranges run along the coast of Baja California, the peninsula west of the Gulf of California. From the north these are the **Sierra Juarez**, **Sierra de San Pedro Martir**, **Sierra Columbia**, and **Sierra de la Giganta**. The Sierra de San Pedro Martir contains the highest peak in Baja, the **Cerro de Encantada**, also known as **Picacho del Diablo** (3070 meters; 10,100 feet). In the mountains of northern Baja grows the boojum tree, which re-

Map 9.5

sembles an upside-down carrot with spines. It puts out leaves only after a rain.

The **Appalachians** follow the coastline of the eastern United States 150 miles inland. Hardwood forests cover these old, rounded mountains. Only in the north is it cold enough for the highest summits to rise above timberline, but the highest peak, **Mount Mitchell** (2009 meters; 6684 feet), tops the **Blue Ridge Mountains** of North Carolina in the south.

In the north the tallest is **Mount Washington** (1917 meters; 6288 feet) in the **White Mountains** of New Hampshire (Figure 9.1). If you drive or walk to the top you will find black spruce forming mats of krummholz. In season the shorter green mats of alpine flowers like diapensia are covered with small blossoms. It is lucky these plants soften the great rock-strewn top of the mountain. Even so it is bleak and cold, for this peak has the worst weather in the United States. This is because it is so far north and so high and because it is located on the tracks of major storms.

You can hike the **Appalachian Trail** for 2000 miles, from **Mount Katahdin** in Maine to **Springer Mountain** in Georgia. On the way it passes through several state and national parks, such as **Adirondack State Park** in New York. If you hike up one of the Adirondacks, such as **Algonquin**, you climb 3000 feet with no switchbacks up a trail of boulders. Thick deciduous forest blankets all except the summits of a few of the peaks. From the top you look off at silvery lakes nestled among rows of scalloped blue-green ridges and at the ski jumps at Lake Placid.

The 840-meter (2800-foot) **Ouachita Mountains** of Oklahoma and Arkansas and the 750-meter (2500-foot) **Ozark Mountains** in those states and Missouri adjoin the southern Appalachians.

The 1170-meter (3900-foot) **Laurentides Mountains** line the Saint Lawrence River in southern Quebec, Canada. This is the northern coniferous forest, so balsam fir is common. If you pop a resin blister on the smooth bark of this tree, it releases the pungent smell of balsam, as strong as turpentine.

Belonging to Canada's Northwest Territories, the Cumberland Peninsula of Baffin Island holds **Auyittuq National Park**, where mountains of granite and ice edge the **Penny Icecap**. The highest peak is **Tete Blanche** (2156 meters; 7074 feet). Access is by air to Pangnirtung.

An icecap crowns most of Greenland, but rock peaks such as

Figure 9.1.   These neighbors of Mount Washington in the White Mountains of New Hampshire show the typical above-timberline summits and rounded contours of the northern Appalachians.
Courtesy of Forest Service Photo Collection, National Agricultural Library.

the highest peak on the island, 3700-meter (12,139-foot) **Gunn-bjorns Fjeld** in the **Watkins Mountains** in the southeast, edge the coasts. The center of the icecap rises gently to 3220 meters (10,825 feet). Fjords connect the icecap to the sea. Access is by air, from Copenhagen to Kangerlussuaq (Sondrestromsfjord) or Narsarsuaq, and then by local air, helicopter, or boat service.

The highest peak in Iceland is **Hvannadalshujukur** (2119 meters; 6929 feet) on the **Oraefajokull Ice Cap** (a volcano crowned with ice), near the southern edge of the huge **Vatnajokull Ice Cap** on the southeast side of the island. North of Iceland, between Greenland and Norway, is the small Norwegian island of Jan Mayen with **Beerenberg** (2277 meters; 8347 feet).

CENTRAL AMERICA

Most people have heard of the great mountain chain of South America, the **Andes**, but few know that Central America has high mountains too. For instance, Guatemala has 13 volcanoes that are over 3000 meters (9843 feet). The highest peak is the volcano **Tajumulco** (4220 meters; 13,812 feet), near the Mexican border and the Pacific. It can be climbed by a five-mile trail from San Sebastian. Two mountain ranges, the **Altos Cuchumatanes** and **Sierra de las Minas**, run across the country from east to west north of Guatemala City. The best weather is from November through April.

Nicaragua is mountainous also, but the highest peak, **Kilambe**, in the **Cordillera Isabella** near the northern border, reaches only 1750 meters (5722 feet).

Costa Rica, adjoining Panama, also contains volcanoes running north-south in chains called the **Cordillera Guanacaste**, **Cordillera Tilaran**, **Cordillera Central**, and **Cordillera de Talamanca. Chirripo** (3900 meters; 12,860 feet) is the tallest. The best weather is from November through April.

Panama has **Volcan de Chiquiri**, also called **Baru** (3461 meters; 11,410 feet), by La Concepción near the Costa Rican border. Low mountains form the spine of the country west of the Panama Canal, with **Cerro Santiago** (2826 meters; 9241 feet) the highest.

You will even find mountains in the islands of the West Indies. The highest peak in the Dominican Republic on the island of Hispaniola is **Pico Duarte** (3175 meters; 10,417 feet). Haiti, which is the west part of the island, contains **La Sella** (2674 meters; 8793 feet), near the southeast coast. Cuba has 1974-meter (6500-foot) **Turquino** in the **Sierra Maestra** on the south coast. Jamaica's highest is 2256-meter (7402-foot) **Blue**

Mountain Peak northeast of Kingston. The most famous mountain in the Caribbean, **Mount Pele** (1477 meters; 4800 feet) on Martinique, erupted in 1902, killing 30,000 people.

SOUTH AMERICA (MAPS 9.6–9.7)

The great chain of the Andes, extending 4600 miles along the Pacific coast of South America, contains both alpine mountains and volcanoes. In the Andes is the highest mountain in the Western Hemisphere, 6960-meter (22,834-foot) **Cerro Aconcagua**. This description of the Andes starts at the north end with Venezuela. The Andes increase in elevation as they go south until they reach their summit at Aconcagua in Argentina, northeast of Santiago and close to the Chilean border. South of there, elevations decrease.

In Venezuela one ridge of the Andes, the **Serrania de Perija**, outlines the Colombian border, and another, the **Cordillera de Merida**, parallels it 150 miles southeast. The highest peak in the Cordillera de Merida is **Pico Bolivar** (5007 meters; 16,523 feet). Dense tropical forest covers the east slope of this range. In the **Sierra Nevada National Park** near Lake Maracaibo, you can take the world's highest and longest cable-car ride to 4741-meter (15,629-foot) **Pico Espejo**.

In Colombia the Andes widen into a triple chain, the **Cordillera Occidental**, **Cordillera Central**, and the **Cordillera Oriental**. The greatest peaks, all in the Cordillera Central, are **Nevado del Huila** (5750 meters; 18,865 feet) and **Nevado del Ruiz** (5319 meters; 17,450 feet), which erupted on November 14, 1985. The highest peak in the Cordillera Occidental is the volcano **Cumbal** (4892 meters; 16,050 feet). Mists often shroud the northern part of the Cordillera Oriental, called the **Sierra Nevada de Cocuy**. This range has several peaks over 5200 meters, with the highest **Alto Ritacova** (5600 meters; 18,372 feet). The only good weather occurs in January and February.

An unusual animal that lives on 45-degree slopes in the Andes from Venezuela to Bolivia but is seldom seen is the spectacled bear. White eye rings give this small bear its name. Spectacled bears eat fruit, nuts, rodents, bamboo, cactus, wood, and the hearts of bromeliads. They build nests of leaves and branches in trees and on the ground.

Map 9.6

From the **Sierra Nevada de Santa Marta** of Colombia you overlook the Caribbean. The peaks of **Simon Bolivar** and **Cristobal Colón** are 5775 meters (18,947 feet) high. From Atanquez near Valledepur, you can hike up the valley of the Donachi River to a view of these peaks. Best weather is from December through March and June through August.

Two Andean chains with volcanoes cross Ecuador. The chief peak in the western chain is **Chimborazo** (6310 meters; 20,702 feet), and in the eastern chain it is **Cotopaxi** (5897 meters; 19,347 feet). The active volcano **Sangay** (5332 meters; 17,493 feet) can be reached from Río Bamba and Aloa. May through September has the best weather.

Twenty named cordilleras of the Andes crowd Peru. Fluted

ridges and cornices of ice cover these, the highest tropical mountains in the world. Formed by the damp climate, this ice draws ice climbers from all over the world.

As you travel south, the main range, the **Cordillera Blanca**, turns into the **Cordillera Huayhuash**, and then to the **Cordillera Occidental**. East of the Cordillera Blanca are the **Cordillera Central** and the **Cordillera Oriental**. Opposite Lima, in the center of the coastline, the **Cordillera Vilcabamba** rises to the east of the main range. Near it congregate the cordilleras **Urubamba**, **Carabaya**, **Vilcanota**, and others. Between the Cordillera Occidental and the **Cordillera Real**, mostly in Bolivia, Lake Titicaca straddles the Bolivian border. The highest peaks in Peru are **Huascaran**, (6768 meters; 22,205 feet) in the Cordillera Blanca and **Yerupaja** (6634 meters; 21,765 feet) in the Cordillera Huayhuash. The highest volcano is **Nevado Coropuna** (6425 meters; 21,079 feet). **Salcantay**, in the Cordillera Vilcabamba, reaches 6271 meters (20,573 feet). **Ausangate** (6372 meters; 20,905 feet) tops the Cordillera Vilcanota. Mountain forests ascend to 10,000 feet with scrub and grass in the drier valleys and the alpine vegetation called puna above that. On the mountain slopes here *Pseudopostoa melanostele*, a rare cactus, has woolly stems resembling bottle brushes made of cotton candy. The best weather is from June through August during the southern winter.

If you ride a bus or hike up to the lakes in **Quebrado Llanganuco**, you will get a magnificent view of the two irregular, ice-draped summits of Huascaran and the south face of **Huandoy**, which is always in shadow. Cliffs, rocks, and tussock grasses surround the lakes. At the lower one twisted quenua trees stand, with their papery red bark.

If you stand on the Cordillera Occidental in western Bolivia you face a maze of ranges to the east, including the Cordillera Real and Cordillera Oriental, across the 3948- to 4000-meter (12,000- to 13,000-foot) plateau of the *altiplano*. The highest peaks are the active volcano **Sajama** (6520 meters; 21,391 feet) in the Cordillera Occidental and **Ancohuma** (6388 meters; 20,958 feet) and **Illimani** (6462 meters; 21,201 feet) in the Cordillera Real.

The Andes form the border between Chile and Argentina. In northern Chile and Argentina a 3948-meter (12,000-foot)

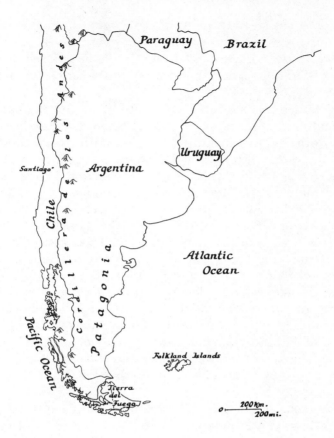

Map 9.7

plateau called the **Puna de Atacama** separates the two main ranges. Isolated volcanoes dot the Puna.

For 1400 miles in southern Chile and Argentina, forests of *Araucaria* and *Nothofagus* dominate the lower mountain slopes. *Nothofagus* (southern or Antarctic beech) is the timberline tree. At higher elevations the species of *Nothofagus* are deciduous; at lower elevations, evergreen.

More than 20 peaks exceed 20,000 feet, including **Aconcagua** (6960 meters; 22,834 feet). From Puenta de Inca you can hike up the Horcones River Valley to a mountain hut at Plaza de Mulas, with a magnificent view of the 10,000-foot south wall of Acon-cagua. Associated ranges are the **Cordillera de Oliva** and the **Cordillera de Ollita** in northern Chile along the border with Argentina, and the **Sierra de Famatina**, **Sierra de Tunuyan**, and the **Sierra del Nevado** in northern Argentina just east of the main range. Again, the southern summer season has the best weather. In the Chilean and Argentine Lake District, 300 miles south of Santiago, the highest peak is **Tronador** (3554 meters; 11,728 feet).

The Andes continue through southern Argentina and Chile, barricading the dry plain of Patagonia on the west. Some refer to the entire region, including the mountains, as Patagonia. The snowline lowers gradually with the higher latitude until in the southern tip of Chile, on the island of Tierra del Fuego, it drops to 700 meters (2300 feet). The most famous mountain in Patagonia is **Fitzroy** (3375 meters; 11,073 feet), which has a 6000-foot sheer face. Fitzroy stands within the Argentinian **Parc Nacional de los Glaciores**, reached by road from Río Gallegos or Santa Cruz. Another group of mountains in Patagonia is the **Torres del Paine**. Here granite cliffs and glaciers fall to milky turquoise lakes surrounded by wildflowers. You may catch a glimpse of the huge red-crested Magellanic woodpecker, the largest woodpecker in the world. The weather in Patagonia and Tierra del Fuego is wet, cold, and windy—never good—but it is a little drier in winter. Rain forest and southern beeches cover the lower slopes of the mountains on the west, while the east side is dry and bare.

Venezuela, Guiana, and Brazil share the **Guiana Highlands**. At **Roraima**, (2772 meters; 9147 feet), the borders of the three countries meet. Other high peaks of the highlands are **Neblina** (3014 meters; 9946 feet) in the northern tip of Brazil and **Auyan-tepuy** (2953 meters; 9688 feet) in Venezuela. On Auyantepuy is the world's highest waterfall. Rivers have dissected the uplifted ancient rock of the highlands into a maze of plateaus and flat-topped mesas called *tepui*, such as Roraima. This is the land Conan Doyle fictionalized in *The Lost World*. Here live many plants endemic to each tableland. Most are unusual, such as a tree-size daisy and a bromeliad with five-foot-long leaves.

A high edge of the Brazilian plateau faces the Atlantic, forming ranges of mountains known as the **Brazilian Highlands**. These ranges include the **Serra do Mar**, **Serra do Chaparao**, **Serra do Espinhaco**, and **Serra Mantiquera** near São Paulo and Rio de Janeiro. The highest peak is **Pico do Bandeira** (2884 meters; 9462 feet) in the Serra do Chaparao near Belo Horizonte.

WESTERN EUROPE (MAPS 9.8–9.12)

The most famous mountain range in Europe is the Alps, which occupy most of Switzerland and parts of France, Germany, Austria, Italy, and Yugoslavia. But you will find several other ranges creasing Europe.

British Isles

In the British Isles the tallest mountain, is **Ben Nevis** (1344 meters; 4406 feet), part of the **Grampian Mountains** just east of the Great Glen in Scotland. You can climb it by trail from

Map 9.8

Achintree, near Fort William. The other high ranges in the British Isles are **Snowdonia** in northern Wales, **McGillicuddy's Reeks** in southwestern Ireland, the **Cumbrian Mountains** in the Lake District of northwestern England, the **Cairngorm Mountains** in the Scotch Highlands, and the **Cuillin Hills** on the Isle of Skye, all with summits of about 1100 meters (3500 feet). Only in the Cairngorms does much alpine tundra grow. This book omits hills of this size in most other countries. But as a training ground for climbers, the British mountains have influenced world mountaineering. These rounded hills can offer mountain climbing because glacial cirques, lined with cliffs, bite into the higher slopes. The famous moors unfurl where the glaciers have scoured away the fertile soil, so that only a few grasses, heaths, and mosses will grow.

Near Capel Durig, Bethesda, and Llanberis in northwest Wales are several peaks in the region called Snowdonia, including the mountain **Snowdon**, also known as Yr Wyddfa (1085 meters; 3560 feet). If you walk along Lyn Llydaw under the spread-out triangle and sloping cliffs of the top of Snowdon you see a treeless world of grass, heather, and outcrops, lime green in spring. A cirque with the frowning dark cliffs of Snowdon and **Y Lliwedd** barricades the head of the canyon.

Windermere, Derwent Water, and other lakes sprinkle the Lake District in the Cumbrian Mountains in England, which contain the highest point in England, **Scafell Pike** (987 meters; 3210 feet). In McGillicuddy's Reeks in Ireland are the Lakes of Killarney and the mountain **Carrantuohill** (1040 meters; 3414 feet).

Scandinavia

A spine of mountains runs along the center of Norway, with the mountains shrinking and the chain narrowing to the north. Great fjords indent the mountains on the western coast. Glaciers descend to 6500 feet in southern Norway. The **Jotunheimen Mountains** in south-central Norway hold the highest peaks, the **Galdhoppigen** (2469 meters; 8098 feet) and **Glittertind** (2472 meters; 8157 feet).

The **Kjolen Mountains** in northern Sweden (Lapland) on the Norwegian border approach the height of those in Norway.

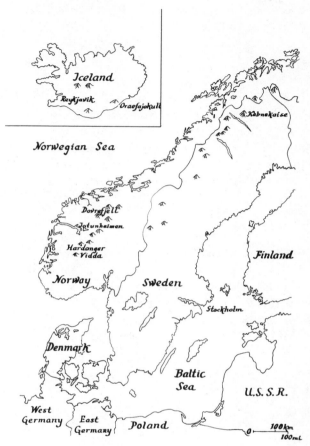

Map 9.9

Kebnekaise, for example, stands 2090 meters (6965 feet). Near it you can hike the **Kungsleden** (the King's Trail) from the Torne Trask south to Ammarnas, northwest of Sorsele. The highest peak in Finland is 1328-meter (4357-foot) **Halti Fell** in the northwest tip of the country. Near it several marked trails surround Lake Kilpisjarvi.

Germany

The Alps form the southern border of West Germany from Lake Constance east to the **Watzmann** (2713 meters; 8900 feet). The named sections of the Alps in Germany are the **Allgauer**

Alps in the west and the **Bavarian Alps** in the east, discussed in a section on the Alps to follow.

France

France has mountains other than the Alps and Pyrenees. The **Jura Mountains** stretch along the French-Swiss border from southeastern France near Geneva to Basel in Switzerland along Lake Geneva and Lake Neuchâtel. Many streams disappear and reappear in this limestone country. The highest point, **Cret de la Neige**, reaches only 1718 meters (5636 feet).

Spain

The highest mountains in Spain, the **Sierra Nevada**, rise out of the Mediterranean southeast of Granada. The highest peak is 3478-meter (11,411-foot) **Mulhacen**. The best weather here is from June through September. This range belongs to the **Sistema Beticos**, a chain that runs from the Balearic Islands (Majorca and Menorca) southwest along the coast of Spain and

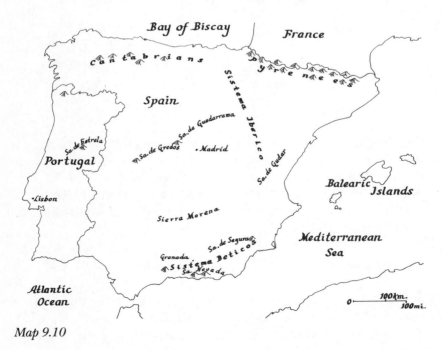

Map 9.10

Map 9.11

emerges south of Gibraltar in the **Rif Mountains** of Morocco. These dry mountains have vegetation similar to that of North Africa. Another section of this range is the **Sierra de Segura**, with **La Sagra** (2381 meters; 7811 feet), north of Huescar. The **Sistema Iberico** runs northwest to southeast in northeastern Spain but rises only to 2404 meters (7887 feet) in the **Sierra de Gudar** east of Cuenca.

In central Spain, northwest of Madrid, are the **Sierra de Gredos**, with **Pico de Almanzor** (2592 meters; 7972 feet), and the **Sierra de Guadarrama**, with **Pico de Penalara** (2430 meters; 7972 feet). South of Madrid an east-west range of hills, the **Sierra Morena**, reaches only 1300 meters (4265 feet).

The **Cantabrians** overlook the northern coast of Spain in a line-with the Pyrenees. The highest, **Torre Ceredo** (2648 meters; 8687 feet), near Arenas, belongs to the 40-kilometer-long **Picos de Europa** group. The best weather is in July and August.

The **Pyrenees** form a barrier between France and Spain, with high passes, 3384-meter (11,000-foot) peaks, and walls of multi-colored limestone. **Pico de Aneto** (3404 meters; 11,168 feet) of the **Montes Malditos**, halfway from the Mediterranean to the

Bay of Biscay, is the highest. You will see a few small glaciers above the snowline at 9000 feet. There is a road along the north side of the range in France called the Route des Pyrenées with access roads branching off, such as one to a trail to the view of the 4900-foot cliffs of the **Cirque de Gavarnie**.

In central Portugal the **Serra da Estrela** near Covilha contains the highest peak in that country, 1993-meter (6539-foot) **Malhao da Estrela**.

The Alps

You may be confused by the names of the ranges in the Alps because they vary with different authors and map makers. Some ranges or areas have more than one name, and small sections of ranges often have individual names too. Look at Map 9.11 as you read this section, and it will help you straighten out the ranges. Because people have lived here for thousands of years,

Figure 9.2. The Alps have a widespread system of mountain huts that allows hikers to travel for several days carrying only their clothes in day packs.
Courtesy of Swiss National Tourist Office.

forest cover has decreased 75 percent from the primeval state. So just below the peaks are many pastures. Timberline varies from 5500 to 7000 feet, with permanent snow at 9000 feet. You have read about and seen pictures of these mountains so often that you may have a picture of the symmetrical tower of the *Matterhorn* in your mind. Climbing most peaks requires mountaineering experience or a guide. Both climbers and hikers stay in mountain huts, instead of backpacking (Figure 9.2).

Western Alps

In France and Italy the **Maritime Alps** draw an east-west arc, with the ends bent northward just north of the Mediterranean. **Argentera** (3297 meters; 10,917 feet), near Saint-Martin, is the highest.

The **Cottian Alps** are also in France and Italy, north of the west end of the Maritime Alps near Biancon and Guillestre. They run north and south; **Monte Viso** (3841 meters; 12,602 feet) is the highest.

The **Dauphine**, near Grenoble, stretch northwest to southeast in France and are northwest of the Cottian Alps. **Barre des Ecrins** (4102 meters; 13,461 feet) in the **Massif du Pelvoux** is the tallest. The **Graian Alps** in France and Italy run southwest to northeast and are north of the Cottian Alps near Aosta. The highest peak is **Gran Paradiso** (4061 meters; 13,323 feet).

Central Alps

The **Mont Blanc Range**, or **Savoy Alps**, in France and Italy west of the **Pennine Alps** near Saint-Gervais and Courmayer holds **Mont Blanc** (4807 meters; 15,771 feet), the highest peak in the Alps. The **Chamonix Aiguilles** are other famous peaks in this section. From Saint-Gingolf you can take a French trail 250 miles along the Swiss and Italian borders through the Alps to Nice on the Mediterranean. The Pennine Alps in Italy and southwestern Switzerland, also called the **Valais**, include 10 of the 12 highest mountains in the Alps. They run southwest to northeast. Two of the peaks are the **Monte Rosa** massif, whose highest point is **Dufourspitze** (4634 meters; 15,203 feet), and the

Matterhorn (4478 meters; 14,690 feet), near Zermatt and Chamonix. You must take the railroad to reach Zermatt because the
road is closed to private automobiles. If you climb the Matterhorn with a guide by the standard route, you will probably
start the climb in the middle of the night from a mountain hut
and be on the top by breakfast. If you are unused to climbing
with ropes, you will wonder, as you tackle cliffs, overhangs, and
ice slopes, how you will ever get down again. From the top you
can look down on the roofs of Zermatt and across at the other
peaks that form a semicircle with the Matterhorn, such as the
four rounded ice buttresses of Monte Rosa and the great finger
of the **Obergabelhorn**.

There are many places in the Alps where Swiss-chalet villages
and scattered groves of spruce, larch, and pine rise up the sides
of U-shaped valleys to green pastures called alps. The pastures
reach up to fluted, sharp peaks or snowy, lumpy ones with
glacier tongues hanging down the walls. One example is the
view from the **Col de Balme** on the **Tour de Mont Blanc** trail on
the French-Swiss border. From here the white summit of Mont
Blanc resembles a mound of ice cream on which a gigantic hand
has made dents and pinched up points and pleats.

The **Bernese Oberland** (or Berner Alps) in Switzerland, north
of the Pennine Alps and east of Geneva, stretch east and west
near Kleine-Schiedegg and Grindelwald. They sweep up to the
Finsteraarhorn (4274 meters; 14,022 feet), **Jungfrau** (4158 meters; 13,462 feet), and **Eiger** (3970 meters; 13,069 feet). A cog
railroad goes up to the Jungfraujoch, not far from the summit of
the Jungfrau.

The **Lepontine** or **Adula Alps** in Switzerland and Italy extend southwest-northeast, north of Lago di Maggiore and west
of the **Rhaetian Alps**. The **Rheinwaldhorn** (3402 meters; 11,162
feet) is the highest in this area.

The **Bernina Alps**, near Saint-Moritz, form a short east-west
range in Italy and southeastern Switzerland. It contains the **Piz
Bernina** (4049 meters; 13,284 feet).

The Rhaetian Alps run southwest to northeast in eastern
Switzerland and Austria, north of the Bernina Alps and also
near Saint-Moritz. **Piz Linard** (3411 meters; 11,190 feet) is the
highest.

The **Glarus** or **Glarner Alps** are north of the eastern end of
the Lepontine Alps, east of the Berner, and north of the Rhae

tian Alps near Zurich. The summit is **Todi** (3614 meters; 11,857 feet).

In the **Ratische Alpen**, a small range west of the center of the Rhaetian Alps near Davos, is the only Swiss national park. Points of interest are **Piz Pisoc** (3154 meters; 10,347 feet) and views of the **Ortler** and Bernina Alps. Here you must stay on marked trails in order to protect the wildlife, which includes chamois and ibex.

The **Alpi Orobie** run east and west in Italy, south of the Bernina Alps and east of Lago di Lecco. **Pizzo di Coca** (3052 meters; 10,013 feet) is the highest.

The **Lechtal Alps**, extending from southwest to northeast in Austria north of the Rhaetian Alps near Lech, climb to **Parseier Spitze** (3036 meters; 9960 feet).

The Allgau or Allgauer Alps in Germany and Austria follow the German border north of the Lechtal Alps and east of Lake Constance. The chief peak is **Hoher Ifen** (2232 meters; 7323 feet).

East of the Bernina Alps near Bolzano, Italy, the Ortles or Ortler Alps run east and west. **Cima Ortles** (3905 meters; 12,792 feet) is the highest peak.

The **Otzal Alps** cluster in Austria and Italy, southwest of Innsbruck and east of the Rhaetian Alps. A cable railway climbs partway up the **Wildspitze** (3772 meters; 12,382 feet).

Eastern Alps

In the Tirol of Austria and Italy, the **Stubai Alps** run northwest to southeast between Innsbruck and the Otzal Alps. The **Zuckerhutl** climbs to 3507 meters (11,499 feet) near Ranalt.

The **Zillertal Alps** are an east-west range in Austria and Italy, southeast of Innsbruck and east of the Brenner Pass. The summit is **Hochfeiler** (3511 meters; 11,516 feet), near Mayrhofen.

The **Dolomites** run southwest to northeast in Italy northeast of Verona. **Marmolada** rises to 3343 meters (10,965 feet). These peaks of white limestone are much climbed by rock climbers because they have milder weather than do the Alps farther west, no glaciers, and short trails to mountain huts. The scenery is beautiful, with many slender spires of layered white limestone above meadows of wildflowers.

The Bavarian Alps in Germany and Austria stretch east and west southeast of Garmisch. The highest peak in Germany, **Zugspitz** (2963 meters; 9721 feet), has trails and a cable railway. You can ride to the summit from Eibsee, near Garmisch.

The **Kitzbuhel Alps** are an east-west range in Austria, east of the Stubai Alps and north of the **Hohe Tauern**. **Kreuzjoch** (2558 meters; 8392 feet) is the summit.

The Hohe Tauern sweep east and west across western Austria, north of Lienz, with **Grossglockner** (3797 meters; 12,461 feet). To the east the Hohe Tauern become the **Niedere Tauern** and rise to **Hochgolling** (2863 meters; 9393 feet).

The **Noric Alps** consist of several subranges north of the Yugoslavian-Italian border. The **Gurktal Alps** (west end of Noric Alps) run east and west. **Eisenhut** (2442 meters; 8008 feet) is the tallest. Other subranges are the **Saualpe**, **Gleinalpe**, **Seetaler Alpen**, and **Koralpe**.

In Austria you can take one of the several marked hiking routes, the **Nordalpiner West-Ost Wanderweg**, to hike clear across the country from Bregenz on the Bodensee in Vorarlberg in the west to Rodaun near Vienna in the east.

The **Carnic Alps** in Austria and Italy range along the Italian-Yugoslavian border east of the Dolomites. They continue as the **Karawanken Range** on the Austrian-Yugoslavian border with **Hohe Warte** or **Mount Coglians** (2780 meters; 9121 feet) the highest.

Italy

The **Apennines**, limestone mountains, wind along the center of the Italian peninsula, beginning near Genoa on the Mediterranean in the northwest, crossing to the Adriatic side of the country near Rome, and ending in the toe of Italy's boot. The highest peak, **Corno Grand** (2912 meters; 9560 feet) is east of Rome in the **Gran Sasso**, a section of the spectacular **Abruzzi** part of the Apennines.

Volcanoes, such as **Mount Vesuvius** (1281 meters; 4201 feet), near Naples, dot Italy. Vesuvius has a chair lift to the top, reached by road from Ercolano. On the island of Sicily **Mount Etna** (3323 meters; 10,902 feet) and on the island of Stromboli, the volcano **Stromboli** (926 meters; 3038 feet), erupt frequently. The highest mountain on Corsica is **Monte Cinto** (2717 meters; 8891 feet), near Salvi on the northwest coast. Corsica, a mountainous island belonging to France, has fjords and alpine scenery but no glaciers. Chestnuts, conifers, and a chaparral called *maquis* cover the slopes. Summers are hot, so June and September are the best months to go there.

Sardinia's major peak is **Punta la Marmora** (1834 meters; 6017 feet) in the **Gennargentu Massif** west of Tortoli. Sardinia, mostly a forested plateau, belongs to Italy.

Yugoslavia

The **Julian Alps** run from the Italian border in northwest Yugoslavia to the Adriatic at Rijeka. The highest peak is **Triglav** (2863 meters; 9393 feet), near Kranjska Gora. To climb Triglav by trail and fixed ropes, take a side road from the Kransjska Gora-Jesenice Road to Mojstrans.

The **Dinaric Alps** run parallel to the Adriatic Sea all along the Yugoslavian coast, from the Julian Alps to Albania. The highest peak is **Djeravica** (2656 meters; 8713 feet) of the **Prokletije Massif** on the Albanian border. Second highest is **Bobotov Kuk** (2522 meters; 8274 feet), of the **Durmitor Massif** north of Titograd. The range has dazzling white limestone walls.

Across the northern edge of Slovenia in Yugoslavia the **Karavanke Mountains** extend the Alps even farther, accompanied on the south by the **Kamniske** and **Savinjske Alpe**. The Karavanke's highest are **Hochstuhl** (2238 meters; 7342 feet), near Franj and Savinjske, and **Grintavec** (2558 meters; 8392 feet), near Plansarsko Jezero.

Albania

Along the northern and eastern borders high mountains barricade Albania from Yugoslavia. The highest, 2757-meter (9068-foot) **Korab**, sits on the eastern border. In the **Albanian Alps** on the northern border near Kopik is **Maje Jezerce** (2694 meters; 8838 feet).

Map 9.12

Greece

The legendary home of the gods, **Mount Olympus** (2917 meters; 9571 feet), the highest mountain in Greece, is located in the north 12 miles from the Aegean Sea near Litochoron. The **Pindos Mountains** run northwest to southeast through the center of Greece, rising to 2637 meters (8652 feet) in **Smolikas** near the Albanian border. Another well-known mountain in this range is **Parnassus** (2457 meters; 8061 feet), near Delphi. You can ascend it from Arahova by road plus chair lift. There are also 8000-foot mountains on the island of Crete; the highest is **Idhi Oros** (2449 meters; 8058 feet).

EASTERN EUROPE

The **Carpathians** extend in a great arc from central Czecho-slovakia northeast through southern Poland. Then they turn southeast through a corner of Russia to the eastern end of the **Transylvanian Alps** in Romania. Some authors include the Transylvanian Alps in the Carpathians. A northern section of this range, the **High Tatras** on the Polish-Czechoslovakian border, has alpine scenery. The highest peak is **Gerlachovsky** (2665 meters; 8730 feet), near Strebske Pleso. The **Low Tatras** crest in **Dumbier** (2043 meters; 6702 feet), near Chopok in Czechoslovakia.

The Transylvanian Alps, a range of forested hills, run east and west in central Romania. In this range, the **Fagaras Massif** contains cirques, aretes, and the highest peak, **Moldeveanu** (2543 meters; 8343 feet), near Rimnicu. The eastern end of the Tran-sylvanian Alps, called the **Bucegi Mountains**, rise to **Mount Omu** (2471 meters; 8238 feet).

In the Transylvanian Alps you walk up from beechwoods at low elevations to spruces, and then stone pines and larches. Finally you reach a dwarfed forest of junipers, rhododendrons, and *Pinus mughus*, a genetically dwarfed pine. Between these trees, wildflowers, many of them endemic, grow in grassy spots. You can look out now at scalloped, fluted summits of rough, crumbly rock, patched with snowbanks but no glaciers. You may catch a glimpse of a chamois leaping up the slopes.

Bulgaria contains the **Balkan** and **Rhodope** mountains. The Balkans, also known as the **Stara Planina**, run east and west across the center of the country. The summit of this gentle range is **Botev** (2376 meters; 7795 feet), near Gabrovo.

In southwestern Bulgaria two scenic branches of the Rhodope Mountains diverge in an inverted V. Just south of Sofia and north of where the V begins, the range is called the **Bulgarian Alps**. In this section the tallest is **Cerni Vrah** (2290 meters; 7513 feet). The northern section of the west side of the V is called the **Rila Range** and the southern section the **Pirin Range**. The east side of the V, just called the **Rhodopes**, includes **Goljam Perelik** (2191 meters; 7188 feet). The major peak in the Pirins is **Vihren** (2914 meters; 9560 feet). **Musala** (2925 meters; 9596 feet), in the Rila Range near Borovets, is the highest mountain in Eastern Europe.

The **Ural Mountains**, 1250 miles (2012 kilometers), long, divide the European and Asian regions of the USSR. They begin at the Kara Sea, an arm of the Arctic Ocean in the north, and run south to just northeast of the Black Sea. In the north, forested peaks with glaciers reach 1895 meters (6214 feet) in **Gora Narodnaya**.

For 600 miles within the USSR the **Caucasus** divides Europe from Asia. The range runs from the north-central coast of the Black Sea to the southern part of the Caspian Sea, reaching 5642 meters (18,510 feet), in **Elbrus**, in the center of the range. You might think you were in the Alps, except that the snowline is higher, the glaciers are smaller, and there are no mountain huts. Because of the influence of the Black Sea, the western end of the range has deciduous forest at low elevations, but the eastern is semidesert and grassland.

ASIA (MAPS 9.13–9.18)

Central Asia has 50 of the highest mountains in the world, with 14 peaks over 8000 meters (26,248 feet). But other parts of Asia have peaks over 16,000 feet. One of these is the Middle East.

Middle East

Most of the mountains of the Middle East have few trees because of the dry climate and long-term human use. What they have are remnants of the Mediterranean type of vegetation. In Turkey the isolated volcano of **Buyuk Agri Dagi**, or **Mount Ararat** (5137 meters; 16,952 feet), rises 14,000 feet out of the lowlands near the Russian-Turkish border. Hanging glaciers and a view of the Caucasus make up for the lack of trees. Now and then someone funds an expedition to search for Noah's Ark up here. The **Cilo-Sat Mountains**, in the southeastern corner, sweep up to **Gelyasin** (4168 meters; 13,675 feet). Another volcano, **Suphan Dagi** (4406 meters; 14,457 feet), sits near Lake Van. The **Pontic Mountains** parallel the Black Sea in the northeast, where **Kackar Peak** reaches 3937 meters (12,917 feet). The **Taurus Mountains** form a semicircle along the south coast. Major peaks are **Demirkazik** (3585 meters; 12,251 feet) and **Erciyas Dag** (3734 meters; 12,848 feet), near Cappadocia.

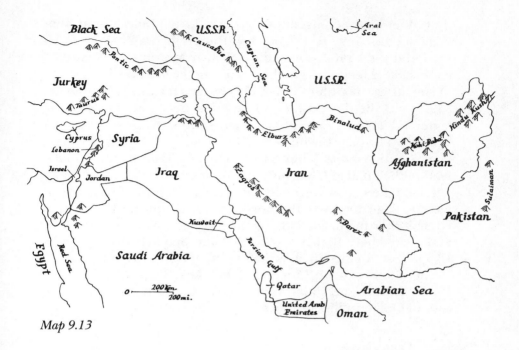

Map 9.13

In northern Iran, the **Elburz Mountains** border the Caspian Sea. The highest peak, **Mount Demavend** (5671 meters; 18,714 feet), near Reineh, is a symmetrical volcano whose crater is filled with ice. Forests cover only the Caspian sides up to 8000 feet. Trails have teahouses along them. The **Zagros Mountains** overlook the Persian Gulf along the western edge of Iran. Only scattered trees grow here. **Zard Kuh**, the highest peak at 4548 meters (14,921 feet), is reached from Isfahan. Southern Iran has volcanoes as tall as 4420-meter (14,500-foot) **Kuh-e Hazaran** near Kerman. In the north the **Binalud Range** faces the Kopet-Dag, across the border in the USSR.

In northeastern Iraq, the other ranges of the Zagros average 2440 meters (8000 feet). The highest peak is **Rawanduz** (3658 meters; 12,001 feet), located where the Iraqi, Iranian, and Turkish borders meet.

In Syria the **Anti-Lebanon Range** follows the Lebanese border. **Mount Hermon** (2814 meters; 9232 feet), southwest of Damascus, is the highest. The **Lebanon Range**, of white limestone and chalk and holding only a few Cedars of Lebanon, runs north-south in the center of the country. **Qurnat as Sawda** (3088 meters; 10,131 feet), northeast of Bsherri, is the highest peak.

On the Sinai Peninsula of Egypt, you can climb **Mount Sinai** (2285 meters; 7497 feet) from Abu Rudeis, by walking up an old road and then 2000 stone steps. Nearby **Mount Katerina** (2637 meters; 8652 feet) is the highest point in the country.

The tallest mountain in Israel is **Mount Jarmaq** (1034 meters; 3393 feet), in the **Gallilee Mountains** near Safadin. A 1754-meter (5754-foot) mountain, **Jebel Ramm**, east of Al Aqabah near Wadi Rum, is the highest in Jordan.

In Saudi Arabia, **Jabal Sawda** reaches 3133 meters (10,279 feet) in the **Jabal el Hijaz** near the Yemen border.

The highest peak in Democratic Yemen is **Jabal Thamir** (2513 meters; 8245 feet), on the border with Yemen north of Aden. Highlands run through the center of Yemen, which is on the Red Sea. Their highest is **Jabal Adur Shu'ayb** (3760 meters; 12,336 feet), in the **Hijaz Asir Mountains** near Zayland.

The chief peak in Oman is **Jabal Ash Sham** (3107 meters; 10,400 feet) in the **Hajar Mountains**, which run parallel to the Gulf of Oman in the northern part of the country.

Central Asia

The **Tian Shan Mountains** extend northeast from the **Pamirs** along the USSR-China border for 400 miles, then turn east and continue for over a thousand miles into Sinkiang, China. **Pik Pobedy**, also called **Victory Peak** (7439 meters; 24,406 feet), southeast of Lake Issyk-Kul, is the highest. Because hot springs warm Lake Issyk-Kul, to over 75°F, it has several resorts. Snow and glaciers allow enough runoff for forests and wildflower meadows in a few places, but most vegetation is steppe and mountain grassland. A flower called the snow lotus, a huge white poppy, has thin, double petals that resemble Kleenex.

The **Altai** run east and west for 1200 miles through the USSR, Mongolia, and China, from the Gobi Desert to the Western Siberian Plain. The highest peak, **Gora Belukha** (4506 meters; 14,783 feet), stands in Siberia near the northern end of the range. The Altai has 32,500 lakes and 1200 glaciers, but there are forests only in the section in Siberia.

The **Khrebet Tannu Ola Range** runs east from the Altai, along the border between the USSR and Mongolia, for 350 miles. The highest peak is 3061-meter (10,043-foot) **Sagly** in the west, southeast of Teli. The stunted trees of taiga cover the northern slopes and the short grasses of steppe the southern.

The Pamirs cluster where three countries join: the USSR, China, and Afghanistan. Other great mountain ranges, the Tian Shan, **Hindu Kush**, and **Kunlun**, extend from this mountain knot. The USSR section climbs to **Pik Communism** (7495 meters; 24,590 feet), near Osh and Nurek. The highest in the Pamirs, **Kongur (Qungur) Tagh** (7719 meters; 25,325 feet), is in the **Mustagh Ata Range** in Sinkiang Province in China. There are a thousand glaciers and wide U-shaped valleys with glacial lakes such as Kara Kul. The valleys between the mountain ranges, called pamirs, are dry and barren, and the slopes have little vegetation. The best season is from June through September.

Three ranges of the Hindu Kush Mountains run northeast to southwest, from the Pamirs along the Afghanistan-Pakistan border to central Afghanistan. There is little vegetation and no forests; the monsoon affects only the eastern range. The highest peak is **Tirich Mir** (7569 meters; 25,130 feet) in the main range. The best access is from Chitral and Gilgit in Pakistan. In Pakistan parallel ranges, such as the **Sulaiman Range**, run south from the Hindu Kush.

In Afghanistan the Hindu Kush are called the **Hendu Kosh** and run from northeast to southwest. They fan out 100 miles north of Kabul into ranges running west, called **Koh-i-Baba, Band-e-Bayan**, and **Safid Kuh**. The highest peak in the Koh-i-Baba is 5143-meter (16,873-foot) **Shah Fuladi** near Bamiyan.

The **Karakoram Range** in Tibet, Kashmir, and Pakistan has 19 peaks over 25,000 feet. Two of these are K 2 (8611 meters; 28,250 feet) and Hidden Peak (8068 meters; 26,470 feet). From the Ladakh Range of the Himalayas, the **Karakorams** extend northwest to the Hindu Kush in Pakistan, cut by the Karakoram Highway, which goes to Kashgar in Sinkiang.

The Himalayas

The **Himalayas** wall off Nepal, Sikkim, Bhutan, and India from Tibet in China. On the west they join the Karakoram and Hindu Kush ranges. The **Great Himalayas**—the highest of several subranges—are a chain of mountain massifs, called *himals,*

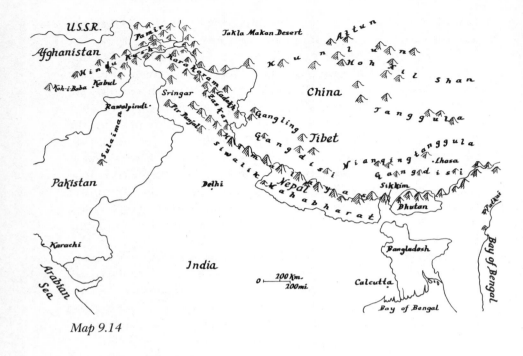

Map 9.14

with deep river gorges on either side. The name Himalaya comes from the Sanskrit *hima* ("snow") and *alaya* ("home"). The 22,700-foot-deep valley of the Kali Gandaki, the deepest valley in the world, divides the **Dhaulagiri** and **Annapurna** himals. In every direction except south, the Himalayas join other mountain ranges to form a great icy maze.

In the 1500-mile-long range stand at least 14 peaks over 8000 meters (26,248 feet), making the Himalayas the highest mountains in the world. We find eight of these on the Nepalese-Tibetan border or in Nepal. Some include the highest and most famous, such as **Everest** (8848 meters; 29,028 feet), **Lhotse** (8501 meters; 27,890 feet), Dhaulagiri (8172 meters; 26,810 feet), and Annapurna (8078 meters; 26,504 feet). The best-known peak in Sikkim, **Kangchenjunga** (8595 meters; 28,208 feet), sits on the Nepalese border. On the Tibetan border in Bhutan is **Kula Kangri** (7534 meters; 24,783 feet). The 14,000-foot snowline in the east rises to 16,500 feet in the west, so in most of the range you see 10,000 feet of mountain above the snowline.

Look at Map 9.14 to get an idea of where the sections of the Himalayas are. Individual ranges of the Himalayas begin in

Pakistan, with the **Hindu Raj** south of Chitral. Here, **Koyo Zom** is 6889 meters (22,603 feet). The Hindu Raj continues in Jammu and Kashmir, India, as the **Pir Panjal**. East of the Pir Panjal are the **Zanskar** and **Ladakh** ranges. The Pir Panjal becomes the **Siwalik Range** as you go southeast, so that the Siwalik Range is in front of the Great Himalayas in the Indian states of Himachal and Uttar Pradesh. A double range in front of the Himalayas continues east into Nepal, where the northern part is called the **Mahabharat Range**.

The main range of the Himalayas, the Great Himalayas, begins in northeastern Pakistan and continues through Kashmir between the Pir Panjal and Zaskar ranges. It follows the Chinese border through Himachal, Uttar Pradesh, Nepal, Sikkim, Bhutan, and Arunachal Pradesh of eastern India to meet the **Hengdu Shan** of China at right angles.

The best weather is in April and May (warm but unsettled) and October and November (cold but clear). Trekking companies offer supervised trips, but if you are an experienced hiker and plan plenty of time to acclimatize to the potentially fatal altitudes, you can arrange your own trips.

If you take a trek in the Himalayas you will hike on trails that were built for travel between villages. These trails often run thousands of feet above a gorge, where a river churns gray with glacial flour, or beside terraced farms and villages with thatched cottages of stone. Suspension bridges wide enough for only one person cross the roiling rivers. Occasional stands of oaks, pines, or Himalayan firs give way to rhododendrons. Much of the original forest in many areas is gone, largely the victim of firewood cutting and the resulting erosion. Above hang the great white walls of the mountains, often 10,000 feet of snow and glaciers. If you take the Everest trek in Nepal and reach the goal of most trekkers, the rocky hill of **Kala Pattar**, you will get a magnificent view of Everest, the gentle pleat of **Pumori**, and the icy fang of **Nuptse**.

India

In countries with fewer mountains, you would consider the **Nilgiri** and **Anamalai Hills** of India mountains because the highest peaks are over 8000 feet. Running east from Udagaman-

dalam in southern India, the Nilgiri Hills rise to **Dodabetta**
(2637 meters; 8647 feet). The Anamalai Hills, southeast of Val-
parai, climb even higher, to **Anai Mudi** (2695 meters; 8841 feet).

Siberia

To climb any mountains in the USSR you need a permit and a
guide. The **Western** or **Zapadnyy Sayan**, north of the Tannu Ola,
runs from west to east to meet the **Vostochnyy Sayan**. The
Western range rises to **Gora Karmosh** (3112 meters; 10,210 feet),
near Idzhim. The Eastern, or Vostochnyy, Sayan is located west
of Lake Baikal and northeast of the **Tannu Ola Range**. Lake
Baikal is 400 miles long, 18 to 50 miles wide, and over a mile
deep. A spreading center may be developing along it. The
Eastern Sayan extends northwest to southeast, with the Western
Sayan touching it at the center at right angles. **Gora Munku-
Sardyk** (3491 meters; 11,453 feet) is the summit. All the ranges
in Siberia are heavily forested. Musk deer live in these forests.
They have tusks but not antlers and are only the size of a large
rabbit.

East of Lake Baikal near Chita, the **Yablonovyy Khrebet** is a
500-mile-long range, which you cross if you ride the Trans-

Map 9.15

Siberian Railroad across Siberia. The range climbs to 1680 meters (5512 feet) at **Mount Kusotuy**.

The **Stanovoy Khrebet** sweeps from just west of the Sea of Okhotsk nearly to the northern end of Lake Baikal. **Skalisty Golets** (2467 meters; 8094 feet), southwest of Chara, is the highest.

The **Verkhoyanskiy Khrebet** runs south from the Laptev Sea of the Arctic Ocean, then turns east, forming a 700-mile-long arc that meets the **Khrebet Suntar Khayata**. The northern section crests at 2959 meters (9707 feet).

The **Khrebet Cherskogo** forms a northwest-to-southeast arc of bare, rounded mountains through northeastern Siberia. The highest peak is **Gora Pobeda** (3147 meters; 10,325 feet), west of Sasyr.

The **Suntar Khayata**, south of the **Chersky Range**, a continuation of the Verkhoyanskiy, reaches 2959 meters (9708 feet) in **Gora Mus Khaya**, east of Rosomakha. This range has glaciers and alpine scenery.

The **Khrebet Sikhote-Alin** parallels the Sea of Japan, in the southeast, for 750 miles. At its north end the range faces Sakhalin Island, and at the south end, near Vladivostok, it faces Hokkaido Island of Japan. The highest peak is **Mount Tardoki-Yani** (2077 meters; 6814 feet). North of this range, along the coast of the Sea of Okhotsk, is the **Dzhugdzhur Khrebet**, with **Gora Topka** (1906 meters; 6253 feet).

The **Anadyr Ranges** near the Bering Strait are the youngest in the USSR. Most of these ranges are low mountains of less than 1524 meters (5000 feet) that cluster west of the Chukotskiy Peninsula. They include two parallel ranges on the Kamchatka Peninsula. Surprisingly, one of them, the **Sredinnyy Khrebet**, has 127 active volcanoes, including **Klyuchevskaya Sopka** (4750 meters; 15,584 feet), the highest active volcano in Eurasia. Another high peak is **Gora Lednaja** (2562 meters; 8405 feet) in the other range, the **Koryakskiy Khrebet**. It is so windy here that Japanese stone pines put out roots part way up the trunks to anchor themselves.

China

In China the **Trans Himalaya** ranges parallel the Himalayas in Tibet. In the west two ranges are the **Nganglong Kangri** and the **Gandise Shan**. In the east are the **Tanggula Shan** and the

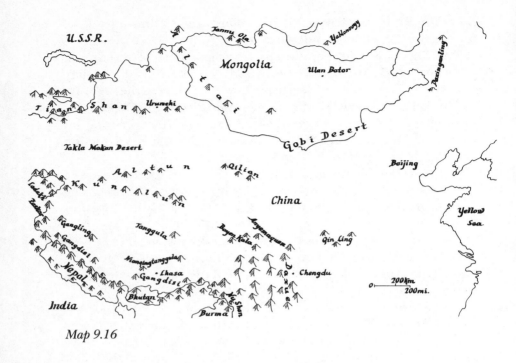

Map 9.16

Nianqingtanggula Shan. The highest peak is **Kangenboge Feng** (6714 meters; 22,027 feet) in the **Gangdise Shan**, northeast of Burang.

The **Kunluns**, or **K'unlun Shan**, extend 1675 miles along the Sinkiang-Tibet border. They tower 4267 meters (14,000 feet) over the surrounding plains. On the west they begin east of the Karakorams as three close-together parallel chains. The highest is **Ulugh Muztagh** (7724 meters; 25,341 feet) in the central part of the main range near Urumchi. Principal ranges in a complex of ranges in the east are the **Altun Shan (Astin Tagh)** on the north and the **Hoh Xil Shan (Ustun Tagh** or **Arka Tagh)** on the south. The Altun Shan continues in Kansu Province as the **Qilian (Nan) Shan**. The **Hoh Xil Shan** runs east into Tsinghai Province, where it becomes the **Bayan Kala (Bayan Kara) Shan**. Northeast of the Bayan Kala Shan is the **Amne Machin**, or **Anyemaquen Shan**, with **Amne Machin** (7160 meters; 23,490 feet).

The **Ta Hsueh Shan (Daxue Shan)**, sometimes called the **Szechuan Alps** or **Great Snow Mountains**, in Szechuan Province,

China, run north and south just west of Chengdu. **Minya Konka**, or **Gongga Shan** (7556 meters; 24,900 feet), south of Kangding, is the highest peak.

Ranges separating the Hwang Ho and Yangtze River are the **Tapa (Daba)**, **Wu Shan**, and **Qin Ling (Tsinling)**, all south of Xian. Highest in the Qin Ling, home of the giant panda, is **Tai Pai Shan** (4067 meters; 13,474 feet).

Korea

Korea has transverse ranges in the north, a central range running north and south, and the **Taeback Range** paralleling the east coast, called the **Hamgyong Sanmaek** in North Korea. The highest peak is **Paektu-san** (2744 meters; 9003 feet), on the Chinese border. The highest in South Korea is **Mount Hallsan** (1950 meters; 6397 feet) on the island of Chejudo, 60 miles south of the mainland.

Japan and Taiwan

Mount Fuji (3776 meters; 12,460 feet) lies 100 kilometers west of Tokyo, Japan, on Honshu Island near Fujijoshida. Northwest of Fuji are the **Southern**, or **Minami, Alps**, with **Kitidake** (3193 meters; 10,471 feet). Thick forest covers these peaks, except above 2500 meters (8000 feet), where slabs of rock emerge. You may see both chamois and monkeys. There are many hot springs, a few at the mountain huts. Farther northwest, the **Northern**, or **Kita, Alps** rise to 3190 meters (10,466 feet) in **Oku-Hotaka** near Kamikochi. The other three islands, Kyusu, Shikoku, and Hokkaido all have mountains, with those of Hokkaido forming a star of ranges. The highest peak on Hokkaido is **Mount Daisetsuzan** or **Asahi Dake** (2290 meters; 7512 feet), near Asahikawa Station. There are nearly 200 volcanoes in Japan, 58 of those active. There is perpetual snow but no glaciers.

The eastern half of Taiwan is mountainous, with 3997-meter (13,114-foot) **Yu Shan**, also known as **Jade Mountain** or **Mount Morrison**, near Ali Shan in a national park. The **Mountain of Harmonious Happiness**, **Hohuan Shan** (3420 meters; 11,220 feet), is also well known for hiking trails, skiing, and hot springs.

Philippines

The active volcano **Mount Apo** (2954 meters; 9689 feet), the highest peak in the Philippines, is on Mindanao, near Davao. On the way up is a hot lake, Lake Agko, that you can swim in. **Mayon Volcano** (2462 meters; 8076 feet), reached from Tabaco on the southeastern end of Luzon, is a perfect volcanic cone; it is so steep you need ropes to climb it. Luzon has a **Central Cordillera**, 3000 meters (9900 feet) high, stretching from Kalinga-Apayo to Benquet along the China Sea. **Pulog** (2934 meters; 9612 feet), near Baguio, is the highest peak on Luzon. The best months for hiking are December through May.

Southeast Asia

A complex of high ranges in northern Burma adjoins the eastern end of the Himalayas. In this knot **Hkakabo Razi** (5881 meters; 19,295 feet) is the highest peak. From here the **Kumon Range** extends south, changing its name to the **Mangin Range** as it goes. Along the border with Arunchal Pradesh, India, in northern Burma, the **Patkai Range** of the **Naga Hills** contains **Saramati** (3286 meters; 12,553 feet). In the **Chin Hills** along the Indian border, **Kennedy Peak**, northwest of Kampetlet, reaches 2704 meters (8871 feet), and **Mount Victoria**, southeast of Tiddim, reaches 3053 meters (10,016 feet).

A national park surrounds the highest peak in Thailand, **Doi Inthanon** (2596 meters; 8514 feet) in the northern part of the country. You can walk or ride a pony to the top, but the Thai prefer that you do this with a guide. Northern Vietnam has the 6000-foot **Chaine Annamitique (Annamese Cordillera)**. North of the Red River lie rugged uplands; **Fan Sai Pan** (3142 meters; 10,308 feet) is southwest of Chapa near the Chinese border. Southern Vietnam has the southern part of the cordillera, which rises to 2598 meters (8524 feet) in **Ngoc Linh**. Kampuchea has **Mount Aural** (1812 meters; 5948 feet) and the **Dangrek Range** in the north and the **Cardamon** and **Elephant** ranges in the south. **Phou Bia** (2818 meters; 9246 feet), southeast of Ban Namcha about 125 miles northeast of Vientiane, is the highest peak in Laos.

Map 9.17

Indonesia, Malaysia, and New Guinea

From its northern tip the island of Borneo climbs to 4101 meters (13,455 feet) at the summit of **Lows Peak**, the highest point on **Mount Kinabalu**. Kinabalu is the only mountain on the island above the jungle. A rectangular peak, it has waterfalls on its sides and spires, rising from slopes of sheet-jointed granite, on top. It is usually foggy around the granite slabs and twisted trees of the summit. On the lower slopes grows the parasitic *Rafflesia*, the largest flower in the world, one meter across.

Pollinated by flies, its blossoms smell like decayed meat. Nine kinds of insectivorous pitcher plants are found on Kinabalu, including one that can hold two quarts of liquid. One species of rhododendron has 12-inch flowers, and there are more than 70 species of orchid. You can reach the mountain from Kota Kinabalu and Ranau. Climbing it requires a guide. North Borneo, called Sabah, is part of Malaysia, so Kinabalu is in Malaysia. On the mainland peninsula of Malaysia, **Gunong Tahan**, near Kuala Tahan, reaches 2187 meters (7175 feet).

All the islands of Indonesia are mountainous with many volcanoes. Outside of West Irian, **Kerintji** (Kerinci), a 3800-meter (12,467-foot) volcano in the **Barisan Range** on Sumatra, is the highest. Java crests in **Semeru** (3676 meters; 12,060 feet), east of Malang near the east end of the island. The summit of Bali is **Agung** (3142 meters; 10,308 feet). On Lombok the high point is **Rindjani** (3748 meters; 12,295 feet). Teak and mahogany cover the lower slopes of the mountain, with pines above. Its crater has a large green lake surrounded by thick forest. There are many hot springs in the area. The island of Sumbawa has **Tambora** (2868 meters; 9410 feet), which blew up in 1815. Celebes holds

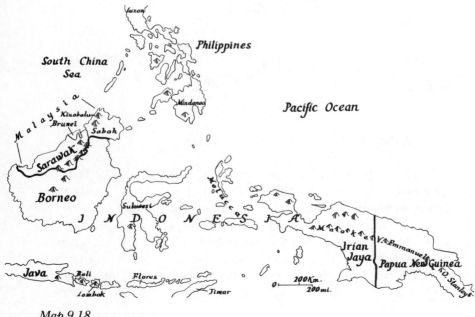

Map 9.18

3505-meter (11,500-foot) **Mount Rantemario** southeast of Todjo. East of New Guinea in the Bismarck Archipelago, the island of New Britain has 2438-meter (7999-foot) **Mount Sinewit**.

In West Irian (Irian Jaya), the western part of the island of New Guinea, the highest mountains are the **Pegunungan Sudriman Range** of the Snow (Maoke) Mountains. They contain the limestone **Puntjak Sukarno**, also known as **Djaya Peak** or **Carstenz Pyramid** (5029 meters; 16,532 feet), near Bioga. The weather is usually stormy but is a little drier between December and April.

In Papua New Guinea, **Mount Wilhelm** (4509 meters; 14,793 feet) can be reached from Kundiwa. The **Owen Stanley Range** in southeastern Papua near Port Moresby has **Mount Victoria** (4073 meters; 13,363 feet). Weather is best from May through September. You will find both of these areas more accessible than those in Irian Jaya. The most famous hike in New Guinea is the **Kokoda Trail**, a historic trail in World War II, from Owens Corner over the Owen Stanley Range to Kokoda near Port Moresby.

AFRICA (MAPS 9.19–9.20)

African mountains differ greatly from each other. **Kilimanjaro** (5895 meters; 19,340 feet), whose glaciers and nested craters make it resemble an angel food cake, contrasts with the sandstone needles of the **Aiguille de Sisse** that bristle out of the desert in the **Tibesti Mountains** of Chad. The cedar forests of the **Middle Atlas** in North Africa contrast with the jungle-clad slopes of **Mount Cameroon** on the west coast. Except in the north, all African mountains between 9000 and 11,000 feet have giant plants similar to those on oceanic islands and reminiscent of the yuccas and Joshua trees of the American southwestern deserts.

North Africa

The **High Atlas Mountains** of northern Africa run east and west through Morocco for 300 miles. The highest peak is **Djebel Toubkal** (4165 meters; 13,661 feet), near Asni and Oukaimeden. The Atlas have deep snow but no glaciers. The streams on the

Map 9.19

north side run into the Mediterranean; those on the south disappear into the desert. Spring and fall are the most comfortable seasons.

In the High Atlas near Djebel Toubkal, you climb from terraced farms and scattered oaks and walnuts of the valleys, past pines and junipers, to clumps of grass and thorny shrubs. You are more likely to see feral house cats than the elusive wild sheep, the moufflon. Above the stone Neltner Hut, acres of charcoal gray and dark red scree and cliffs lead up to peaks like Toubkal, with cirques, crumbling cliffs, and rounded summits. It is hot with no water in summer.

The Middle Atlas, northeast of the High Atlas, near Ifrane, reaches 3290 meters (10,794 feet) in **Djebel Bou Naceur**. Cedar forest and stream gorges give these mountains an alpine appearance. The **Anti Atlas**, southwest of the High Atlas, near Tafraout, rise to **Djebel Aklim** (3304 meters; 10,839 feet).

In Algeria two ranges, the **Atlas Saharien** and the **Atlas Tellien**, continue the Atlas Mountains. Ouarensis is the access point for a national park in the Tellien Atlas surrounding **Djebel Ouarensis** (1830 meters; 6000 feet), but the highest in the Tellien Atlas is **Lalla Khedidja** (2308 meters; 7572 feet). Sixty miles south, the **Atlas Saharien** climbs to the 2235-meter (7333-foot) **Djebel Aissa** at the west end near Aflou. The range diminishes into Tunisia as the **Great Dorssal Range**, beginning with **Djebel Chami** (1544 meters; 5065 feet) at the Algerian border. Spring is the best season.

Sometimes called the **Rif Atlas**, the **Rif Mountains** parallel the Mediterranean in Morocco and ascend to 2342 meters (7680 feet) in **Djebel Tidighine** near Melilla. At Taza Gap you can see the division—between the white rock of the Rif Mountains on the north and the red rock of the Middle Atlas on the south—that marks the end of the Sistemos Beticos, which began in Spain.

A heap of boulders, **Mount Tahat** (2918 meters; 9573 feet), is the highest point in the basaltic **Ahaggar**, or **Hoggar**, **Mountains** in southern Algeria. Volcanic, unearthly peaks of the Plateau of Assekem, they are reached from Tamranasset. People have gone up Tahat on camels. The best weather is from November through April because it gets to 120°F in summer.

In northern Chad the extinct volcanoes of the **Tibesti Mountains** reach 3415 meters (11,204 feet) in **Emi Koussi**. They are composed of crumbly conglomerate rock. Best weather is from November through April.

Reached from Kas, **Jebel Marra** (3088 meters; 10,131 feet) is the summit of the **Darfour Mountains** in central-western Sudan. The highest mountain in the Sudan is **Mount Kinyeti** (3237 meters; 10,620 feet) on the southern border near Nyertete.

West Africa

Mount Cameroon, an active volcano in Cameroon on Africa's southwest coast, rises to 4100 meters (13,350 feet), near Doula. Because it's near the coast the rain is almost constant (400 inches per year on the west side of the mountain), but you will find November through March drier. You can hike up the mountain with a guide on a trail from Buea near Doula, as did the British explorer Mary Kingsley in 1896. The **Massif de l'Adamaoua** defends the northwestern border of Cameroon with peaks as high as 2679 meters (8789 feet).

Southern Africa

The **Drakenburg Mountains** extend along the east coast of South Africa from the Cape to Transvaal. In Lesotho you see them as an escarpment 100 miles long and 1219 meters (4000 feet) high. **Thabana Ntlenyana** (3482 meters; 11,425 feet), the highest point in the range, is in Lesotho, well back from the edge of the escarpment. The mountains are good for walking any time of year, even though there is some snow in winter.

The granite domes of the **Mlanje Mountains** top the Shire Highlands in Malawi south of Lake Malawi. The highest is **Sapitwa** (3050 meters; 9847 feet), reached from Blantyre. The best season is from April through November. A continuation of these mountains runs east into Mozambique, where the high point is **Namuli**, 2419 meters (7936 feet).

East Africa

The **Virunga** volcanoes smolder in eastern Africa where the countries of Uganda, Rwanda, and Zaire join. Only two are active. The highest is **Karisimbi** (4507 meters; 14,782 feet) on the border between Rwanda and Zaire near the north end of Lake Kivu. The Virunga and another East African range, the **Ruwenzori Mountains** are wetter than the mountains on the east side of the Great Rift Valley, so the vegetation is more luxuriant.

Dian Fossey studied the mountain gorillas that live on the Virunga volcanoes. These gorillas eat bitter plants such as vines, wild celery, bamboo shoots, and wood nettles. They communicate with each other by more than 20 distinct sounds, and their favorite vocalization, resembling a burp, means contentment. A silverback male acts as dictator for each group. The Ruwenzori were named the **Mountains of the Moon** about A.D. 100 by Ptolemy. The 60-mile-long range, a fault block of Precambrian rock, runs north and south along the border of Zaire and Uganda between Lake Edward and Lake Albert. It has ten peaks

Map 9.20

over 16,000 feet. **Margherita** (5109 meters; 16,763 feet), in the **Mount Stanley Group**, tops the range near Lake Bujuku. Because of the wet, foggy weather, tree groundsel, lobelia, giant heaths, and giant everlasting reach their largest sizes and densest stands here below permanent snow, which begins at 15,000 feet. The weather is a little better from December to mid-March and from June through August.

Kilimanjaro is a dormant volcano located in Tanzania, southwest of the border with Kenya and east of the Serengeti Plain (Figure 9.3). It has two summits, **Kibo** (5895 meters; 19,340 feet) and **Mawenzi** (5148 meters; 16,980 feet). The best weather is from August through October. Those in good condition can take a five-day hike to the summit of Kibo and back from the Marangu Gate, reached by road from Mombasa. Another volcano, **Mount Meru** (4566 meters; 14,979 feet), is 40 miles southwest of Kilimanjaro near Arusha.

The highest peak in the **Kipingere Range** in southern Tanzania northwest of Lake Malawi is **Rungwe** (2901 meters; 9713 feet). The **Livingstone Range**, with **Mount Chamembe**, or **Jamimbi** (2398 meters; 7870 feet), borders the Lake Nyasa Rift Valley at the north end of the lake.

Mount Kenya, the plug of an old volcano, covers 150 square miles in the center of the country named for it. A glacier-hung notch called **Gate of the Mists** separates the highest point, **Batian** (5199 meters; 17,065 feet), from a sister summit, **Nelion** (5188 meters; 17,021 feet). There are clusters of knifelike aguilles near the two summits. The dry seasons are from mid-January through February and from late August through September.

At about 11,000 feet on Mount Kenya you come out of the moss-draped tree heaths onto grassland pillowed with tussocks of coarse grass. Ahead, amid lichen-coated boulders, beckon the

Figure 9.3.   Nested craters on the summit of Kilimanjaro in Africa show a pattern typical of volcano summits.
Courtesy of American Geographical Society Collection, University of Wisconsin—Milwaukee Library.

tufted, branching forms of giant groundsels. Here the pointed, jagged tops of the mountain's two summits, plastered with glaciers, peek over a ridge. Unless you have climbing experience and a guide, you climb only to a viewpoint called **Point Lenana**.

Mount Elgon, another extinct volcano, lies on the Uganda-Kenya border north of Lake Victoria. The highest point is **Wagagai** (4321 meters; 14,178 feet) in Uganda. The summit of Elgon has a crater five miles across and 2000 feet deep with a marsh in it. Hundreds of caves pit the side of the mountain. To one named Kitum, elephants and other animals come to lick minerals from the walls.

Fifty miles southwest of Mount Kenya stand the **Aberdares Mountains**. These high, grassy hills rise to **Ol Donyo Lasatima**, (3994 meters; 13,120 feet).

In northern Ethiopia, near Debarek, the **Semyen Mountains**, one of eight mountain groups in the country, reach 4620 meters (15,158 feet) in **Rasdajan (Ras Dashan)**. These mountains, remnants of a shield volcano, form a 4000-foot escarpment that runs for over 20 miles. The best weather is from September through February.

Islands Near Africa

Off the coast of Morocco lie the Canary Islands, which belong to Spain. Tenerife has a 3718-meter (12,128-foot) volcano, **Pico de Tiede**, with a cable railway up it. On Gran Canaria, **Pico de las Nieves** (1949 meters; 6394 feet) is the highest peak.

The highest point on Bioka (Fernando Po), 25 miles off Cameroon on the west coast of Africa, is **Pico de Santa Isabel** (3008 meters; 9869 feet). The best weather occurs from November through March.

The highest peak on Madagascar, in the Indian Ocean off the coast of Africa, is **Maromokotro** (2870 meters; 9436 feet) in the **Massif du Tsaratanana** at the north end of the island.

The highest peak in Sri Lanka (Ceylon) is **Pidurutalagala** (2524 meters; 8280 feet). A trail to the summit leads from the resort of Newara Eliya, southeast of Kandy.

The island of Reunion, in the Indian Ocean 420 miles east of Madagascar, rises to **Piton de Neiges** (3069 meters; 10,069 feet). May through October has the best weather.

Pico de Fano on Fogo of the Cape Verde Islands, 300 miles off the coast of West Africa, is 2829 meters (9281 feet). These islands are hot with little rain but high humidity.

AUSTRALIA AND THE PACIFIC (MAP 9.21)

Australia and the Pacific Islands also have many types of mountains, from the glacier-covered New Zealand Alps to the vegetation-mantled pinnacles of Tahiti.

Australia

If you had enough time you could follow the **Great Dividing Range** of Australia, an ancient, gentle range that runs along the entire east coast of the continent, from the pointed northern tip

Map 9.21

of Queensland to Victoria on the south coast. The range culmi-
nates at the south end in the **Snowy Mountains (Australian
Alps)**, which rise to 2228 meters (7310 feet) in **Mount Kosciusko**.
Sections of the range have individual names, such as the **Blue
Mountains** near Windsor. Snow here melts each summer. One of
the most scenic parts of the range is the **Warrumbungles** in New
South Wales, where blade-shaped peaks like the **Breadknife**
display 1000-foot cliffs. The best weather is from November
through April. None of the other Australian ranges reach 5000
feet, and many are arid and inhospitable. The highest of these is
1510-meter (4954-foot) **Mount Ziel** of the **Mcdonnell Ranges** in
central Australia.

If you hiked up **Mount Kosciusko**, you would see rolling hills
covered with varieties of eucalyptus except for the bare ski runs
and the highest 1000 feet, which is above timberline. As you
walk, tall stringybark, candlebark, and mountain ash give way at
4000 feet to twisted snow gums, with their red-, cream-, and
brown-streaked bark (Figure 9.4). You may catch a glimpse of a
crimson rosella, a parrot with red and lavender feathers that
often is found among snow gums. All of these trees are *Eucalyptus.* Eucalyptus leaves have two layers of cells instead of one
and stomata on both sides, so they resemble two leaves pasted
together back to back. From the open tussock grassland of the
summit of Mount Kosciusko you will see small blue lakes
nestled among boulders and grass and the Snowy River beginning in a glacial cirque.

The rugged peaks of Tasmania reach 1617 meters (5305 feet)
in **Mount Ossa**. Rain forest, made impenetrable by thickets of
five-foot high saxifrage, nicknamed the horizontal, chokes the
western slopes. The stems of this shrub are weak, and wherever
they flop over to the ground, roots grow. The best weather is
from November through April. Cradle Mountain-Lake Sinclair
National Park in central Tasmania has alpine flowers and the
highest mountains. Nearby, Frenchman's Cap National Park offers a peak of white quartz for climbing.

Because of frigid year-round temperatures and travel restric-
tions, only mountaineering expeditions climb the mountains of
Antarctica. Highest are the **Vinson Massif** (5139 meters; 16,860
feet) and **Mount Tyree** (4965 meters; 16,290 feet) in the **Sentinel
Range** of the **Ellsworth Mountains** in western Antarctica. An
active volcano, **Erebus,** reaches 4024 meters (13,202 feet).

Figure 9.4.   Snow gum, a eucalyptus with red-, cream- and brown-streaked bark, is the timberline tree in Australia.
Courtesy of Promotion Australia.

New Zealand

The **Southern Alps** of New Zealand extend for 450 miles north and south along South Island. The highest is **Mount Cook** (3764 meters; 12,349 feet) in Mount Cook National Park, one of several parks on the South Island. Because of the high precipitation and cold weather, glaciers begin at the bases of the peaks. The Tasman Glacier is 18 miles long. The highest of the several volcanoes on North Island is 2797-meter (9175-foot) **Ruapehu** in Tongariro National Park near Lake Taupo. Its crater holds a warm-water lake. Best weather is from November through April. To tramp the walking tracks in some of the national parks, you need advance registration to stay in the hotel-like huts. It is much easier and quicker to arrange to stay in the simpler huts as a "freedom walker," a tramper who carries his or her own bedding, food, and cooking pots.

Above the **Milford Track** on the South Island hang the braided white threads of waterfalls. On the lower parts of the trail beeches are draped with moss, vines, and lichens. On **Mac-Kinnon Pass** you come out on alpine grassland, where two-inch white buttercups raise clusters of bloom into a misty sky below the dark faces of surrounding peaks. A parrot, the kea, dark green with orange underwings, may beg for a bit of lunch or chew on your hiking boots. This bird nests in tunnels under the rocks at timberline, eating roots, leaves, insects, dead sheep, and occasionally attacking sick and dying ones. Similar, but flightless, as are many New Zealand birds, is the rare 24-inch-long kakapo, which lives in the beech forests but walks up into the tundra to eat snow grass.

Pacific Islands

Some of the smaller Pacific islands have high mountains for their sizes. An example is the Solomon Islands, located in the western Pacific east of New Guinea. The highest summit is **Mount Makarakomburu** (2447 meters; 8028 feet) on Guadalcanal. **Mount Tabemasana** (1888 meters; 6195 feet) on Espiritu Santo is the highest peak in the New Hebrides Islands. On Tahiti, the largest of the Society Islands, the major mountain is **Mount Orohena** (2322 meters; 7618 feet). There are several access trails from the road around the island, but ropes are needed to climb it. On the island of Savai'i in Samoa is a mountain called **Mauga Silisili** (1857 meters; 6094 feet), south of Aopo.

Hawaii

The Hawaiian Islands are the high points in a 1600-mile ridge of volcanoes rising from the ocean floor. The greatest of these, **Mauna Kea** (4205 meters; 13,796 feet), rises 32,000 feet from the ocean floor, the highest such rise in the world. **Mauna Loa** (4169 meters; 13,680 feet), which erupts periodically, is the world's largest active volcano. On its flank belches the continuously active crater of **Kilauea**. **Haleakala**, on the island of Maui, northwest of Hawaii, climbs to 3055 meters (10,025 feet) in **Red Hill**. These peaks feature dense tropical vegetation at low levels and bare black lava sprinkled with a few endemics like the silversword higher up.

In Hawaii we are almost back to where we started on our round-the-world tour of mountains. You have read about mountain natural history and where the mountains of the world are located. Now it is time for you to go out in the field and observe for yourself. It is time to go hiking with a new understanding of the mountain environment and a new eagerness to learn even more about what you see.

Appendix

MAP AND GUIDEBOOK SOURCES

There are hundreds of guidebooks in English to trails in the United States and several dozen to trails in other countries. Space prohibits listing them. Look in *Books in Print* in your library, or ask to see the catalogs your local bookstore or backpacking store use if they don't carry what you need. Here are some sources of maps and guidebooks:

Alpenbooks, P.O. Box 761, Snohomish, Washington 98290. Hundreds of hiking, white-water, and climbing guidebooks from all over the world. Also mountaineering history.

Bradt Enterprises Inc., 95 Harvey Street, Cambridge, Massachusetts 02140. Maps, hiking guidebooks.

Branch of Distribution, U.S. Geological Survey, Box 25286 Federal Center, Denver, Colorado 80225. Topographic maps of the United States.

Edward Stanford Ltd., 12-14 Long Acre, London, England WC2E 9LP. World's largest map supplier.

Geography and Map Division, Library of Congress, Washington, D.C. 20540. Photocopies of uncopyrighted maps, no list.

Internationales Landkartenhaus, Postfach 80 08 30, Schockenridstr., 40A, D-7000 Stuttgart 80, West Germany. Two-volume catalog of topographic and scientific maps from all over the world.

Libreria Alpina, Via C. Coronedi-Berti, 4, Bologna, Italy 40137. Italian-language catalog of maps of countries.

Michael Chessler Books, P.O. Box 4267, Evergreen, Colorado 80439. Hiking and climbing guides, mountaineering classics.

Rand McNally, 8255 N. Central Park Avenue, Skokie, Illinois 60076-2970. World maps and guidebooks sold in retail stores.

NATURAL HISTORY AND MOUNTAIN ADVENTURE TRIPS

Many other companies offer natural history and adventure trips in the United States and in other countries. Before signing up for a trip ask the company for names and addresses of a few of their clients, so you can write to them and see how they liked the trips.

Above the Clouds Trekking, P.O. Box 398, Worcester, Massachusetts 01602. Trekking off the beaten track in the Himalayas, North America, Europe, Andes, Japan, Yemen, Romania, and Indonesia. Emphasizes wildlife and culture; led by experts on the countries.

Alaska Discovery, 369-S South Franklin, Juneau, Alaska 99801. Courses offered through the University of Alaska on kayak, river raft, canoe; natural history and fish and wildlife trips led by certified Alaska wilderness guides. Award by American Travel Writers. Has Forest and Park Service contracts.

American Alpine Institute, 1212 24th P-86, Bellingham, Washington 98225. Trekking, mountaineering, skiing, and backpacking trips and instruction in high-altitude physiology, mountaineering, and expedition and rescue skills led by professional mountaineers, skiers, and educators in the North Cascades, Alaska, Peru, Bolivia, and Nepal.

American Museum of Natural History Discovery Tours, Central Park West at 79th Street, New York, New York 10024. Natural history cruises, led by museum naturalists, to various parts of the world. The tours are open to museum members (all those who subscribe to *Natural History*).

Colorado Mountain School, Box 2106, Estes Park, Colorado 80517. Family mountaineering instruction and nordic skiing trips year-round in Colorado, Alaska, Mexico, the Andes, the Alps, British Columbia, and the Yukon. Led by expert mountain guides. Rated excellent by the U.S. Department of Interior.

Colorado Outward Bound School, 945 Pennsylvania Street, Denver, Colorado 80203-3198. One of several branches of Outward Bound in the United States and Britain. Instruction in backcountry travel and mountaineering. Mountaineering, rafting, and nordic skiing trips led by outdoor experts in Colorado and Utah. Challenges your courage to develop confidence.

Earthwatch, Box 403, Watertown, Massachusetts 02272. Research expeditions in natural history and archaeology·all over the world. Led by scientists, who are assisted by the volunteers who pay to go on the trips.

Geo Expeditions, P.O. Box 3656, Sonora, California 95370. Wildlife observation on Land Rover and rafting trips in Africa, South America, Mexico, Indonesia, and India led by experts in the regions of the trips, some with doctorates in natural history fields.

Himalayan Travel, P.O. Box 481, Greenwich, Connecticut 06836. Trekking or rafting trips in the Himalayas, Sri Lanka, Burma, Thailand, Peru, and Africa, emphasizing interaction with cultures. Led by a travel agency that employs expert mountaineers.

Mountain Travel, 6420 Fairmount Avenue, El Cerrito, California 94530. Adventure travel graded by difficulty on all continents of the world. Trekking, natural history, mountaineering, overland, and other trips led by people expert in the regions.

National Outdoor Leadership School (NOLS), P.O. Box AA, Lander, Wyoming 82520. Wilderness skills, mountaineering, kayaking, backpacking, photography, and natural history taught on trips in Wyoming, Mexico, Washington, Alaska, and Kenya by skilled professionals who are graduates of NOLS instructors course.

Nature Expeditions International, P.O. Box 11496, Eugene, Oregon 97440. Natural history and culture taught by people with M.A.'s, Ph.D's, college teaching experience, and knowledge of the countries. Trekking and day hiking trips in the Himalayas, New Guinea, Andes, Baja, Australia, Tanzania, and Hawaii.

Questers Worldwide Nature Tours, 257 Park Avenue South, New York, New York 10010-7369. Naturalist-led day hiking, trekking, and canoeing trips all over the world, featuring observation of natural history, culture, and customs.

Sierra Club, Outing Department, 730 Polk Street, San Francisco, California 94109. Backpacking, burro, pack, ski, raft, kayak, outdoor cleanup, and trail-maintenance trips in the United States and other countries for Sierra Club members.

Sobek's Expeditions, Box 1089-21, Angels Camp, California 95222. Trips make adventure available to all. Trekking, cycling, skiing, sailing, rafting, canoeing, overland, natural history, climbing, kayaking, backpacking, horseback, and llama-packing trips on all continents, offered by a variety of companies including Sobek. Trips graded by difficulty.

Wilderness Travel, 801-N Allston Way, Berkeley, California 94710. Trekking, raft, yacht, canoe, bicycle, and four-wheel drive trips in South America, Alaska, Himalayas, Europe, East Africa, Australia. Led by those with in-depth knowledge of countries and their natural history.

A FEW MOUNTAIN ENVIRONMENTAL EDUCATION CENTERS AND PROGRAMS

Laboratory of Ornithology, Cornell University, 159 Sapsucker Woods Road, Ithaca, New York 14850. Correspondence courses in ornithology and bird photography taught by college professors.

Mountain Research Station, University of Colorado, Nederland, Colorado 80466. Courses in flora, climatology, ecology, wildland management, and environmental science taught by college professors. Also ecological research.

National Audubon Society Expedition Institute, Northeast Audubon Center, Sharon, Connecticut 06069. Environmental education offering high school and college degrees. Bus, canoe, or backpacking trips in the United States and Canada taught by faculty of Lesley College and expert wilderness guides.

The Nature Place, Colorado Outdoor Education Center, Florrisant, Colorado 80816. Courses, workshops, and conferences in natural history, history, art, and photography taught by professional botanists, ornithologists, geologists, and environmental educators.

Wilderness Extension, University of California, Davis, California 95616. Extension courses in fields of natural history, anthropology, and natural resources taught in California, Peru, Japan, Africa, and New Guinea by instructors at U.C.-Davis.

Yellowstone Institute, Box 117, Yellowstone National Park, Wyoming 82190. Courses in geology, archaeology, botany, zoology, photography, and history taught by college teachers with Ph.D's, ranger naturalists, and noted photographers.

TRAILS FOR THE HANDICAPPED

Only a few countries as yet have trails designed for the handicapped. In the United States in many campgrounds and picnic sites in national forests and state and national parks there are paths modified for wheelchair use, but there are only a few hiking trails that wheelchairs can travel. There are even fewer trails with braille markings. You can obtain a list of the appropriate trails in each national forest from its supervisor's office. The most up-to-date list for national parks can be obtained from each park's headquarters. You might also consult *Access National Parks, A Guide for Handicapped Visitors* (Washington D.C.: National Park Service, 1978).

Several trails for the handicapped in Great Britain are listed in the book *The Countryside and Wildlife for Disabled People,* by Anthony Chapman, published by the Royal Association for Disability and Rehabilitation, 25 Mortimer St., London W-1, England. In addition, there is a book that gives helpful ideas for handicapped travelers, such as wilderness courses available to them: *Access to the World: A Travel Guide for the Handicapped,* by Louise Weiss (New York: Facts on File, 1983).

Bibliography

Arno, Stephen, and Hammerly, Ramona, *Timberline: Mountain and Arctic Forest Frontiers* (Seattle: The Mountaineers, 1984).

Bailey, Ronald H., *Glacier* (Alexandria, Virginia: Time-Life Books, 1982).

Billings, W. D., *Plants, Man and the Ecosystem* (Belmont, California: Wadsworth Publishing, 1970).

Cleare, John, *The World Guide to Mountains and Mountaineering* (Exeter, England: Webb & Bower, 1979).

Cronin, Edward W., Jr., *The Arun: A Natural History of the World's Deepest Valley* (Boston: Houghton Mifflin Co., 1979).

Cvancara, Alan M., *A Field Manual for the Amateur Geologist* (Englewood Cliffs, N.J.: Prentice-Hall, 1985).

Daubenmire, Rexford, *Plant Geography* (New York: Academic Press, 1978).

Eicher, Don; McAlester, A. Lee; and Rottman, Marcia, *The History of the Earth's Crust* (Englewood Cliffs, N.J.: Prentice-Hall, 1984).

Ives, Jack D., and Barry, Roger G., eds. *Arctic and Alpine Environments* (London: Methune, 1974).

Jerome, John, *On Mountains* (New York: Harcourt, Brace, Jovanovich, 1978).

Kelsey, Michael, *Climbers and Hikers Guide to the World's Mountains* (Springville, Utah: Kelsey Publishing, 1984).

Kormondy, Edward J., *Concepts of Ecology* (Englewood Cliffs, N.J.: Prentice-Hall, 1984).

McPhee, John, *In Suspect Terrain* (New York: Farrar, Straus & Giroux, 1983).

Miyashiro, Akiho; Aki, Keiifi; and Sengor, A. M. Celal, *Orogeny* (New York: John Wiley & Sons, 1982).

Odum, Eugene, *Fundamentals of Ecology* (Philadelphia: W. B. Saunders Co., 1971).

Perry, Richard, *Mountain Wildlife* (Harrisburg, Pa.: Stackpole Books, 1981).

Plummer, Charles C., and McGeary, David, *Physical Geology* (Dubuque, Iowa: Wm. C. Brown, 1985).

Press, Frank, and Siever, Raymond, *Earth* (San Francisco: W. H. Freeman and Company, 1982).

Price, Larry, *Mountains and Man* (Berkeley: University of California, 1981).

Prinz, Martin; Harlow, George; and Peters, Joseph, eds. *Simon & Schuster's Guide to Rocks and Minerals* (New York: Simon & Schuster, 1978).

Reifsnyder, William, *Weathering the Wilderness: The Sierra Club Guide to Practical Meteorology* (San Francisco: Sierra Club, 1980).

Ricciuti, Edward R., *Wildlife of the Mountains* (New York: Harry N. Abrams, Inc., 1979).

Roth, Charles, *The Plant Observer's Guidebook: A Field Botany Manual for the Amateur Naturalist* (Englewood Cliffs, N.J.: Prentice-Hall, 1984).

Roth, Charles, *Wildlife Observer's Guidebook* (Englewood Cliffs, N.J.: Prentice-Hall, 1982).

Saigo, Roy H., and Saigo, Barbara, *Botany: Principles and Applications* (Englewood Cliffs, N.J.: Prentice-Hall, 1983).

Strahler, Arthur, *Physical Geology* (Cambridge, Mass.: Harper & Row, 1981).

Van Andel, Tjeerd H., *New Views On An Old Planet* (Cambridge, England: Cambridge University Press, 1985).

Walter, Heinrich, *Vegetation of the Earth and Ecological Systems of the Geo-biosphere* (New York: Springer-Verlag, 1979).

Wright, H. E., Jr., and Osburn, W. H., eds. *Arctic & Alpine Environments* (Bloomington: Indiana University Press, 1968).

Index